Get Ready! for Social Studies
U.S. HISTORY

Books in the *Get Ready! for Social Studies* Series:

Essays, Book Reports, and Research Papers
Geography
Government and Citizenship
U.S. History
World History

Nancy White and Francine Weinberg, series editors, have been involved in educating elementary and secondary students for more than thirty years. They have had experience in the classroom as well as on dozens of books and electronic projects. They welcome this partnership with parents and other adults to promote knowledge, skills, and critical thinking.

Get Ready! for Social Studies
U.S. HISTORY

Erin Ash Sullivan

Series Editors
Nancy White
Francine Weinberg

McGraw-Hill
New York   Chicago   San Francisco
Lisbon   London   Madrid   Mexico City
Milan   New Delhi   San Juan   Seoul
Singapore   Sydney   Toronto

Library of Congress Cataloging-in-Publication Data applied for.

McGraw-Hill

A Division of The McGraw-Hill Companies

Copyright © 2002 by The McGraw-Hill Companies, Inc. All rights reserved. Printed in the United States of America. Except as permitted under the United States Copyright Act of 1976, no part of this publication may be reproduced or distributed in any form or by any means, or stored in a database or retrieval system, without the prior written permission of the publisher.

1 2 3 4 5 6 7 8 9 0   QPD/QPD   0 9 8 7 6 5 4 3 2

ISBN 0-07-137763-8

This book was set in Goudy Oldstyle by North Market Street Graphics.

Printed and bound by Quebecor/Dubuque.

McGraw-Hill books are available at special quantity discounts to use as premiums and sales promotions, or for use in corporate training programs. For more information, please write to the Director of Special Sales, Professional Publishing, McGraw-Hill, Two Penn Plaza, New York, NY 10121-2298. Or contact your local bookstore.

 This book is printed on recycled, acid-free paper containing a minimum of 50% recycled, de-inked fiber.

Contents

Introduction

In recent years, the media have told us that many students need to know more about history, geography, and government and to improve their writing skills. While schools are attempting to raise standards, learning need not be limited to the classroom. Parents and other concerned adults can help students too. *Get Ready! for Social Studies* provides you with the information and resources you need to help students with homework, projects, and tests and to create a general excitement about learning.

You may choose to use this book in several different ways, depending on your child's strengths and preferences. You might read passages aloud, you might read it to yourself and then paraphrase it for your child, or you might ask your child to read the material along with you or on his or her own. To help you use this book successfully, brief boldface paragraphs, addressed to you, the adult, appear from time to time.

Here is a preview of the features you will find in each chapter.

Word Power

To help students expand their vocabulary, the "Word Power" feature in each chapter defines underlined words with which students may be unfamiliar. These are words that students may use in a variety of contexts in their writing and speaking. In addition, proper nouns and more technical terms appear in boldface type within the chapter, along with their definitions. For example, the word decade is defined as "period of ten years" on a "Word Power" list. The word **cartography** would appear in boldface type within the chapter and be defined there as "the science of mapmaking."

What Your Child Needs to Know

This section provides key facts and concepts in a conversational, informal style to make the content accessible and engaging for all readers.

Implications

This section goes beyond the facts and concepts. Here, we provide the answers to students' centuries-old questions, "Why does this matter?" and "Why is this important for me to know?"

Fact Checker

A puzzle, game, or other short-answer activity checks children's grasp of facts—people, places, things, dates, and other details.

The Big Questions

These questions encourage students to think reflectively and critically in order to form a broader understanding of the material.

Skills Practice

Activities provide the opportunity for children to learn and to apply reading, writing, and thinking skills basic to social studies and other subjects as well. These skills include learning from historical documents, map reading, identifying cause and effect, comparing and contrasting, and writing analytically and creatively.

Top of the Class

In this section, creative suggestions help students stand out in class. By taking some of these suggestions, students can show their teachers that they have been putting in the extra effort that means the difference between average and excellent performance.

The book you are now holding in your hand is a powerful tool. It will help you boost your child's performance in school, increase his or her self-confidence, and open the door to a successful future as a well-educated adult.

Nancy White and Francine Weinberg

CHAPTER 1
Prehistory and Early Native American History before European Contact
30,000 B.C.–A.D. 1492

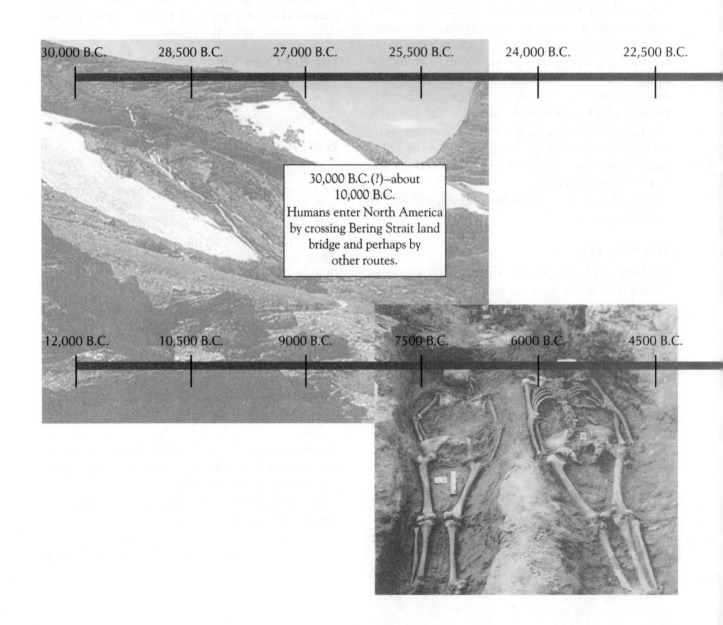

| 30,000 B.C. | 28,500 B.C. | 27,000 B.C. | 25,500 B.C. | 24,000 B.C. | 22,500 B.C. |

30,000 B.C. (?)–about 10,000 B.C.
Humans enter North America by crossing Bering Strait land bridge and perhaps by other routes.

| 12,000 B.C. | 10,500 B.C. | 9000 B.C. | 7500 B.C. | 6000 B.C. | 4500 B.C. |

This timeline provides an overview of the prehistoric period and the period of early Native American settlement in North America. The chapter provides a narrative that describes the development of various cultures and civilizations and discusses their significance.

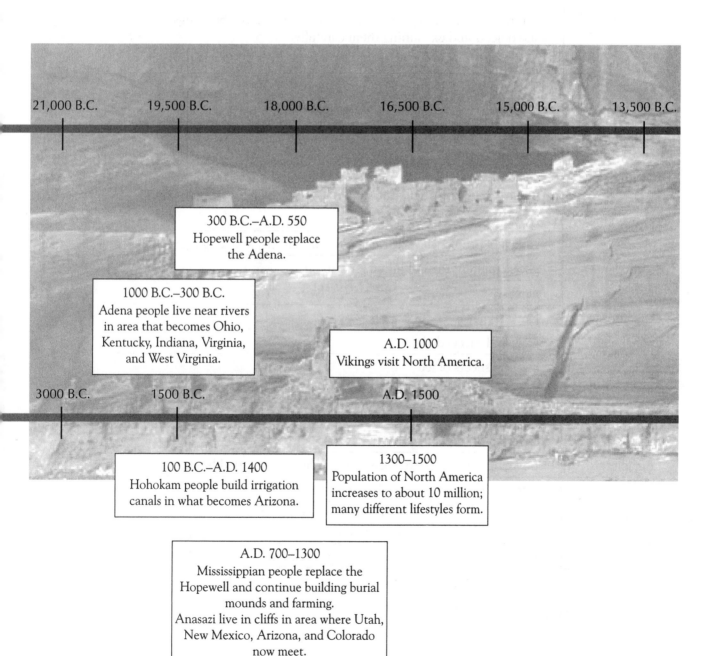

21,000 B.C.   19,500 B.C.   18,000 B.C.   16,500 B.C.   15,000 B.C.   13,500 B.C.

300 B.C.–A.D. 550
Hopewell people replace
the Adena.

1000 B.C.–300 B.C.
Adena people live near rivers
in area that becomes Ohio,
Kentucky, Indiana, Virginia,
and West Virginia.

A.D. 1000
Vikings visit North America.

3000 B.C.   1500 B.C.   A.D. 1500

100 B.C.–A.D. 1400
Hohokam people build irrigation
canals in what becomes Arizona.

1300–1500
Population of North America
increases to about 10 million;
many different lifestyles form.

A.D. 700–1300
Mississippian people replace the
Hopewell and continue building burial
mounds and farming.
Anasazi live in cliffs in area where Utah,
New Mexico, Arizona, and Colorado
now meet.

3

Word Power

The words on the following chart are underscored in the section called "What Your Child Needs to Know." Explain their meanings to your child as needed when they come up in reading or discussion. Keep this list handy for you and your child to use.

Word	Definition
archaeological	referring to *archaeology*, the science of digging up old buildings and objects and examining them carefully
arid	dry
artifacts	objects made or changed by human beings
artisans	people who work skillfully with their hands at a particular craft
compromise	agree to accept something that is not exactly what you originally wanted
continent	one of the seven large land masses on Earth: North America, South America, Africa, Europe, Asia, Australia, and Antarctica
cultivated	grown
cultures	groups of people with the same customs, beliefs, and language
descendants	one's children, their children, and so on
dwellings	homes
expedition	long journey
flourished	grew and succeeded
glaciers	gigantic sheets of ice
inhabited	lived in
insulation	material that keeps heat from escaping and cold from entering
irrigation	system of transporting water for crops
nomadic	traveling from place to place, without having a settled home
prehistoric	belonging to a time before history was recorded
resources	things that a place has and can use to its advantage (for example, the natural resources coal and oil)
ritual	set of actions that one performs at a ceremony
spiritual	having to do with the soul or religion
stereotype	overly simple picture or opinion about a group of people

What Your Child Needs to Know

You may choose to use the following text in several different ways, depending on your child's strengths and preferences. You might read the passage aloud; you might read it to yourself and then paraphrase it for your child; or you might ask your child to read the material along with you or on his or her own.

Glacier

THE EARLIEST HUMANS IN NORTH AMERICA

The story of American history does not begin with the Revolution or the Pilgrims or even the first colony at Jamestown, Virginia. The story goes back much further. It begins with the prehistoric people who made their way to North America many thousands of years ago.

Where Did They Come from and How?

Some scientists claim that people first arrived on the continent we now call North America nine thousand years ago; other scientists say the arrival was more like thirty thousand years ago. In either case, much of Earth back then was in the midst of an ice age, and much of the water supply had frozen into glaciers. As a result, sea levels dropped, and areas formerly (and presently) covered by water became dry land that humans could cross on foot.

One such area was the Bering Strait, the narrow strip of ocean that separates northeastern Asia from North America. Sea levels dropped in this area more than three hundred feet (ninety meters), leaving an open land bridge for people to use in walking from one continent to the other.

These early people were nomadic **hunter-gatherers.** They traveled from place to place and ate the fruits and vegetables they could find. They also followed large animals such as the woolly mammoth and killed them with primitive but effective stone weapons.

Not all scientists agree, however, that the Bering Strait was the first or only entrance to

North America. Recent findings of ancient bones and artifacts at archaeological sites all over North America suggest that early people may have come here from a variety of places and by a variety of routes—not just via the Bering Strait. For example, when scientists examined the ninety-three-hundred-year-old bones of "Kennewick Man"—a skeleton found in what is now Washington state—they claimed that physically he resembled people from Polynesia and South Asia, not people from

Skeletons about a thousand years old, found in Southwest.

ancient northeastern Asia. In addition, some scientists think that early people may have come to North America from Asia or from Pacific islands not by foot but rather in hide-covered canoes. These people might have then sailed along the coast of the Americas and stopped on land for food and shelter when necessary.

What Did They Find?

These early arrivals inhabited a North America very different from the continent that we know today. Shorelines extended farther than they do now because of lower sea levels. Dense forests lined the coasts. As mentioned before, abundant vegetation as well as animals, such as saber-toothed cats and woolly mammoths, provided food. Then, once those animals became extinct, people started hunting bison.

During the period from about 8000 B.C. to about 1000 B.C., the nomadic people in North America gradually developed a more settled way of life. Small villages sprang up, and people began farming instead of relying on what food they could find. Some of the earliest cultivated plants were corn, rice, and squash.

NORTH AMERICAN CULTURES FROM 1000 B.C. TO A.D. 1300

During the twenty-three hundred years from about 1000 B.C. to A.D. 1300, human populations expanded significantly in North America. Many cultures developed and flourished. Here we discuss a few of them.

Mound Builders

The **Adena** (ah DEE nuh), one of the first cultures in North America, lived from about 1000 B.C. to 300 B.C. on riverbanks in today's central and southern Ohio, Kentucky, Indiana, Virginia, and West Virginia. Most of what people today know about the Adena is from their burial mounds. These rounded mounds of earth range from twenty feet (six meters) to more than three hundred feet (ninety meters) wide. Inside, archaeologists have found such artifacts as spear points, smoking pipes, copper bracelets, and stone tablets.

Scientists reason that Adena society was very well organized, given the amount of planning and

work that the mound building must have required. At Grave Creek Mound in West Virginia, for example, scientists have calculated that Adena people must have moved more than sixty thousand tons of earth by the basket load.

While the Adena hunted and gathered available plants, they did some simple farming of corn, beans, and squash. They also ranged beyond their own lands to trade with other groups. Bones collected from burial mounds suggest that the Adena were large people, with women as tall as six feet and some men reaching seven feet.

By about 300 B.C., the Adena culture had begun to fade, and the **Hopewell** culture arose. The Hopewell incorporated many elements of Adena culture, such as burial mounds for their dead. The Hopewell also developed more advanced farming techniques, cultivating corn, barley, squash, and sunflowers. Artifacts from Hopewell sites suggest that these people were also active traders and imported valuable goods such as copper, silver, shells, and alligator teeth from all over North America. In addition, they were skilled craftspeople; they carved designs and shapes of animals on tools and worked with metals such as iron, copper, and silver. But by the sixth century, their culture had also begun to decline.

The **Mississippian** Mound Builders (A.D. 700–1300) followed the Hopewell and built towns along the banks of the Ohio, Missouri, and Mississippi rivers. These people also incorporated many elements of the cultures that had preceded them. Like the Adena and the Hopewell, they used gigantic mounds to bury their dead; but they also built mounds for other purposes, such as for temples where they would worship. The rich soil along the riverbanks made farming easy, and the Mississippians became expert growers of the "Three Sisters"—corn, beans, and squash. As the Mississippians flourished, their population grew, and by A.D. 1100 **Cahokia** (kuh HOH kee uh), in what is now Illinois, was the largest town in North America, with perhaps as many as twenty thousand inhabitants.

The Mississippians' greater wealth meant these people had time to focus on more than just survival, so they created art. Carvings and pottery found in burial mounds show detailed work, frequently with patterns of birds and serpents. By about 1300, this culture had begun to decline; at the same time, more modern Native American cultures were beginning to develop.

Cultures of the Southwest

While the mound-building cultures were developing in the eastern part of North America, other cultures were developing in the Southwest. The **Hohokam** (hoh hoh KAM) lived from 100 B.C. to A.D. 1400 in what is now southern Arizona. They probably had moved here from **Mesoamerica** (Mexico and Central America), and they created a culture that bore many similarities to the cultures of the Inca (see Chapter 2) and the Maya. Like those people, the Hohokam lived in a hot, <u>arid</u> climate and had to develop tools and systems that would ensure their survival.

The Hohokam were not nomadic; therefore, they had to find a way to grow crops successfully in a difficult climate. Their solution was a complex series of canals for <u>irrigation</u>. Some canals, which brought water from a river to their fields, were as long as ten miles. The Hohokam planted corn, beans, and squash together because each plant, they realized, helped the others to grow and survive. Cotton was another regular crop.

Efficient farming techniques gave the Hohokam time for amusement. Archaeological sites in the Tucson Basin show remains of an ancient ball court made of stone with rings at either end. This ruin is not unlike our modern-day basketball courts.

The Hohokam also developed advanced art techniques and were among the first cultures in North America to create etched art. <u>Artisans</u> carved images and designs into smooth shells (acquired from trade with groups on the California coast). Then the Hohokam soaked the shells in the acidic juice of the saguaro cactus, which deepened the carving and left the image raised.

By about A.D. 700, the **Anasazi** (an uh SAH zee) began to flourish nearby in today's Four Corners region, where Utah, New Mexico, Arizona, and Colorado meet. The Anasazi created apartment-building-style <u>dwellings</u>, built into the sides of steep cliffs. The outer walls of the dwellings were **adobe**—bricks of mud and water baked dry in the sun.

Anasazi dwellings

The Anasazi's well-designed homes served them very well. The adobe bricks provided excellent <u>insulation</u> from the scorching desert heat. And the location against the cliffs protected the Anasazi from enemy raiders. Instead of entrances on the ground floor with interior stairs to upper floors, outside ladders provided access to the second and third floors. During attacks, people drew the ladders inside their homes to keep out unwanted visitors. These impressive dwellings also contained underground rooms called **kivas** (KEE vahz), where the men performed sacred <u>spiritual</u> ceremonies.

Anasazi culture flourished for hundreds of years, but the circumstances of its decline remain a mystery. By 1300, few traces of the people or culture remained.

The Vikings

North America was not entirely isolated from Europe during this period. Though most people think Christopher Columbus "discovered" the "New World" in 1492, the **Vikings** had been exploring the open seas centuries before. The Vikings were superb sailors and fierce soldiers who journeyed from their homes in northern Europe in search of new lands and riches. Around A.D. 1000, **Leif Eriksson** led an expedition from Greenland to North America. Artifacts at Baffin Island, Labrador, and Newfoundland support the theory that Vikings landed—and perhaps settled—in at least three different places.

NATIVE AMERICAN CULTURES FROM 1300 TO 1500

This period is known as the golden period of Native American cultures. At this time, just before Europeans arrived in North America, the native population was about 10 million.

Tribes of people developed their own solutions to the challenges of shelter, food, worship, art, and music. Contrary to the stereotype that all Native Americans rode horses, wore feathered head-dresses, hunted buffalo, and lived in tipis, tribes in each region developed distinctive cultural styles closely tied to the land on which they lived. Here are a few examples.

The Southwest

During this time, the **Pueblo** and **Hopi** (HOH pee) tribes of the Southwest, possibly descendants of the Hohokam and Anasazi people, lived in apartment-like dwellings that were made of adobe and built into the sides of steep cliffs. They, too, employed special farming techniques to combat the dry climate and focused primarily on the successful trio of corn, beans, and squash.

The Hopi had a system of religious beliefs that centered around **kachinas** (kuh CHEE nuhz), or spirits, that represented various elements in nature. For six months of every year, the Hopi believed, the kachinas lived in the distant, snowcapped mountains; for the other six months, according to the Hopi, the spirits lived with the people in the villages.

While tribes such as the Hopi and the Pueblo carried on the apartment-dwelling traditions, other southwestern tribes developed a more isolated way of life. For example, the **Navajo** (NAH vuh hoh) became sheep farmers, using the animals for meat as well as wool. Sprinkled far apart on the land, their eight-sided homes, called **hogans** (HOH gahnz), left plenty of room for the herds to graze. The Navajo also became excellent weavers

and created rugs of detailed patterns and vivid colors.

Farther West

To the west, in what is now California, tribes developed a culture well suited to their mild climate. For these people, the comfortable temperature and abundant supply of food from ocean and forest led to a relatively easy way of life. Tribes like the **Chumash** (SHOO mash) in southern California built simple shelters, called **aps,** out of rushes and reeds, while the **Miwok** (MEE wok) of northern California built bark homes called **umachas.** Most tribes hunted and fished, and they ground acorns into fine flour for flatbreads and soups.

Many tribes also had **sweathouses,** or structures where fires were built to create intense heat for the people inside. After sitting in the sweathouse for a long period of time, people would run outside and jump into the ocean or a nearby river. The sweathouses not only served to keep village inhabitants clean but also were part of a sacred ritual that was central to the spiritual life of the people.

The Plains

The Native Americans of the plains region faced their own set of challenges. The climate and land of the plains—currently, the central part of the United States—made life hard for the inhabitants. It could be extremely hot and humid during the summer and windy and freezing during the winter. The wide, grassy plains lacked trees for shelter and vegetation for food, and the land was not well suited for crops or farming.

As a result, plains tribes such as the **Cheyenne** (sheye AN) were nomads, traveling to hunt their primary source of food and shelter—the buffalo. During this period, millions of buffalo roamed the plains, as opposed to the few thousand alive today. It is a well-known part of Native American tradition that every part of the buffalo was used: the meat for food; the hide for shelter and clothing; the bones for tools, toys, and needles; even the brains, which yielded a substance for tanning the buffalo hides.

The home of the plains tribes was called a **tipi.** A tipi is a cone-shaped shelter consisting of a semicircle of sewn buffalo hides wrapped around a supporting structure of long wooden poles. Families who traveled together set up their tipis by a riverbank during the winter or in a ring on the plains during the summer; all of the entrances faced east to greet the morning sun.

Plains tribes first traveled on foot and used dogs to transport most of their goods in heavy bundles. (In later years—during the 1500s, which are described in Chapter 2—the plains tribes' lives changed with the arrival of the "sacred dog," the horse. The horses that these tribes discovered were the wild descendants of horses ridden by the Spaniards, who had brought them to the Americas. The plains tribes—the **Blackfoot** tribe in particular—soon became excellent riders of horses, and their success in hunting buffalo increased dramatically.)

Northwest Coast

The tribes of the northwest coast were among the most prosperous of all the Native American groups. The sea gave them an unlimited supply of food, to which they added vegetation from the surrounding forests. For transportation, they built long, heavy canoes that could carry up to forty men on long trading journeys.

Tribes such as the **Chinook** (shuh NUK) and the **Makah** (muh KAH) lived in solid wooden plank homes, which were arranged in rows, with the chief's home in the center. Northwest coast tribes were extremely concerned with social structure, and each village was firmly divided into the social classes of slave, commoner, and noble. The wealthiest members of the village might occasionally hold a **potlatch,** an extravagant party of hearty meals and entertainment. The host of a potlatch would prove his wealth and power by giving a valuable gift to each guest.

Northwest coast tribes made tall and intricately carved **totem poles.** While totem poles served many different purposes, they often told a family's history, honoring important people and events.

Eastern Woodlands

Like the cultures on the opposite coast, the people of the eastern woodlands region—along the Atlantic Coast, and as far north and west as Minnesota and Michigan—had many natural resources available to them. Big game like deer and bear roamed the forests, oceans were rich with fish, and the forests provided trees and plants that could be eaten.

Tribes such as the **Mohawk** and the **Seneca** lived in villages; farmed corn, beans, and squash; and added meat or fish to their diets. During the winters, these natives lived in bark-covered shelters called **wigwams.** During the summers, they lived in vast, wooden lodges called **longhouses,** each of which could fit as many as nine families inside. Eastern woodlands societies were **matriarchal;** that is, women selected the leaders, and people lived in the longhouses of their female relatives.

The eastern woodlands tribes were among the first to meet the Europeans who came to America in the late 1400s and beyond (see Chapters 2 and 3). Members of these tribes showed the new settlers how to farm the land and manage their crops successfully.

It is possible that the eastern woodlands tribes also provided the European settlers with a model of how to compromise politically. Five New York–area tribes—the Mohawk, the Seneca, the **Oneida** (oh NEYE duh), the **Onondaga** (ah nuhn DAW guh), and the **Cayuga** (kay YOO guh)—had been at war for many years; finally in the late 1500s, two leaders, named **Hiawatha** and **Deganawida,** brought the tribes together as the **Iroquois** (ihr ruh KWOI) **League.** Then women in each of the five tribes selected ten men to serve on a **Great Council,** which helped to resolve conflicts and set goals for the group.

! Implications

> To answer the question, "Why does all this matter?" or "What does it mean?," share the following insights with your child.

This chapter has dealt with many prehistoric people—people who did not know how to write, so they could not leave written stories and records for their descendants. Therefore, it is not surprising that scientists are not sure *when* people arrived and *where* they came from. Some sentences in the preceding pages use expressions such as "Recent findings . . . *suggest*" and "Some scientists *think*. . . ."

Amid all the incomplete and sometimes conflicting evidence lies an important lesson: in the study of history—and, especially, prehistory—we must always be open to discovering or hearing about new information. Maybe a newly found skeleton or a new technology can give us additional information about a skeleton or artifact found decades ago. The new information, in turn, makes us reexamine what we think we know and, sometimes, forces us to come up with new theories. For example, at one time, we thought the first inhabitants came to North America only nine thousand years ago and all came from one place; now we hear that the first inhabitants may have arrived much earlier and probably came from various parts of the world.

Another important lesson from this chapter is seeing how cultures are alike and how they are different. The chapter mentions, for example, that the early mound builders influenced the later ones; the same is true about the early and the later cliff-dwelling settlers. But the chapter teaches also that people in one area often develop a different lifestyle from the people in another area.

Think about the following question. Since 1492—the end date of this chapter—have people in one part of this country become more alike or more different from people in another part of this country? Read on to find out.

 # Fact Checker

To check that your child knows or can find the basic facts in this chapter, here is a map for children to fill in. Have them write the name of each tribe from the following list in the correct region of the map. Encourage them to fill in the map further with names of other tribes.

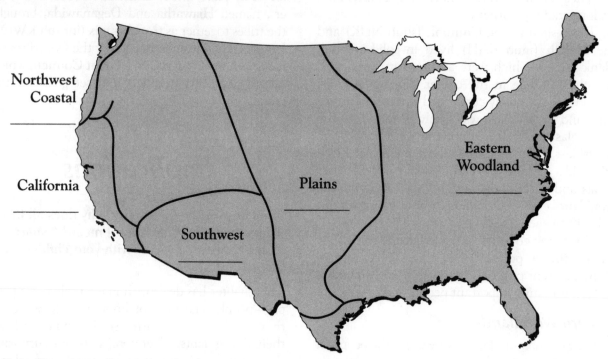

Tribal regions before European arrival

Tribes

Pueblo   Chumash   Cheyenne   Makah   Mohawk

Answers appear in the back, preceding the index.

? The Big Questions

The following questions encourage your child to think critically rather than simply recall facts. If necessary, review the specific information from the preceding pages that will help your child make the necessary inferences to come up with reasonable answers.

1. Explain whether you agree or disagree with the following statement—and tell why: "The United States is a country of immigrants."
2. How do we know anything about the people who lived here hundreds and thousands of years ago?
3. According to this chapter, what did ancient people probably think about first: (a) food, (b) art, or (c) sports and games? Why?

Suggested Answers

1. *At first, the statement may sound false. Usually, we think only of recent arrivals as immigrants to the United States. But this chapter suggests that human life did not begin here; people always immigrated here. All of us—even those of us who can trace back our families' presence here for hundreds of years—are current immigrants or descendants of immigrants.*
2. *This chapter talks repeatedly about finding ancient sites with weapons, jewelry, pottery, and buildings. Scientists and historians examine these finds to figure out when ancient people lived and what their lives were like.*
3. *According to this chapter, food seems to have been the most important thing to ancient people. Only after they had found, hunted, or grown enough food did they have time left over to make art and engage in games.*

Skills Practice

The following activities give your child practice in applying the skills basic to social studies. For some of the activities, your child may need to review the information in the preceding pages.

A. COMPARING AND CONTRASTING CULTURES

The following information and questions will give your child an opportunity to see similarities and differences between his or her life and the lives of Native American children who lived a thousand years ago.

Anasazi children went through an initiation rite. An **initiation rite** is a ceremony that welcomes young people as full adult members of a group. An uncle on the mother's side of an Anasazi family took a boy on his first visit to the community kiva (previously described). There the adult began to teach the boy myths and songs so that one day he could pass this information on to his own nephews.

Now think about how *your* family passes on traditions and how its methods are like and unlike the Anasazi's. Family traditions may be moral (for example, helping older people), religious (for example, reading from a sacred book), or otherwise cultural (for example, learning how to prepare an ethnic food). Answer the following questions, comparing and contrasting your family to Anasazi families.

1. In your family, who teaches the child the tradition?
2. At what age does a child in your family begin to learn the tradition?
3. Is the tradition linked to a ceremony or place, as the Anasazi one was linked to the kiva?
4. What does your family think will become of the tradition in the future?

Evaluating Your Child's Skills: In order to complete this activity successfully, your child must answer the questions about your

family and also mention how your family's practice resembles or differs from the Anasazi experience. If your child has trouble with comparison/contrast, copy the following chart (without the answers) and help him or her to fill in the boxes.

	Anasazi Family	*My Family*
teacher	uncle	
age when lessons begin	about 12	
place of ceremony	kiva	

B. READING BAR GRAPHS

An important skill for learning social studies (as well as most other subjects) is interpreting visuals—for example, graphs such as the one that follows.

In talking about the early people who lived here, the chapter mentions many times that they farmed corn, beans, and squash. All these hundreds—even thousands—of years later, those three crops are *still* a part of many diets in the United States. Here are the results from three families who were asked, "On how many days in July and August did you eat fresh corn, beans, and squash?" Examine the bar graph carefully, and answer the three questions about it.

Questions

1. Which family most frequently ate corn? Beans? Squash?
2. Which family came closest to eating all three foods the same number of times in July and August?
3. A person looking at the graph said, "Boy! The Chins must love squash!" Do you agree or disagree with that conclusion? Why?

Answers

1. *Corn: The Ortiz family ate the most.*
   Beans: The Strauss family ate the most.
   Squash: The Chin family ate the most.
2. *The Strauss family came closest.*
3. *The person's conclusion may be right because the Chins ate squash on forty-five days. Maybe, though, the children hate squash but had to eat it because the parents grew a bumper crop and they could not waste food.*

Evaluating Your Child's Skills: **In order to answer the first two questions correctly,**

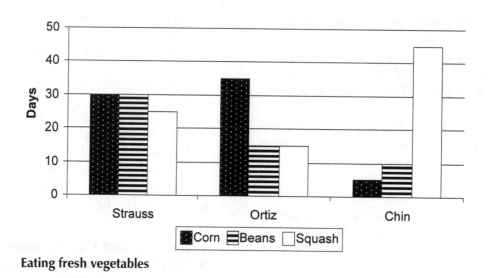

Eating fresh vegetables

your child needs to understand what each bar stands for. If necessary, tell him or her, "The first bar means that the Strauss family ate corn on thirty days." Then ask the child to tell you what the other bars mean. To answer the third question fully, the child has to realize that numbers can be misleading and that there's danger in coming to conclusions without all the facts. The activity calls for important reasoning skills.

 # *Top of the Class*

Children interested in delving more deeply into the topics covered in this chapter can choose one or both of the following activities. They may do the activities for their own satisfaction or report on what they have done to show that they have been seriously considering very early America.

A POINT TO PONDER: BONES

Suggest to your child that he or she raise the following issue in class.

All Americans face difficult questions regarding the ancient past of this land. When archaeologists in the United States find bones of a person who lived and died here hundreds or thousands of years ago, to whom should they give the bones? Should the bones go to scientists and historians who may learn more about our past by examining and testing the bones, or should they go to a Native American group for reburial and religious ceremonies?

BOOKS TO READ AND RECOMMEND IN CLASS

Suggest that your child read either the fiction or the nonfiction book from the following list and respond to it by giving an oral or written critique in class.

Bruchac, Joseph. *Children of the Longhouse.* New York: Dial Books, 1996. The novel features eleven-year-old boy-and-girl twins who live in a Mohawk village before contact with Europeans. The *Booklist* review says: "Bruchac explains the roles of men and women, teaching practices, family relationships, and customs. . . . Although the information overshadows the story at times, middle readers interested in traditional practices will find this clear and easy to understand."

Dewey, Jennifer Owings. *Stories on Stone.* Boston: Little, Brown, 1996. This nonfiction book deals with ancient rock art. *Booklist* says, "What could be a dry and difficult subject is made enjoyable in a brief, readable text surrounded by Dewey's soft monochromatic illustrations. . . . [The book] will provide background knowledge for families who are planning to visit the Southwest."

CHAPTER 2
The Age of Exploration
1492–1609

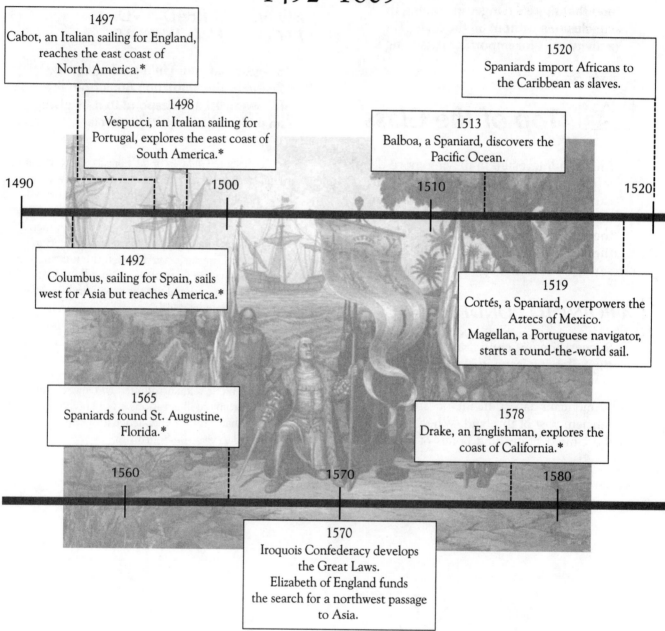

1497
Cabot, an Italian sailing for England, reaches the east coast of North America.*

1498
Vespucci, an Italian sailing for Portugal, explores the east coast of South America.*

1520
Spaniards import Africans to the Caribbean as slaves.

1513
Balboa, a Spaniard, discovers the Pacific Ocean.

1490   1500   1510   1520

1492
Columbus, sailing for Spain, sails west for Asia but reaches America.*

1519
Cortés, a Spaniard, overpowers the Aztecs of Mexico.
Magellan, a Portuguese navigator, starts a round-the-world sail.

1565
Spaniards found St. Augustine, Florida.*

1578
Drake, an Englishman, explores the coast of California.*

1560   1570   1580

1570
Iroquois Confederacy develops the Great Laws.
Elizabeth of England funds the search for a northwest passage to Asia.

*This name was not used at the time of exploration.

This timeline provides an overview of the period called the Age of Exploration. On the next page, a map illustrates important expeditions. Then a narrative describes the Age of Exploration in greater detail and discusses its significance.

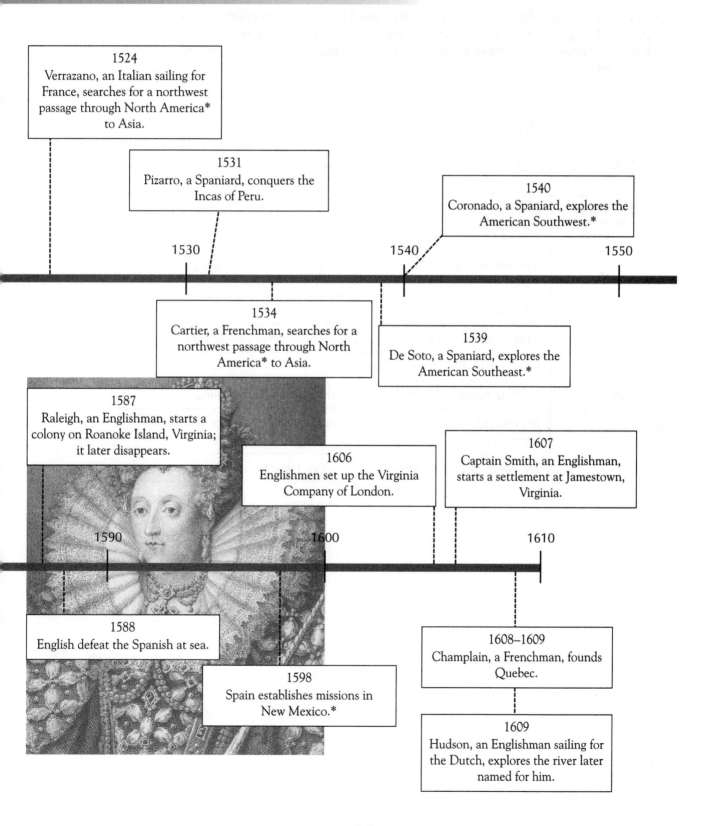

1524
Verrazano, an Italian sailing for France, searches for a northwest passage through North America* to Asia.

1531
Pizarro, a Spaniard, conquers the Incas of Peru.

1540
Coronado, a Spaniard, explores the American Southwest.*

1530

1540

1550

1534
Cartier, a Frenchman, searches for a northwest passage through North America* to Asia.

1539
De Soto, a Spaniard, explores the American Southeast.*

1587
Raleigh, an Englishman, starts a colony on Roanoke Island, Virginia; it later disappears.

1606
Englishmen set up the Virginia Company of London.

1607
Captain Smith, an Englishman, starts a settlement at Jamestown, Virginia.

1590

1600

1610

1588
English defeat the Spanish at sea.

1598
Spain establishes missions in New Mexico.*

1608–1609
Champlain, a Frenchman, founds Quebec.

1609
Hudson, an Englishman sailing for the Dutch, explores the river later named for him.

Word Power

The words on the following chart are underscored in the section called "What Your Child Needs to Know." Explain their meanings to your child as needed when they come up in reading or discussion. Keep this list handy for you and your child to use.

Word	Definition
astrolabe	instrument once used to determine position of a ship in relation to the sun or stars
circumnavigating	going completely around
colony	area of land that has been settled by people from another place
compass	instrument used for determining the directions north, east, south, and west
founded	established a town, city, or other settlement
jade	a mineral, usually green, valued as an ornamental stone for carvings
navigator	person who directs a ship's course
porcelain	ceramic material like that used for dishes; also called *china*
quadrant	instrument similar to the astrolabe; once used by astronomers and navigators
strait	narrow passage of water connecting two large bodies of water

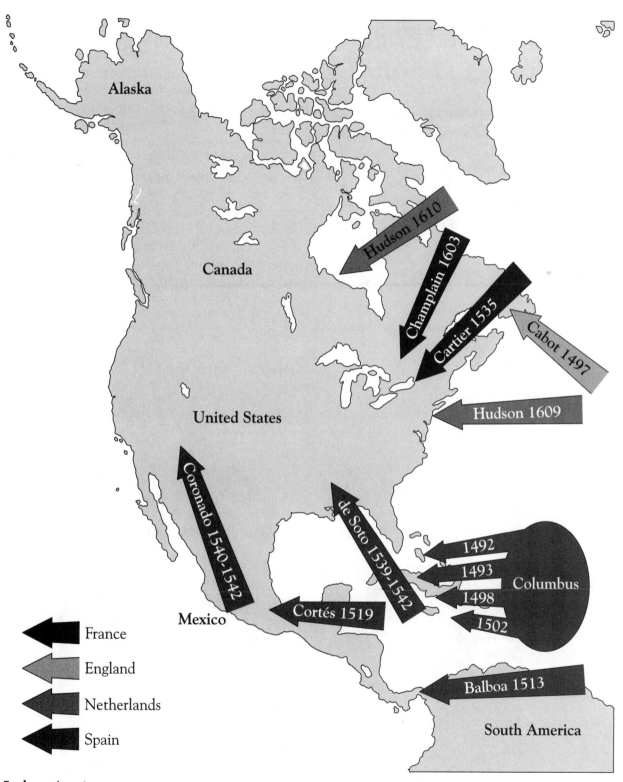

Alaska

Canada

United States

Mexico

South America

Hudson 1610

Champlain 1603

Cartier 1535

Cabot 1497

Hudson 1609

Coronado 1540-1542

de Soto 1539-1542

Cortés 1519

1492
1493
1498
1502

Columbus

Balboa 1513

France

England

Netherlands

Spain

Explorers' routes

What Your Child Needs to Know

You may choose to use the following text in several different ways, depending on your child's strengths and preferences. You might read the passage aloud; you might read it to yourself and then paraphrase it for your child; or you might ask your child to read the material along with you or on his or her own.

DISCOVERY AND EXPLORATION BEGIN

Everyone learns that in 1492 **Christopher Columbus** "discovered" America. What do we mean when we say *discovered*? The Americas, of course, were already home to many millions of native people. Therefore, when we say *discovered*, we do not mean that these lands were completely unknown or uninhabited before Columbus's voyage. Rather, we mean that Europeans did not previously know of these lands.

What we call the Age of Exploration lasted a little more than one hundred years, from the time Christopher Columbus discovered the New World in 1492 to the time when Henry Hudson sailed up what we now call the Hudson River in 1609. But it was the Venetian **Marco Polo** who really started it all back in 1298, when his book, *Description of the World*, became the most widely read book in Europe. In his book, Polo told of his overland travels to China, where he had served the Mongol ruler **Kublai Khan** (koo blah KAHN) for close to twenty years. For the Khan, Polo had traveled farther, made notes of what he saw, and returned with the information. When he later came back to Venice, he brought with him ivory, <u>jade</u>, jewels, <u>porcelain</u>, silk, spices, and other treasures.

CHRISTOPHER COLUMBUS

As a result of Polo's book and increased trade between Italy and Asia, Italians a couple hundred years later were becoming rich from importing and

Nineteenth-century illustration of Columbus taking possession of the new country

selling spices, silk, jade, gold, and jewels. But over-land travel to Asia was difficult and very expensive. Merchants began to wish for an easier and cheaper way to get there and back.

In the 1490s, the great Italian <u>navigator</u> Christopher Columbus reasoned that, since the world was round (a fact widely accepted by educated people of the time), one could reach Asia by traveling west over water rather than east over land.

Recent advances in shipping included a new kind of ship called the **caravel,** which, unlike ships used up until then, could sail against the wind. As a result, Columbus figured that a long westward voyage would be possible. In addition, improvements in navigational tools—such as the <u>compass</u>, <u>astrolabe</u>, and <u>quadrant</u>—made it possible to navigate and sail safely outside the sight of land.

Columbus, of course, had the right idea. The only mistake he made was believing that Japan was much closer to the west coast of Spain than it really is and that there was nothing in between the continents of Europe and Asia. So when **Queen Isabella** and **King Ferdinand** of Spain agreed to pay for his voyage, Columbus traveled west over the Atlantic Ocean and reached islands that are part of what we now call the West Indies; he believed he had arrived in the Spice Islands (now called the Moluccas) in the East Indies of Asia. This mistake by Columbus is why he called the people there "Indians."

Columbus returned safely from his first voyage and made a second a year later. Columbus's voyages began an age of exploration and discovery that had far-reaching effects on the history of the United States and the world.

AFTER COLUMBUS

In 1497, **John Cabot** (an Italian named Giovanni Caboto) sailed for King Henry VII of England and also attempted to reach Asia by sailing west, but he chose a more northern route than Columbus's. Instead of Asia, Cabot reached either the island of Newfoundland or Cape Breton Island, now a part of Nova Scotia. Although he did not find the riches he had hoped for, Cabot believed, as had Columbus, that he had reached Asia.

In 1499, **Amerigo Vespucci** (uh MAIR ruh *goh ve SPOO chee*), an Italian sailing for the Portuguese, reached and explored the coast of South America. Unlike earlier explorers, Vespucci realized that the land he had reached was a vast continent, unknown as yet to anyone in Europe. "This land is a whole new world," he said. In 1507, a German geographer and mapmaker named the land *America* for Amerigo.

Vasco Núñez de Balboa (vaz KOH NOO nyez duh boul BOH uh), a Spanish explorer, leading an expedition to Central America, arrived at what is now Panama in 1513. From there, he saw the east shore of the Pacific Ocean and realized that to reach Asia a traveler from Spain would have to cross a second ocean.

In 1519, the Portuguese navigator **Ferdinand Magellan** (muh JEL len) searched for a <u>strait</u> connecting the Atlantic and Pacific oceans. Such a strait would provide a water route through America to Asia. He found what he was looking for at the southern tip of South America. This body of water—the Strait of Magellan—now bears his name. Magellan died in 1521, but one of his five ships succeeded not only in reaching Asia but in <u>circumnavigating</u> the globe and returning to Spain three years after it had left.

Magellan had found a long southwest passage to Asia. But many people still thought that a shorter northwest passage might exist. Looking for such a passage, **Giovanni da Verrazano** (joh VAH nee dah *vair* ruh ZAH noh) explored the east coast of North America in 1524 but did not get far. Ten years later, the Frenchman **Jacques Cartier** (zhahk KAR tee ay) also failed to find a northwest passage but explored the St. Lawrence River to what is now **Montreal.**

Others who joined in the search for the northwest passage were the Englishman **Henry Hudson** and the Frenchman **Samuel de Champlain** (duh sham PLAYN). Neither found the passage. However, Hudson, sailing for the **Dutch East India Company,** explored the Hudson River Valley and the area that came to be New York City. (*Dutch* is the adjective for the country known both as Holland and the Netherlands.) As a result of Hudson's trip, the Dutch set up trading posts on Manhattan Island, which they called **New Amsterdam,** and along the Hudson River. Champlain discovered the Great Lakes and founded the city of **Quebec** on the St. Lawrence River. He set up trading posts to exchange European goods for fur, but because Champlain attacked the Iroquois, those Indians became longtime enemies of the French.

CONTROLLING THE NEW WORLD

Many explorers saw the New World merely as an obstacle to reaching Asia. But to others, America was a worthwhile goal in itself. For example, the Spaniard **Juan Ponce de León** (WAN POHN say day le OHN) was, according to legend, searching for the Fountain of Youth, when he landed in **Puerto Rico** and in **Florida.** He claimed them both for Spain.

Legends of the Seven Cities of Cíbola (SEE boh lah), cities supposedly built of gold, and of El Dorado, a fabulously rich Indian king, spurred further exploration. **Hernando Cortés** (ur NAN doh kor TEZ), who had taken part in the Spanish conquest of **Cuba,** led an expedition from Cuba to **Mexico** to seek gold, claim land, and develop trade with the **Aztec Indians.** Cortés and his troops destroyed the Aztecs' city of **Tenochtitlán** (tay nawch teet LAHN), kidnapped and killed the emperor **Moctezuma** (mok tuh ZOO muh), and took control of all central Mexico.

Later, in 1531, **Francisco Pizarro** (puh ZAR roh) conquered **Cuzco,** the **Inca** capital of what is now Peru. Pizarro opened the way for Spanish settlers to immigrate to Peru to mine gold and silver. Another Spaniard, **Francisco Vásquez de Coronado** (vaz KWEZ day *kor* ruh NAH doh), led an expedition in search of cities reported by explorers and Indians to be rich in gold. Setting out from Mexico, early in 1540, he explored the American Southwest and crossed the Rocky Mountains. From 1539 to 1542, **Hernando de Soto** (ur NAN doh duh SOH toh) explored the American Southeast up to the Mississippi River. By the 1540s, Spain had claimed land from what is now Kansas to the tip of South America.

In 1570, **Queen Elizabeth** of England, worried about Spanish power in America, funded an expedition by **Martin Frobisher** (FROH bee shur), who explored the Atlantic coast of Canada. In 1577,

she sent **Francis Drake** on a sea voyage to loot Spanish ships and colonies along the Pacific coast of South America. Drake sailed through the Strait of Magellan and north along the Pacific coast of South America; he continued to what is now San Francisco Bay. Fearing an attack by the Spaniards if he sailed south again, Drake sailed home by way of the Pacific and Indian oceans, and became the first Englishman to circumnavigate the globe. He was later knighted, and in 1588, when Drake led England in defeating the Spanish navy, or **Armada,** he cleared the way for English colonization in the New World.

In 1585, another favorite of Queen Elizabeth's, **Walter Raleigh** (RAW lee), began sending expeditions to America and spent a fortune trying to establish an English colony there. His settlers landed in what is now North Carolina and explored the coast as far as present-day Florida. Raleigh named the entire region **Virginia** and established a settlement in **Roanoke** (ROH uh nohk) in 1587. This settlement mysteriously disappeared; its settlers,

Queen Elizabeth I

now referred to as the Lost Colony, left only the word CROATAN carved on a tree.

In 1606, a group of Englishmen created the **Virginia Company of London,** and **King James** granted the company the right to start up a colony in Virginia. The colonists received tools, weapons, medicines, and seeds—for which they would repay the company in gold and crops. A year later, the Virginia Company sent **Captain John Smith** to establish a settlement at **Jamestown.**

! Implications

To answer the question, "Why does all this matter?" or "What does it mean?," share the following insights with your child.

The Europeans who discovered that there was, indeed, a "New World" in the Atlantic Ocean between Europe and Asia changed the course of history. After all, it is that New World that eventually became the United States and all the other countries of North America and South America.

But the voyages of those early explorers also caused immediate changes in the lives of all people in both the old world and the new. Europeans benefited from these changes, but the Native American populations suffered greatly. When Columbus returned home from his voyages, he brought back and introduced to Europeans corn, potatoes, tomatoes, chili peppers, pumpkins, beans, peanuts, tobacco, pineapples, and turkeys. Later, European countries acquired new lands to settle. From the Europeans, native people contracted diseases—smallpox, measles, typhus, and influenza—that had not previously existed among them. These diseases wiped out millions of natives in the course of the next two hundred years.

In addition, European settlers cleared forests in order to build villages and plant crops. These forests had been the homes of many wild animals that the Native Americans hunted and depended on for food. Colonists who came to settle the New World brought with them and introduced to the Native Americans horses, cattle, and sheep, as well as seeds and cuttings for growing wheat, onions, and other European crops. But these gains did not make up for the losses in lives, land, and animals.

Perhaps the most significant tragedy of this period was the spread of slavery. While slavery existed in other parts of the world before Europeans populated the New World, it became more widespread. In the Caribbean, Europeans treated the native people as slaves. When many of the natives died of diseases or conflicts, the Europeans replaced laborers by forcibly bringing people from Africa. The evil of slavery would become even more widespread on the North American continent.

✔ Fact Checker

To check that your child knows or can find the basic facts in this chapter, here is a puzzle using proper nouns discussed in the preceding pages.

EXPLORERS PUZZLE

Fill in the boxes using the following clues. Each answer is a name from this chapter.

Across

4. Englishman who established a colony that disappeared
5. Spanish explorer who crossed the Rocky Mountains
6. Spaniard who conquered the Incas
8. Englishman who established the colony Jamestown
10. Name of the "Lost Colony"
11. Venetian who explored China for Kublai Khan
12. French explorer who founded the city of Quebec

Down

1. Italian explorer for whom America was named
2. First European to see the Pacific Ocean
3. English queen who financed voyages of exploration
5. Spaniard who conquered the Aztecs
7. English pirate who defeated the Spanish Armada
9. First explorer to circumnavigate the globe

Answers appear in the back, preceding the index.

The Big Questions

The following questions encourage your child to think critically rather than simply recall facts. If necessary, review the specific information from the preceding pages that will help your child make the necessary inferences to come up with reasonable answers.

1. What were the two main reasons Europeans explored lands across the Atlantic Ocean?
2. How did science and technology make it possible to explore far-off places?
3. What do you think were the best effects of European exploration of the Americas?
4. What do you think were the worst effects?

Suggested Answers

1. *They wanted a better way of trading with Asia; they wanted to establish power and colonies in the New World.*
2. *Developing a new kind of ship and navigating tools allowed explorers to cross the Atlantic Ocean.*
3. *Europeans established New World settlements that eventually led to the development of the United States of America; Europeans learned about new plants and animals.*
4. *Native Americans contracted diseases that killed many of them; European settlers cleared land that had been hunting grounds; slavery became more widespread.*

Skills Practice

The following activities give your child practice in applying the skills basic to social studies. For some of the activities, your child may need to review the information in the preceding pages.

A. LEARNING FROM PRIMARY SOURCES

Either read to your child or ask your child to read the passage on page 24 about October 12 and October 13, 1492. Christopher Columbus wrote the passage in the ship's log. The American poet William Carlos Williams translated it into English. Ask your child to read or listen carefully so that he or she can figure out from this passage what Columbus thought of the people he met.

Question

What do you think Columbus thought about the people he found where he landed? What do you think the native people may have thought of Columbus?

Possible Answers

• *Columbus went ashore in an armed boat. He may have thought that he would need protection from the people he saw on land.*
• *Then Columbus gave the people cheap gifts. He may not have respected the people very much.*
• *Columbus describes the young men's bodies. It seems that he thought the young men looked healthy.*
• *Columbus describes the canoes. It seems that he admired them.*
• *The natives seemed friendly toward Columbus. They brought gifts. They didn't seem to have weapons with them.*

Evaluating Your Child's Skills: In order to answer the preceding question successfully, your child will need to go beyond specific information to make inferences. If your child has trouble with this skill,

On Friday, the twelfth of October, we anchored before the land and made ready to go on shore. Presently we saw naked people on the beach. I went ashore in the armed boat. . . . And we saw the trees very green, and much water and fruits of diverse kinds. Presently many of the inhabitants assembled. I gave to some red caps and glass beads to put round their necks, and many other things of little value. They came to the ships' boats afterward, where we were, swimming and bringing us parrots, cotton threads in skeins, darts—what they had, with good will. . . .

On Saturday, as dawn broke, many of these people came to the beach, all youths [young men]. Their legs are very straight, all in one line and no belly. They came to the ship in canoes, made out of the trunk of a tree, all in one piece, and wonderfully worked, propelled with a paddle like a baker's shovel, and go at a marvelous speed.

demonstrate for him or her how you would arrive at one of the answers.

Talk through your own thought process. For example, you might point to the third sentence in the passage and say, "I see here that Columbus went ashore in an armed boat. Why did he mention that the boat was armed? He must have thought that there was a possibility that the native people would be hostile."

B. SUPPORTING GENERALIZATIONS WITH SPECIFICS

Ask your child to define *generalization* and *specifics*. Then give your child the following generalizations that can be made from the map. Have him or her support each generalization with specifics from the map.

1. Many European countries explored the New World.
2. More explorations of the New World took place after 1500 than before.
3. Spain and England sent out the most expeditions.

Answers

1. *England, France, the Netherlands, and Spain all explored the New World.*

2. *Only four explorations took place before 1500, but nine explorations took place after 1500.*
3. *According to the map, Spain sent out eight expeditions, and England sent out two expeditions. The other countries sponsored fewer expeditions.*

Evaluating Your Child's Skills: In order to complete this activity successfully, your child will need to select appropriate facts to support each generalization. If he or she has trouble, reword your instructions as a question as follows: "What specific pieces of information from the filled-in map will prove the truth of each general statement?"

C. READING A TIMELINE

With your child, look at the title of the timeline and at the horizontal section from 1490 to 1530 of the timeline on the opening pages of Chapter 2. Ask your child the following questions, and help him or her with the answers as necessary.

1. What do the horizontal line and each vertical marker and numbers stand for?
2. Reading the horizontal line from left to right, do the years go forward or backward?
3. How many years are there between two consecutive short, vertical lines?

4. How many years does the whole horizontal line represent?

5. Which two explorations took place between 1495 and 1500? According to this timeline, which explorations occurred from 1500 to 1510?

Answers

1. *The horizontal line stands for the period from the year 1490 to the year 1530. Each number with its vertical line stands for a year, or date.*
2. *The years go forward. They advance chronologically from earlier dates to later dates.*
3. *Ten years*
4. *40 years*
5. *Between 1495 and 1500, Cabot explored the east coast of North America, and Vespucci explored the east coast of South America. According to this timeline, no explorations took place between 1500 and 1510.*

Evaluating Your Child's Skills: In order to complete this activity successfully, your child will need to interpret a graphic representation by focusing on a variety of details and then extracting information. If your child needs help with any of the answers, isolate for him or her the part of the timeline to focus on.

 # Top of the Class

Following are a variety of activities children can do on their own or share in class to show that they have been seriously considering the topic of European exploration of the New World.

A POINT TO PONDER OR RAISE IN CLASS

Suggest to your child that he or she raise the following issue in class.

Why was it Europeans and not Asians who set off to explore the New World? Why didn't people from the east coast of Asia set out east across the Pacific Ocean to reach the coast of what is now California?

BOOKS TO READ AND RECOMMEND IN CLASS

Suggest that your child read one of the following books and respond to it by giving an oral or written critique in class.

Aronson, Marc. *Sir Walter Raleigh and the Quest for El Dorado.* Clarion, 2000.

Columbus, Christopher. *The Log of Christopher Columbus' First Voyage to America in the year 1492 as Copied Out in Brief by Bartholomew Las Casas.* Little, Brown, 1989.

Greene, Carol. *Marco Polo: Voyager to the Orient.* Childrens Press, 1987.

Humble, Richard. *The Voyage of Magellan.* Watts, 1989.

Osborne, Mary Pope. *The Story of Christopher Columbus, Admiral of the Ocean Sea.* Dell, 1987.

WEB SITES TO EXPLORE

By typing in the name of any explorer, your child can use a search engine to find a wealth of Web sites that provide in-depth information.

One of the many Web sites for Henry Hudson, www.georgian.net/rally/hudson, provides extensive biographical information, historical context, pictures, timelines, letters, and more.

QUICK RESEARCH

With your child, use an encyclopedia, the Internet, or a library to find out more about one or more of the following topics.

Find at least two more facts about any of the following items.

| caravel | quadrant | Roanoke |
| astrolabe | compass | |

CHAPTER 3

Early Settlement and the Thirteen English Colonies
1607–1732

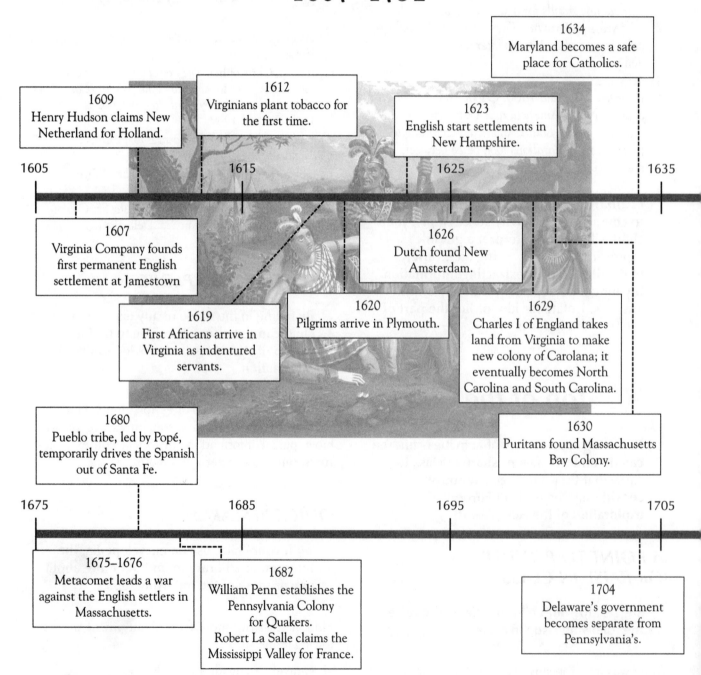

1634
Maryland becomes a safe place for Catholics.

1609
Henry Hudson claims New Netherland for Holland.

1612
Virginians plant tobacco for the first time.

1623
English start settlements in New Hampshire.

1605   1615   1625   1635

1607
Virginia Company founds first permanent English settlement at Jamestown

1626
Dutch found New Amsterdam.

1619
First Africans arrive in Virginia as indentured servants.

1620
Pilgrims arrive in Plymouth.

1629
Charles I of England takes land from Virginia to make new colony of Carolana; it eventually becomes North Carolina and South Carolina.

1680
Pueblo tribe, led by Popé, temporarily drives the Spanish out of Santa Fe.

1630
Puritans found Massachusetts Bay Colony.

1675   1685   1695   1705

1675–1676
Metacomet leads a war against the English settlers in Massachusetts.

1682
William Penn establishes the Pennsylvania Colony for Quakers.
Robert La Salle claims the Mississippi Valley for France.

1704
Delaware's government becomes separate from Pennsylvania's.

This timeline provides an overview of the period during which the thirteen colonies took shape. In the next pages, a narrative describes the development of each colony and discusses the significant events of the period.

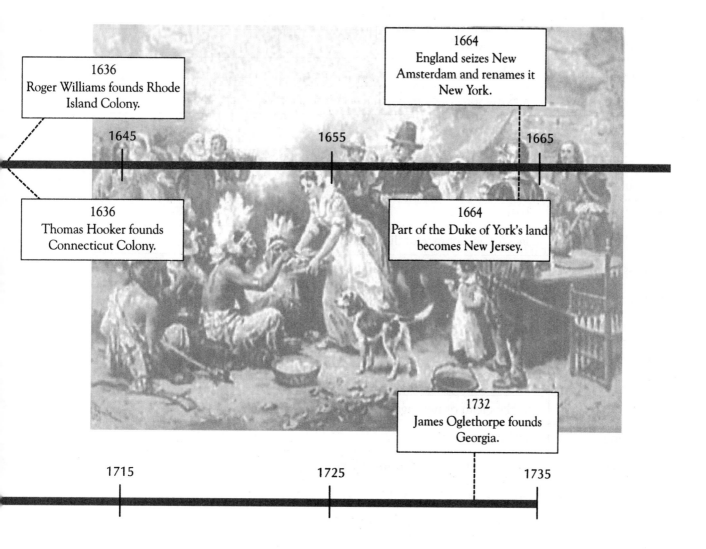

1636
Roger Williams founds Rhode Island Colony.

1664
England seizes New Amsterdam and renames it New York.

1645

1655

1665

1636
Thomas Hooker founds Connecticut Colony.

1664
Part of the Duke of York's land becomes New Jersey.

1732
James Oglethorpe founds Georgia.

1715

1725

1735

Word Power

The words on the following chart are underscored in the section called "What Your Child Needs to Know." Explain their meanings to your child as needed when they come up in reading or discussion. Keep this list handy for you and your child to use.

Word	*Definition*
banished	sent away and forbidden to return
brutal	cruel and violent
consequences	results
converting	making someone change his or her religion or other beliefs
dissenter	someone who disagrees
emigrate	leave one's home country and move to a new country
ensured	made certain that something would happen
fundamental	basic
intolerance	lack of acceptance of different opinions or lifestyles
massacres	brutal killings of a large number of people
merged	joined together to form something new
peers	people who are equal
peninsula	piece of land surrounded by water on three sides
persecuted	punished unfairly
purify	make clean or new again
rotating	switching around
sacrifice	act of giving up important things
savages	wild people without culture or manners
tolerated	accepted opinions and lifestyles of others

What Your Child Needs to Know

European explorers returned home from the "New World" to tell of a vast territory ready for settlement and mining. Of course, Native Americans who had been living there for centuries had already settled much of the land. But Native American culture was so different from "old world" culture that most Europeans dismissed the Native Americans as <u>savages</u> with no human rights. Europeans arrived in North America ready to claim this rich new land for themselves; they had little regard for the people who were already there.

THE JAMESTOWN COLONY, 1607

In the early 1600s, some English businessmen believed that North America contained rich gold mines. They wanted to send colonists to find the mines, but none of the men was rich enough to support an expedition on his own. Their solution was to combine their money in an outfit called the Virginia Company of London, which then received from King James a charter that allowed them to establish a colony. In December 1606, a boat left London for Virginia carrying 105 male colonists.

They arrived in April of 1607 and founded the colony of Jamestown, which they named for their king. They thought the <u>peninsula</u> they had selected for the colony was an excellent site that would be easy to defend. However, the land was swampy, making farming difficult. It was too hot in the summer and too cold in the winter. And the area was full of mosquitoes carrying the often deadly disease malaria.

The colonists contributed to the difficulties themselves. Many of them were gentlemen who had been attracted to the colony by the promise of gold. They were not used to hard work, and they were untrained in other essential skills such as farming and hunting. Instead of building homes and tending crops, most of the first colonists spent their days looking for gold. By the fall of 1607, half of the colonists had died, and the colony was in deep trouble.

John Smith and Pocahontas

Rescue came in the form of colonist Captain John Smith. Taking charge, he forced the others to raise crops and tend livestock. His rough ways made him unpopular, but his efforts <u>ensured</u> their survival.

Smith also made a name for himself another way. The Jamestown colony was on land that belonged to a collection of Native American tribes called the **Powhatan** (*poh* huh TAHN). Their leader **Wahunsonacock** (wah hun SUN uh *kok*) was also called Powhatan, and he controlled a vast area of land. The Powhatan were concerned about the Europeans settling on their land, but they did want to trade for European goods such as blankets and tools, so they <u>tolerated</u> the new arrivals for a while. But when John Smith refused to trade the Powhatan guns, they captured him.

Popular legend says that the Powhatan laid Smith's head on a rock and prepared to kill him, but before they did, Pocahontas (*poh* kuh HAHN tus), Chief Powhatan's favorite daughter, laid her head on Smith's and saved his life. Historians think this story was an exaggeration by Smith. Whatever the true story was, Smith became an honorary member of Powhatan's family.

Still the Jamestown colonists' struggles were not over. After Smith left for England in 1609 because of an injury, the Powhatan prevented colonists from leaving or entering the settlement. The colonists soon ran out of food and were unable to go to the forest to hunt. That winter became known as the **Starving Time.** Although the European population of Jamestown had increased to five hundred before the Starving Time, a new boatload of settlers arriving in the spring of 1610 found only sixty still alive.

Nineteenth-century illustration of Pocahontas saving the life of Captain John Smith

John Rolfe's Tobacco Crop

At last, in 1614, a settler named John Rolfe developed a new kind of tobacco leaf that became popular in England. Tobacco was a valuable crop that the colonists could sell at a profit and keep their colony going. In the same year, John Rolfe married Pocahontas, and their marriage led to a few years of peace with the Powhatan. Pocahontas eventually traveled with Rolfe to England, where she died of the disease smallpox a few years later.

Self-Government in Jamestown

For the first ten years or so of Jamestown, the Virginia Company kept control of the colonists. Then in 1619 the Virginia Company set up a government in Jamestown modeled on the English **Parliament,** the body that made laws and advised the king. The new body in Virginia was called the **House of Burgesses.** It consisted of elected white male representatives who voted on important matters. Many people other than these white males did not have the right to vote for the representatives, but setting up the House of Burgesses was at least a first step toward giving the colonies some power to govern themselves.

New Faces in Jamestown

The year 1619 brought two other firsts to Jamestown. One was the first boatload of European women, brought over as wives for the colonists. Husbands paid for their wives' voyages in tobacco. The first boatload of Africans also arrived that year. Unlike the Africans that would follow them, these people arrived as **indentured servants.** A colonist paid for each indentured servant's voyage; in return, the indentured servant had to work for that colonist for four to seven years before receiving his or her freedom. The Africans on that first ship eventually got their freedom and became members of the community. The ones who followed were not so fortunate.

THE PILGRIMS IN MASSACHUSETTS, 1620

At this time in England, some people were dissatisfied with the Church of England, and they wanted to "purify" it. These people were called **Puritans,** and many of them were persecuted for their beliefs.

Some Puritans, called **Separatists,** felt that they had to leave—or separate from—England so that they could worship freely. At first, a group of Separatists went to Holland. But parents began to worry that their children were not maintaining the English ways, so they decided to <u>emigrate</u> to Virginia, where other English people had settled.

In 1620, a boat called the *Mayflower* carried just over a hundred passengers across the ocean. Half of them were Separatists, who referred to the other half of the group as Strangers. All of them were Pilgrims, travelers on a long journey toward better lives. After a miserable, stormy, sixty-six-day voyage, the Pilgrims realized they had been blown off course and found themselves in Cape Cod Bay. They came to shore at today's Provincetown, Massachusetts, moved on, and founded the colony of **Plimouth** (now spelled *Plymouth*).

Before getting off the boat, the Pilgrims signed an agreement called the **Mayflower Compact.** During the journey, the Strangers and the Separatists had had trouble getting along. Therefore, they created the Mayflower Compact, a document that established an elected government to help the Pilgrims settle differences and govern themselves.

Help from the Wampanoag

Like the Jamestown colony, the Plymouth colony had a rocky start. Because of cold, hunger, and disease, fewer than half the settlers survived the first winter. This period, again, was called the Starving Time.

Luckily for the Pilgrims, among the Wampanoag (*wahm* puh NOH ag) people who lived in about thirty communities around Plymouth were three men who helped the newcomers prepare for the next autumn and winter. The chief **Massasoit** (mah suh SOIT) and the Pilgrims' governor **John Carver** signed a treaty that kept the peace for more than fifty years. The two other Wampanoags were **Samoset** (SAH muh *set*) and **Squanto** (SKWAHN toh), who spoke English and showed the Pilgrims how to farm and where to hunt. (They had learned English from Englishmen who had earlier sailed and traded in the Wampanoag region but had not settled. Squanto had even been to England.)

By the fall of 1621, the Pilgrims had a successful harvest. They invited their Wampanoag friends to the first **Thanksgiving** feast, which, according to new governor **William Bradford,** lasted for three days.

Puritan Life in the Massachusetts Bay Colony

The Pilgrims' success encouraged the Englishman **John Winthrop** to lead another, much larger, group of Puritans to Massachusetts to form the Massachusetts Bay Colony in 1630. As in Plymouth, Puritan life there included much work and <u>sacrifice</u>. According to Puritan beliefs, people were supposed to work hard and live by a series of strict rules. After six days of working from sunrise to sunset, Puritan families spent Sundays in church, where they prayed and listened to sermons that often lasted for hours. People who did not live by the community's rules were punished.

The Puritans' strict rules and hard work contributed to the colony's success. When settlers discovered that the rocky, thin soil would not provide much more food than what they needed to survive, they devoted themselves to other ways of earning a living in order to help the colony. Some hunted and traded furs, while others started shipbuilding businesses. Those who wanted to fish or trade turned to the sea for their living.

Puritans often built their settlements around a **common,** a grassy central area where animals could graze. Near the common stood a church and a meeting hall. The hall was the site of regular town meetings, where the men gathered to vote on community issues.

Close by stood a school. An important part of Puritan religious belief was that people should read the Bible on their own. So these early settlers passed laws requiring each settlement to hire a teacher. This decision was another first for the colonies: free public education.

NEW ENGLAND COLONIES, 1623 TO 1636

Soon people from Plymouth and the Massachusetts Bay Colony moved farther afield, and John Smith of Virginia fame began to call this region *New England.* (Plymouth and the Massachusetts Bay Colony eventually <u>merged</u> to form one colony.) While some people left in order to claim more land, many left because of religious and political differences with leaders in the original Puritan settlements. The leaders, who had taken people

First Thanksgiving, **by Jean Louis Gerome Ferris, 1863–1930, photo 1920**

out of England because of religious <u>intolerance</u> there, were now themselves not tolerant of anyone who disagreed with their beliefs and traditions.

Rhode Island

Roger Williams was a Puritan minister who disagreed with the Puritan leaders in Massachusetts because they lacked tolerance for others' religious beliefs. In 1636, Williams spoke out against this intolerance; Puritan leaders brought him to trial and <u>banished</u> him. Rather than allowing himself to be shipped back to England, Williams escaped south.

Here, in what would become Rhode Island, the **Narragansett** (*nar* uh GAN set) tribe sheltered him during the cold winter. Then he bought land from them so that he could found his own settlement called *Providence*. Williams's respect for the Narragansett ensured a lasting peace between the tribe and the new colonists. In addition to promising all settlers freedom of worship, Williams's colony also set up an elected government.

Another <u>dissenter</u> named **Anne Hutchinson** soon arrived in Rhode Island, where she started a settlement known as Portsmouth (PORT smith). She, too, had been banished from Massachusetts for disagreeing with some of the Puritans' beliefs and for daring to speak her mind. Her behavior horrified some people; after all, women during this period did not share the rights of men and, in fact, were considered the property of their fathers or husbands.

Connecticut and New Hampshire

Soon, King James gave two friends gifts of land: one parcel became the colony of New Hampshire, and the other was the area we call *Maine* today. (Maine was never one of the original colonies; it was part of Massachusetts until it became a state in 1820.)

In 1636, a Puritan minister named **Thomas Hooker** led followers south to a new colony called Connecticut. While they, too, disagreed with some of the Puritan beliefs, their primary reason for leaving Massachusetts was that it was getting crowded, and they wanted more land.

King Philip's War, 1675 to 1676

Colonists such as Hooker thought that they were heading to vast areas of land free for the taking, but the Native Americans who lived there became angry that settlers were eating up their land. As fences appeared and livestock overtook formerly unspoiled wilderness, these natives saw their way of life disappearing.

When Massasoit, the chief of the Wampanoag, died, his son **Metacomet** took over. In an effort to bring the two cultures closer together, Massasoit had also given his son a European name, Philip.

Metacomet did not want to keep the peace that his father had established. He wanted to preserve his people's lands. So in 1675, he launched a two-year war of raids and brutal massacres. Eventually, Metacomet was captured and killed, and the colonists "won" the war. It was the last time that the New England tribes tried to defend their lands.

THE MIDDLE COLONIES, 1626 TO 1682

The colonies that grew up along the middle section of the Atlantic Coast were New York, New Jersey, Pennsylvania, and Delaware.

New York and New Jersey

The explorer Henry Hudson sailed for the Dutch West India Company. He was looking for a northwest passage through America to Asia when in 1609 he sailed up what is now called the Hudson River. He stopped at an island inhabited by the **Mannahatta** (*man* nuh HAT tuh) tribe, claimed it and the surrounding territory for the Netherlands, and named the area **New Netherland.**

Hudson did not pay for the land he claimed, but in 1624 Dutch settlers, led by **Peter Minuit** (MIN yoo wit), purchased the island from the Mannahatta for $24. According to the historian Kenneth C. Davis, the purchase price was "two boxes of trade goods—probably hatchets, cloth, metal pots, and bright beads—worth sixty Dutch guilders. At the time, that equaled 2,400 English cents, which has come down in history as the famous twenty-four-dollar figure."

In 1626, the Dutch founded the city of **New Amsterdam** on the island of Manhattan. In the 1640s, **Peter Stuyvesant** (STEYE vuh sunt) became its governor. He was a harsh man who was unpopular with the colonists. He was so disliked, in fact, that in 1664, when the **Duke of York** arrived to claim the city and its surroundings for England,

the colonists surrendered without the English having to fire a single shot. The duke renamed the colony after himself.

That same year the duke gave a parcel of his new property to two friends, **George Carteret** (car tuh RET) and **John Berkeley;** this land became the colony of New Jersey. Both New York and New Jersey were royal colonies that had governors appointed by the king or other royals; in addition, they had elected governments that made important decisions.

Pennsylvania and Delaware

In 1682, an Englishman named **William Penn** founded Pennsylvania. Penn was a member of the Society of Friends, called **Quakers,** a religious group that the English persecuted. William Penn wished to create a colony where all people could worship freely and where all people could take part in the elected government, regardless of their religion.

Penn showed great respect toward the **Lenni Lenape** (*le* nee LE nuh pee) tribe that had been living on the land already. Legend says that as he set up his colony, he made a peaceful agreement with their leader to buy no more land than he could walk in three days. Pennsylvania's capital city, **Philadelphia,** was a well-planned city, and soon it became the largest city in all of the colonies.

European claims on Delaware were more complicated than on Pennsylvania. Delaware went from Dutch to English ownership several times (with a brief period of control by Sweden). Then for more than twenty years Penn considered Delaware a part of Pennsylvania. Only after 1704 did Delaware become a separate colony.

Life in the Middle Colonies

Life in the middle colonies was quite different from life in New England. The climate was milder and the soil richer than in New England; as a result, it was easier to grow crops for profit. Because of the region's abundant crops of wheat, oats, and rye, it became known as the breadbasket of the colonies.

The middle colonies also became a center for manufacturing. Colonists opened factories that produced glass, leatherworks, ironworks, and shoes. New York and Philadelphia, major port cities, became bustling centers of trade.

Perhaps the biggest difference between New England and the middle colonies lay in the population. While New England was peopled primarily with Puritans, the middle colonies hosted a mix of different ethnic backgrounds and religions. Jews came from Portugal, a large Scots-Irish population settled in this region, and many religious groups from Germany came to Pennsylvania. Because the Germans' language was called *Deutsch*, these people came to be known as the Pennsylvania Dutch. Africans, many of whom were slaves, also entered the region.

THE SOUTHERN COLONIES, 1634 TO 1732

The successful colonization of Virginia set the stage for other colonies in the South. Like Virginia, most of the southern colonies came to rely on tobacco as their primary source of income.

Tobacco posed particular problems for owners of large farms, or **plantations.** After a few years of growing tobacco in the same places, the soil lost its nutrients and needed to rest before it was healthy enough to support crops again. This situation meant that farmers needed additional land for rotating crops. Tobacco farming also required a great deal of cheap, hands-on labor. Plantation owners soon discovered that the most profitable way to farm tobacco was to use slave labor.

Not Just the South

While slavery occurred mostly in the South, it also played a role in northern and middle colonies. Merchants from Boston and New York were often part of one or more **triangles of trade,** which tied them into the business of slavery. A merchant might sail from Boston or New York to West Africa, where he would trade rum, iron, and guns for gold, ivory, and slaves. He would take the new cargo to the West Indies or to the southern colonies, where he would trade for supplies needed back in New England or in the middle colonies.

The colonies of the South did not share the rigid life of the New England Puritans or the more worldly feel of the Middle Atlantic colonies. Most

Southern plantation owners enjoyed an easygoing pace of life. Future leaders such as Thomas Jefferson, George Washington, and Patrick Henry lived in the South during this period and carried on a lively exchange of ideas with their peers.

Maryland, the Carolinas, and Georgia

After Virginia, Maryland was the next southern colony to be founded, in 1634. **Lord George Calvert** established the colony as a safe place for Catholics, who were enduring persecution back in England. In 1629, the English king **Charles I** took land from Virginia to create a new colony named after himself—Carolana. Later, the name changed to Carolina, and eventually the area became two colonies, North and South Carolina. Both colonies consisted mostly of plantations and small farms; their major crops were rice and **indigo,** a plant that makes blue dye.

Finally, in 1732, Georgia became the last colony. **James Oglethorpe** founded Georgia as an alternative to **debtor's prison.** During this period, people who could not pay their bills were sent to jail until they could find the money for their creditors.

Oglethorpe's idea was to have the debtors work off their debts in the new colony. His idea was not successful, but soon people of many different religious and cultural backgrounds settled the area.

Georgia also served an important political purpose. As the southernmost colony, it formed a buffer zone between the English colonies and the Spanish colonies to the south.

By 1732, there were thirteen English colonies in North America. All of them had some form of elected self-government.

SPANISH SETTLEMENTS

While the English were busy colonizing the east coast of North America, the Spanish were conquering the Southwest. (As mentioned in Chapter 2, back in 1513, the Spaniard Ponce de León had claimed Florida for Spain.) Like the English, the Spanish were interested in using their colonies to make money, but they also took the land with the idea of <u>converting</u> the local people to Christianity.

During the 1670s, the Spanish set up settlements in New Mexico, near Santa Fe. As they took control of the area, they forbade the local Pueblo tribe to worship in their own way and demanded that they follow Christian traditions. In 1680, a Pueblo leader named **Popé** led a rebellion that drove the Spanish out of New Mexico for twelve years. However, the Spanish eventually created many successful settlements and **missions,** or churches, throughout the Southwest and along the California coast.

FRENCH SETTLEMENTS

The French were also busy making their own inroads in North America in the 1600s. With the founding of Quebec in 1608, the French had established the region of **New France,** which would soon stretch from Quebec in the north to **New Orleans** in the south.

Attempts to create lasting settlements became difficult in the northern part of New France because of ongoing conflicts with the Iroquois. But east of the Mississippi River, French settlers put up forts and trading posts to sell the **pelts,** or animal skins, that many of them hunted and trapped. French explorers roamed throughout the Midwest, visited the Great Lakes, and traveled down the Mississippi and St. Lawrence rivers. In the late 1600s, **Robert La Salle** (lah SAL) claimed the Mississippi valley for **King Louis XIV** of France; he named the land **Louisiana.**

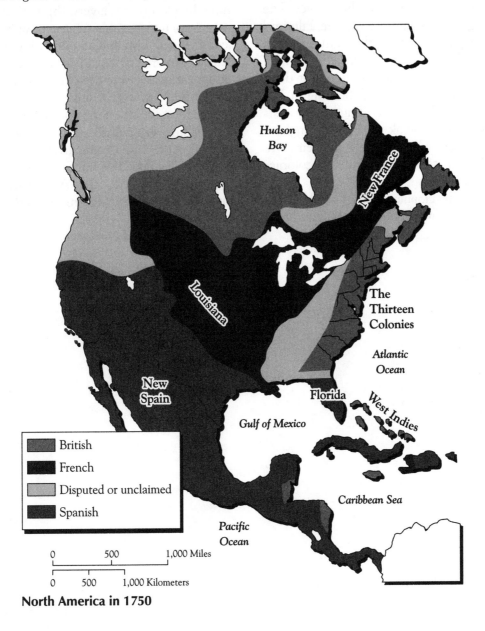

North America in 1750

! Implications

For lovers of American history, the founding of the thirteen colonies is truly the start of it all. Among everything that happened in the English colonies between 1607 and 1732, four developments set the stage for what the colonies would become.

First, and maybe foremost, the English colonists learned that they could look after themselves. The House of Burgesses in Jamestown, the Pilgrims' Mayflower Compact, and even the Puritans' town meetings were all instances in which ordinary men chose their leaders and voted on important decisions—but still under the eye of the king in England. In the years ahead, some English colonists would feel they should break totally with England and live in the New World entirely on their own. Their practice in self-government as colonies would help them greatly.

The second development that would have major consequences was the Puritans' decision to provide education for all children—a brand-new idea. When masses of ordinary people know how to read and write, they can communicate with more people, complain about their government more effectively, and make changes.

Third, freedom of religion was also a big new idea for people used to the English system of government. When Roger Williams and William Penn founded their colonies by inviting people of all faiths, they were establishing a fundamental idea for the future United States of America.

Fourth, the rise of slavery in the South during this period was a development that would cause great pain for the future country for a very long time. In addition to slavery, this period saw the beginning of unforgivable treatment of Native Americans. As colonists spread out and took more land, Native Americans began to see their way of life disappearing. Despite their best attempts to defend their land, they were losing.

In the next chapters, you will see how all the seeds that were planted during this period—self-government, public education, freedom of religion, and unequal treatment of people based on race—grew into the American Revolution and American life in the nineteenth century and beyond.

Fact Checker

COLONIAL PUZZLE

(1) For each numbered item fill in the missing word, one letter to a blank. (2) Copy each numbered letter in your answers onto the corresponding numbered blank at the bottom of the puzzle. You will spell out the name of a period Jamestown colonists went through from 1609 to 1610 and Plymouth colonists experienced from 1620 to 1621.

1. The name of the first permanent English colony in America was __ __ __ __ __ __ __ __ __.
                                                                                    11

2. The Native American who is said to have saved Captain John Smith's life was __ __ __ __ __ __ __ __ __ __.
                                                                                    9

3. The Pilgrims who arrived in Massachusetts in 1620 had hoped to land in __ __ __ __ __ __ __ __.
                                                                                 5

4. The name of the ship that the Pilgrims came over on was the __ __ __ __ __ __ __ __ __.
                                                                    3   12

5. The name of the second permanent English colony in America was originally spelled __ __ __ __ __ __ __ __.
                                                                                        6   2

6. The Native Americans who lived where the Pilgrims landed were the __ __ __ __ __ __ __ __ __.
                                                                                       7   8

7. The name of one of the Native Americans who helped the Pilgrims was __ __ __ __ __ __ __.
                                                                          1

8. The settlers who started Massachusetts Bay Colony practiced the __ __ __ __ __ __ __ religion.
                                                                      4 10

Period from 1609 to 1610 and 1620 to 1621:

__ __ __ __ __ __ __ __ __ __ __ __
1 2 3 4 5 6 7 8   9 10 11 12

Answers appear in the back, preceding the index.

 # The Big Questions

1. What were the main reasons Europeans came to America in the 1600s?
2. In some cases, the relationships between the Europeans and the Native Americans in the

original thirteen colonies started out friendly. Why did the relationships turn sour so often?

3. King James I of England in the early 1600s described tobacco as a "stinking weed." He went on to say that tobacco was "hateful to the nose, harmful to the brain, and dangerous to the lungs." Tell what you know about the American tobacco business as it developed in the United States in the four hundred years since James made his comment.

Suggested Answers

1. *In the East, Europeans came in the 1600s to make money and to live somewhere with religious freedom. In the West, Europeans came with an additional goal—to convert the Native Americans to Christianity.*

2. *The relationship between colonists and Native Americans started out friendly because neither group threatened the other group. As the number of Europeans increased and as they took over more and more land, the natives felt their own lifestyle was in danger.*

3. *Tobacco has become a major industry in which many tens of thousands of people work. Some work in the growing fields, some in advertising agencies, and some in many other sites. Tobacco has taken on symbolism; it has brought its user sophistication or ridicule, depending on the historical period. Legal suits have criticized the tobacco industry for creating serious and expensive health problems.*

Skills Practice

The following activities give your child practice in applying the skills basic to social studies. For some of the activities, your child may need to review the information in the preceding pages.

A. THE EARLY COLONISTS AS PROBLEM SOLVERS

The following activity will focus your child's attention on the resourcefulness of the early colonists. After your child has completed the chart, you might point out that one problem colonists did not solve was their displacing of Native Americans.

The Europeans who wanted to start colonies and those who settled in the colonies faced difficulties all along the way. For each problem listed on the chart, tell what solution these people came up with.

Problem	*Solution*
1. None of the businessmen inEngland who wanted to start a colony in America had enough money to cover the costs.	
2. The Puritans who had moved from England to Holland were unhappy there.	

Problem	Solution
3. The Separatists and the Strangers did not get along well on the long voyage from England, yet they were going to have to live together in America.	
4. The soil in Massachusetts was not rich enough to allow all the colonists to become farmers.	
5. Roger Williams was banished from Massachusetts but didn't want to go back to England.	
6. The colonists who lived in New Amsterdam disliked their Dutch leader, Peter Stuyvesant.	
7. By planting tobacco on the same land every year, the colonists in the South were ruining the soil.	

Answers

1. *The men joined to form the Virginia Company, each one of them putting money into the company. The company, rather than any one man, received a charter from the king to set up a colony. Later, they would all share the profit made by the company.*
2. *These people needed to move to a place where they could practice their religion and a place where people also practiced English customs. They thought America might be such a place and organized themselves to go there.*
3. *The Separatists and the Strangers knew that everyone needed to have a voice in decision making. They agreed to elect the people who would be in charge. The agreement was called the Mayflower Compact.*
4. *They needed to figure out other ways to make a living. Either by doing a job like one they did earlier in England or by trying something new, they came up with other sources of income.*
5. *Williams had to get away and find another place to settle where he would welcome people of all beliefs. He escaped south, bought land from the Native Americans, and set up a new colony.*
6. *The Dutch colonists welcomed the English, who would take control away from Stuyvesant.*
7. *The planters needed to give their soil a rest, so they would have to find additional land to plant on.*

> **Evaluating Your Child's Skills:**   In order to complete this activity successfully, your child must think about each problem, identify a positive goal for the person or group who had the problem, and figure out how to achieve that goal. If your child has trouble thinking about abstract historic characters, suggest that he or she put himself in the shoes of these characters. What would *your child* do if he or she personally faced these problems?

B.   DOING RESEARCH: PLACE NAMES

> An important social studies skill is learning where to look to find answers. This activity gives your child a chance to use a few sources of information.

39

Select three of the following places in the United States, and find out how each got its name: (1) Connecticut, (2) Delaware, (3) Georgia, (4) the Hudson River in New York, (5) Maryland, (6) Massachusetts, (7) Plymouth in Massachusetts.

You may find the answers in one or more of the following printed or electronic books: a regular dictionary, a dictionary of geographical terms, an encyclopedia, a history or geography textbook.

Answers

1. *Connecticut: name from Algonquian word meaning "place of the long river"*
2. *Delaware: named after Baron De La Warr, the first English colonial governor of Virginia*
3. *Georgia: named after George II, king of England from 1727 to 1760*
4. *Hudson River: named after the explorer Henry Hudson*
5. *Maryland: named after Queen Henrietta Maria, wife of Charles I, king of England from 1625 to 1649*

6. *Massachusetts: name from the Algonquian words meaning "at the big hill," referring to the Blue Hills near Boston*
7. *Plymouth: named for the seaport in southwest England, from which the Mayflower had departed*

Evaluating Your Child's Skills: In order to complete this activity successfully, your child may have to check more than one source. Some, but not all, popular dictionaries and encyclopedias give information about origins of place names. If your child has trouble finding answers, model the role persistence plays in doing research.

C. LEARNING FROM A PRIMARY SOURCE

Read your child the following passages that William Bradford (1590–1657) wrote about the Pilgrims' experience with Indians. Ask how Bradford's opinion changed and why.

Before Bradford got to know an Indian:
"All this while the Indians came skulking about them, and . . . when any Indian approached near the Pilgrims the Indians would run away; and once they stole away the Pilgrims' tools where they had been at work and were gone to dinner."

After Bradford knew Squanto for a while:
". . . Squanto continued with the Pilgrims and was their interpreter and was a special instrument sent of God for their good beyond their expectation. He directed them how to set their corn, where to take fish, and to procure other commodities, and was also their pilot to bring them to unknown places for their profit, and never left them till he died."

Evaluating Your Child's Skills: In order to complete this activity successfully, your child must be able, first, to detect the distrust that Bradford expresses by describing the Indians as "skulking" (or stealthy or slinking) and, second, to see how grateful Bradford later was for Squanto's help. Getting to know one particular Indian dispelled the negative stereotypes Bradford first had.

 Top of the Class

Children interested in delving more deeply into the topics covered in this chapter can choose one or more of the following activities. They may do the activities for their own satisfaction or report on what they have done to show that they have been seriously considering colonial America.

A POINT TO PONDER: CONFLICTING STORIES

If your child has seen the Disney movie about Pocahontas or has read a version of the story in another source, help him or her uncover the debate about the "true" story.

What have you read or watched about Pocahontas and Captain John Smith? Follow these steps:

1. On the Internet or in your library, find a newspaper or magazine review of the Disney movie from the 1990s. What did the reviewer say about the movie version of what happened between Pocahontas and Smith?
2. What does the Powhatan Web site www.powhatan.org/pocc.html say happened?
3. Look in a recently published encyclopedia to get an objective report about Pocahontas and Smith.
4. Summarize what you've learned in your research.

WRITING A CHILDREN'S STORY

Here's an opportunity for your child to share what he or she has learned with a younger child.

Write a story about the Pilgrims from the time they set out in the *Mayflower* until they celebrated the first Thanksgiving. Write the story so that children who are in kindergarten can understand it.

DISCUSSING VOTING RIGHTS

Discussing the following text with your child will help him or her understand how much has changed in American elections since the early days of Jamestown.

Beginning in 1619, this chapter explains, elected white male representatives voted on matters of importance to the colonists in Jamestown. But none of the following people could vote: men without property, slaves, servants, single women, wives, Catholics, free blacks, Indians, criminals, and the insane. How have voting rights changed over time? Find out who can vote today in a local, state, or national election in the United States.

CHAPTER 4
The Fight for Independence
1732–1783

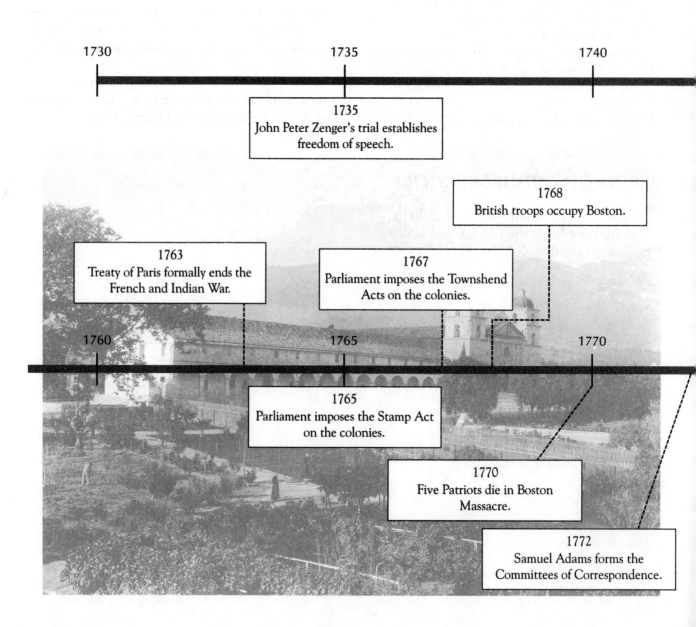

1730   1735   1740

1735
John Peter Zenger's trial establishes freedom of speech.

1768
British troops occupy Boston.

1763
Treaty of Paris formally ends the French and Indian War.

1767
Parliament imposes the Townshend Acts on the colonies.

1760   1765   1770

1765
Parliament imposes the Stamp Act on the colonies.

1770
Five Patriots die in Boston Massacre.

1772
Samuel Adams forms the Committees of Correspondence.

This timeline provides an overview of the events that occurred during the fight for independence in the United States. In the following pages, a narrative describes the causes of the Revolution and the important events of the Revolutionary War.

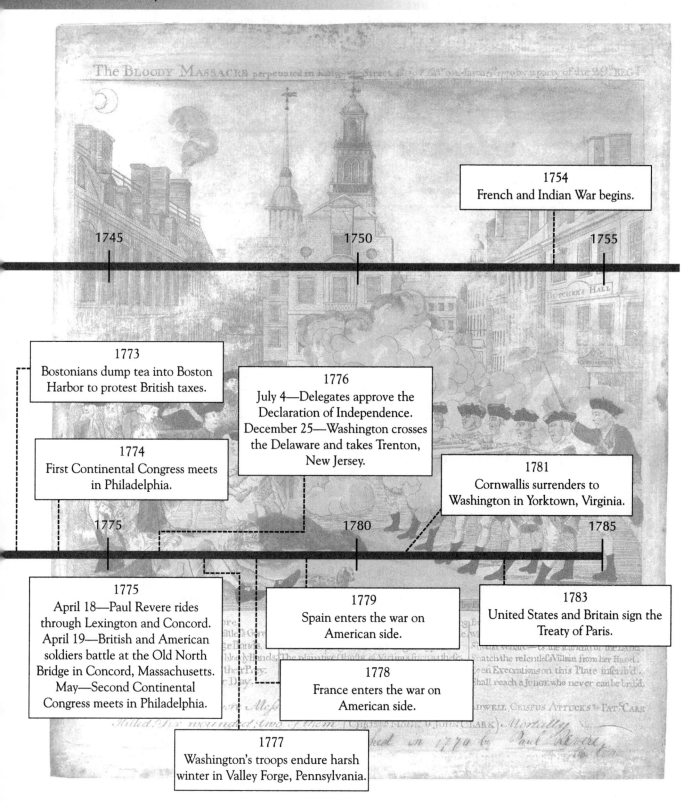

1754
French and Indian War begins.

1745   1750   1755

1773
Bostonians dump tea into Boston Harbor to protest British taxes.

1776
July 4—Delegates approve the Declaration of Independence.
December 25—Washington crosses the Delaware and takes Trenton, New Jersey.

1774
First Continental Congress meets in Philadelphia.

1781
Cornwallis surrenders to Washington in Yorktown, Virginia.

1775   1780   1785

1775
April 18—Paul Revere rides through Lexington and Concord.
April 19—British and American soldiers battle at the Old North Bridge in Concord, Massachusetts.
May—Second Continental Congress meets in Philadelphia.

1779
Spain enters the war on American side.

1783
United States and Britain sign the Treaty of Paris.

1778
France enters the war on American side.

1777
Washington's troops endure harsh winter in Valley Forge, Pennsylvania.

Word Power

Word	Definition
acquitted	declared innocent
allies	people on the same side in a conflict
boycotted	refused to buy something as a way of making a protest
corrupt	bad; dishonest
delegates	representatives
engraving	picture produced by cutting a design into metal
fertile	good for growing things
fortified	made stronger against attack
humiliating	making a person or a group of people look foolish
mercenaries	soldiers who fight for money
proclamation	statement or law
reinforcements	new, fresh soldiers
repealed	undone
silversmith	person who makes things out of silver
skirmish	small battle or fight
surveyor	one who measures an area in order to make a map or plan
tax	in addition to the price of an item, money that must be paid to a government
traitor	someone who aids the enemy of his or her country
troops	armed forces; soldiers
villain	scoundrel; criminal

What Your Child Needs to Know

You may choose to use the following text in several different ways, depending on your child's strengths and preferences. You might read the passage aloud; you might read it to yourself and then paraphrase it for your child; or you might ask your child to read the material along with you or on his or her own.

By 1732, North America was, for Europeans, no longer the unknown territory it had been only 150 years before. France, Spain, and England all claimed territory on the continent, and each of these countries wanted to find and keep the riches of the New World for itself.

Spain had been active in the Southwest since the early 1500s, establishing missions to convert the local tribes to Christianity. In 1769, a Spanish missionary named **Father Junípero Serra** (hoo NEE puh roh SAIR ruh) started missions along the California coast. Spain also claimed Florida and founded the town of St. Augustine there in 1565.

In the north, France had claimed Quebec, the Great Lakes region, and the land near the St. Lawrence River. Then in 1673, **Jacques Marquette** (zhahk mar KET) and **Louis Jolliet** (loo WEE zhahl YAY) set out to find the Northwest Passage through North America to Asia but ended up exploring the Mississippi River. Inspired by Marquette and Jolliet, Robert La Salle continued south. In 1682 he found its **mouth,** or the place where the river flowed into a larger body of water—the Gulf of Mexico. He named the Mississippi Valley *Louisiana.* Fur traders and settlers founded cities across the region, including St. Louis and Detroit.

Back east, the colonists had settled and cultivated most of the territory claimed along the Atlantic Coast by Britain. (England's name had changed in 1707 to *Great Britain.*) The settlers had begun to think of themselves as Americans, but many still felt a tie with Britain, and it was only natural for them to expect help from Britain when some colonists, hungry for more land, expressed interest in moving west. But interest in the fertile area known as the Ohio River Valley brought the British into conflict with the French.

Mission of Santa Barbara, California

THE FRENCH AND INDIAN WAR, 1754 TO 1763

England, France, and Spain had battled over land in North America several times in the first half of the eighteenth century. These wars culminated in the French and Indian War.

In 1754, the French built **Fort Duquesne** (doo KAYN) on the Ohio River where Pittsburgh is today. The British claimed this land as part of Virginia and sent a twenty-one-year-old <u>surveyor</u> named **George Washington** along with 150 <u>troops</u> to tell the French to leave. When the French refused, Washington led a successful attack on the fort. This <u>skirmish</u> started the French and Indian War. Although the French recaptured their fort, the event singled out Washington as a military hero.

As expected, Major **Edward Braddock** arrived from Britain to lead American troops against the French and the **Huron,** their Indian <u>allies</u>. Braddock was used to traditional European methods of fighting; he marched rows of uniformed soldiers onto an open field. He was unprepared for the French and Native American fighters, who hid in the woods and shot from behind in surprise attacks.

The British were losing the war, and they needed Native American help in order to win it. They finally received the help of the Iroquois, who considered the Huron their enemy. Furthermore, in exchange for help from the Iroquois, the British promised to protect their lands from colonists.

With the Iroquois on their side, the British defeated the French in a final battle in Quebec in 1759. When France signed the **Treaty of Paris** in 1763, it lost most of its lands in the New World. England now controlled Canada as well as the Ohio Valley and other land east of the Mississippi River. At the end of the war, Britain's **King George III** issued an important <u>proclamation</u>. It said that lands east of the Mississippi River belonged to the colonists and that lands west of the Mississippi were for Native American tribes. European settlers who had already moved into the western region would have to leave.

This proclamation was Britain's attempt to honor its agreement with the Iroquois. However, King George's plan to limit colonists to a specific area probably reflected Britain's concerns that protecting colonists in the western territories would be too difficult and expensive.

The king's ruling was not popular with many colonists. They had already settled most of the good land along the Atlantic; many newcomers wanted the western lands for themselves and didn't care that these lands already belonged to the Native Americans. The **Proclamation of 1763** was shaping up as the first of many British acts that would make Americans think about breaking away from the crown.

THE ROAD TO A WAR OF INDEPENDENCE, 1763 TO 1775

A Taste of Freedom

Back in 1735, New Yorkers had established the right of free speech in a landmark court case. A newspaper editor and printer named **John Peter Zenger** faced a trial by jury because he had criticized the <u>corrupt</u> New York governor in his newspaper. Zenger's lawyer argued that all people should have the right to speak freely as long as they are speaking the truth. The jury <u>acquitted</u> Zenger. Americans throughout the colonies would continue to champion the right of free speech during the next forty years, during which time they harshly criticized Britain and eventually declared their independence.

"No Taxation without Representation"

The British Parliament, the lawmaking body, was heavily in debt from the French and Indian War and decided that the American colonies should pay some of it off. So in 1765, Parliament passed the **Stamp Act,** which called for placing a stamp on every piece of paper—newspaper, writing paper, playing cards—purchased in the colonies. The stamp proved that the consumer had paid the British government a <u>tax</u> for the item. Colonists protested this tax, and Parliament <u>repealed</u> it the following year.

Soon to follow, however, were the **Townshend Acts,** which taxed lead, glass, paper, paint, and tea that the colonists imported from Britain. The outraged colonists <u>boycotted</u> all British goods. This time, British merchants demanded repeal of the taxes, and Britain did eliminate some in 1770.

Colonists were upset by the burden of heavy taxes—and angry because Britain had imposed the taxes without their consent. British citizens in Britain voted for Parliamentary representatives who could speak for them. Colonists, however, had no representative to protect their interests in Parliament. Their protest slogan became "no taxation without representation."

The Boston Massacre

To make matters worse, Parliament sent British troops into Boston beginning in 1768 to enforce the taxes. Bostonians were furious. The anger boiled over in March 1770, when some unarmed colonists began annoying a group of British soldiers. In the confusion, the soldiers began firing; when it was all over, the attack had caused twelve American casualties: five dead and seven wounded. One of the dead was **Crispus Attucks** (A tuhks), a former slave. Some say Attucks was the first African American to give his life for his country.

Samuel Adams was a Boston colonist who supported American independence. He called this event the Boston Massacre; then he took an

Bloody Massacre Perpetrated in King Street, Boston, engraving by Paul Revere, 1770

engraving of the event made by his friend, silversmith **Paul Revere** (ruh VIHR), and sent copies of it throughout the colonies to publicize the British action.

Adams didn't stop there. In 1772, he formed the **Committees of Correspondence,** groups of men from all over the colonies who corresponded, or wrote letters, to keep each other informed of important events. Their goal was to bring the colonies together to protect their rights.

The Boston Tea Party

By 1773, the British still had not repealed the Boston tea tax. One night, a group of rebels dressed as Mohawks climbed aboard trading ships in Boston Harbor. These ships held British tea waiting to be taxed and unloaded. The rebels tossed crate after crate of tea into the harbor.

Britain's response was to close Boston Harbor until the colonists paid for the tea. As a result, food and supplies could not enter or leave the harbor, and thousands of people whose livings relied on the shipping business were out of work. In addition, Parliament insisted that the colonists provide food and shelter for the British soldiers in the colonies. Colonists called these actions the **Intolerable Acts.**

The First Continental Congress

The dramatic events in Massachusetts led the members of the Committees of Correspondence to gather for the first time in 1774 in Philadelphia, Pennsylvania. The delegates came from every colony except Georgia. They called themselves the First Continental Congress (the word *continental* suggests "from the North American colonies on the continent," and *congress* means "assembly" or "meeting"). The congress aimed to protest the Intolerable Acts and to find a way to protect colonists' rights.

Two major decisions came out of the First Continental Congress. The delegates sent King George a petition that asked him to allow the colonies greater control over their own government. They also decided that each colony should gather an army of **minutemen,** soldiers who could be ready at a minute's notice should war break out.

While some members of the Continental Congress were eager to keep but improve America's relationship with Britain, most were **Patriots,** people who believed that the colonies should break away and govern themselves. Among the Patriots was **Patrick Henry,** one of the country's most famous public speakers. Henry's famous words in support of a **militia,** a volunteer force for emergencies, and a fight for independence have come down to us through the ages: "Is life so dear or peace so sweet as to be purchased at the price of chains and slavery? Forbid it, Almighty God—I know not what course others may take; but as for me, give me liberty, or give me death!"

Paul Revere's Ride

The colonists prepared for war with Britain. They thought war was the only way to gain self-rule and freedom. In Concord, Massachusetts, the minutemen hid weapons and gunpowder. Nearby in Lexington, Samuel Adams and **John Hancock,** another Patriot, were hiding because they knew the British considered them dangerous rebels. Paul Revere found out that British troops planned to seize the weapons in Concord and arrest Adams and Hancock. So on April 18, 1775, Revere began his famous "midnight ride" to Concord and Lexington to warn the Patriots that the British troops were on their way.

Riding with Revere were **Billy Dawes** and **Dr. Samuel Prescott.** Though the British captured Revere and Dawes at Lexington, Prescott rode on to Concord to warn the rest.

On the morning of April 19, the British arrived in Lexington and Concord. After a brief skirmish in Lexington, someone at the Old North Bridge in Concord fired the famous "shot heard round the world"—the shot that started the American Revolution.

Once again, British troops fought in the traditional way. The rebels, however, used the tactics they had learned during the French and Indian War. Hiding behind bushes and trees, the minutemen fired on the red-coated British, finally forcing the British to retreat to Boston.

THE REVOLUTIONARY WAR, 1775 TO 1783

The action in Massachusetts and growing unrest all over the colonies led to the **Second Continental Congress** in May of 1775. The delegates returned to Philadelphia, and among them were some of the most famous Americans of the period.

Benjamin Franklin (1706–1790) was well known and the oldest member of the group. He had made his fortune as a newspaper printer. He was also the author of *Poor Richard's Almanack*, an annual book full of useful information and witty sayings. Franklin was a scientist and an inventor, too: he conducted a famous kite experiment to prove that lightning and electricity are related, and he invented an efficient wood-burning stove that today still bears his name—the Franklin stove.

Thomas Jefferson (1743–1826) was the youngest to attend the congress. A member of the House of Burgesses, Jefferson came from a wealthy plantation-owning family in Virginia; he was a talented writer, musician, architect, and inventor.

George Washington (1732–1799) was also a member of the congress. Like Jefferson, he came from a Virginian farming family and was a member of the House of Burgesses. Washington had become famous during the French and Indian War; colonists admired him for his strong leadership abilities.

The Second Continental Congress made a number of historic decisions. The members decided to form a Continental Army, and they named George Washington as commander-in-chief. They also set up a post office so that the colonies could communicate better, and they chose Ben Franklin as postmaster general.

Members of the congress realized that fighting Britain, the country with the most powerful army in the world, would be difficult, so they decided to make peace with the Native American tribes and ask for the support of foreign countries such as France and Spain. Finally, the congress sent to King George one last document, called the **Olive Branch Petition,** which asked him to recognize and honor their requests. But the king refused even to read it. At that point, the congress moved on to its last—and perhaps most important—decision: appointing a committee that included **John Adams,** Ben Franklin, and Thomas Jefferson to create a document that would declare the independence of the colonies from Britain. Jefferson wrote the document based on the committee's ideas.

The First Battles

Even before Jefferson finished the document, the first battles of the Revolutionary War established America as a force to be reckoned with. While the British had well-trained troops and plenty of supplies, the Americans, although lacking training and supplies, were fighting on their own land for a cause that they passionately believed in.

From the western territory of New Hampshire, where Vermont is today, **Ethan Allen** led his **Green Mountain Boys** in a successful raid on **Fort Ticonderoga** on Lake Champlain in May of 1775. By capturing this British fort, Allen cut off a major supply route for the British from Canada.

The **Battle of Bunker Hill** took place in Boston the following month. In the middle of the night, American troops climbed Breed's Hill and surprised the British troops when they woke in the morning. The two sides fought hard for both Breed's Hill and Bunker Hill; while the Patriots eventually "lost" the battle and had to retreat, it was at great cost to the British, who counted many casualties.

In June of 1776, the Patriots finally drove the British out of Boston. **Henry Knox** used oxen to drag heavy cannon down from the fort at Ticonderoga. The Americans pointed the cannon at the British in Boston and made them retreat.

The Declaration of Independence

Meanwhile, delegates were working hard on the document they called the Declaration of Independence. After consulting with other members of his committee, Jefferson wrote a draft of the document in two days.

It presented groundbreaking ideas, some of which actually had occurred earlier to British thinkers. The first major idea was that all men are created equal and have the right to "Life, Liberty, and the pursuit of Happiness." The declaration also stated that people create governments to preserve those rights. It argued that King George had not protected the colonists' rights, had taxed without representation, had closed down assemblies, and had kept troops in the colonies to control but not to aid the colonists. Finally, the document declared that the combined colonies now formed the independent country of the **United States of America.**

It is interesting to note that in his original draft of the Declaration of Independence, Jefferson also argued against slavery. However, other committee members removed this section in order to ensure that delegates from the southern colonies would go along with the document. The delegates approved the Declaration of Independence on July 4, 1776.

Members of the War Effort

The new nation received a great deal of help. Many individual Europeans believed in America's cause and came to join in the fight. The **Marquis de Lafayette** (mar KEE duh lah fay ET) arrived from France when he was only nineteen; he volunteered his services to the Continental Army and soon became an adviser to Washington. **Baron Friedrich von Steuben** (von STOO ben) was a German who came to America to drill and train the troops.

Women were also busy supporting the war effort. Some women stayed at home and took over the jobs of farming and running businesses. Some became nurses. Some, such as Molly Hays, even went to the front and brought pitchers of water to thirsty soldiers; she acquired the nickname **Molly Pitcher. Deborah Sampson** also joined the battle; she disguised herself as a man and served as a soldier for three years.

Some African Americans sided with the British, who promised freedom to those slaves who fought for them. Others chose to support the Americans. A few years into the war, the Continental Army forbade African Americans to serve because Southerners were afraid that if slaves were armed, they would rebel against their owners. However, this law soon changed, and many African Americans continued in the fight.

Difficult Times for the Patriots

After Bunker Hill and Fort Ticonderoga, things went badly for the Americans. General **William Howe** led the British Army into New York and New Jersey and forced the Continental Army to retreat to Pennsylvania. The British had added to their troops by hiring German mercenaries, called **Hessians** (HE shinz) to fight on their side.

In September of 1776, the British captured a twenty-one-year-old schoolteacher named **Nathan Hale,** who had been spying for the United States.

Legend says that before he was hanged, he spoke these famous words: "I regret that I have but one life to lose for my country."

There was one bright moment for the Americans on Christmas night, 1776. Washington secretly led troops across the Delaware River to **Trenton,** New Jersey, where he captured a group of Hessian soldiers. A week later, he defeated a British force in Princeton and took back New Jersey for the Americans.

In October of 1777, the Americans won another important battle when they defeated British General **John Burgoyne** (bur GOIN) at **Saratoga,** New York. Burgoyne planned to take the Hudson River Valley, but the Americans camped on a <u>fortified</u> bluff high above the entrance to the city. It was impossible for the British soldiers to defend themselves during the battle, and they surrendered.

The British continued to win many battles, however, and the Americans, ill equipped to begin with, were in desperate need of soldiers and supplies. Their low point came when they set up camp in **Valley Forge,** Pennsylvania, during the winter of 1776 to 1777. Washington and his troops spent one of the coldest winters in history in drafty cabins with few supplies. Thousands of troops died from hunger and disease. But Washington was at his best. He encouraged and inspired his troops, while von Steuben drilled them. The men who survived were a united, well-trained, loyal group of soldiers, ready to defend their country.

Help from the French

Help on a large scale arrived just in time. American delegates had gone to Paris to seek aid from the French. While the French were not particularly interested in preserving the ideals of democracy, they were interested in <u>humiliating</u> the British, who had defeated them in the French and Indian War. The Americans' victory at Saratoga convinced the French that the Patriots did indeed have a chance of winning, and in 1778 they agreed to send troops and supplies to America.

Heroes and Villains

The war dragged on, and many Americans made names for themselves as heroes. One was **George Rogers Clark,** who led men into the Ohio Valley and captured three forts for the Americans. At **Fort Vincennes** (vin SENZ) Clark had only 150 men with him. He ordered them to confuse the enemy by yelling and screaming as they fired into the fort. Inside, it seemed to the British that a much larger army was attacking, and they surrendered.

On the sea, **John Paul Jones** led the new American navy. His boat was the *Bonhomme Richard,* named for Poor Richard from Franklin's *Poor Richard's Almanack.* In 1779, Jones fought a famous battle with the British ship *Serapis;* when it seemed that the Americans would have to surrender, Jones famously declared to his enemies, "I have not yet begun to fight!" It was the *Serapis* that eventually surrendered, and Jones's ship won the battle.

Benedict Arnold started out as an American hero but ended as the war's most famous <u>villain</u> and <u>traitor</u>. Arnold, respected for his brilliance and bravery, was a top leader in the Continental Army. However, some began to question the way he spent military funds. Angered by this, he began spying for the British and arranged to hand over the New York fort at **West Point.** When the Americans captured British Major **John André** with the plans, they discovered the plot. André was hanged, but Arnold escaped to Britain and eventually died of old age.

The End of the War, 1778 to 1781

With France joining the war in 1778 and Spain following in 1779, the Continental Army held out against the British.

The British then decided to move south. They believed that there they would find more **Loyalists,** people true to Britain. As they headed south, British troops kept winning big battles in cities such as Savannah, Georgia, and Charleston, South Carolina, but the Americans kept holding on.

The major turning point in the war came at **Guilford Courthouse** in North Carolina. Here American troops fought British troops led by General **Charles Cornwallis;** though the Americans lost the battle, Cornwallis suffered the loss of many troops and supplies.

In this weakened state, Cornwallis marched on to **Yorktown,** Virginia. American soldiers and their French allies surrounded the city, and

French warships closed off the harbor. Unable to defend himself or receive new <u>reinforcements</u>, Cornwallis surrendered to Washington on October 19, 1781. It was the last battle of the war. Two years later, in 1783, England and the United States signed a second **Treaty of Paris,** an agreement declaring that the United States was now free to govern itself.

 # Implications

To answer the question, "Why does all this matter?" or "What does it mean?," share the following insights with your child.

People who believed passionately in a cause fought and won the Revolutionary War. But these people included many outside the military. An important lesson of this chapter is that people must organize, plan, and work together in order to achieve political goals. Samuel Adams's Committees of Correspondence may have seemed no more than a group of people writing letters, but they were the start of something big. People who share information and communicate thoughtfully can accomplish a great deal.

The Declaration of Independence is another wonderful example of careful thought and planning. Jefferson and his committee members plus the other delegates who acted as editors considered all the issues and created a powerful written statement that changed the world forever. No country had ever before established itself on the principles of "Life, Liberty, and the pursuit of Happiness." And the language of the Declaration was just general enough to leave room for further interpretation in the future. "All men are created equal" eventually led the way to freedom for African Americans and equality for women.

A new country needs a strong but fair government to keep it together. Chapter 5 shows how our country's founders set up a government.

✓ *Fact Checker*

To check that your child knows or can find the basic facts in this chapter, here are multiple-choice questions about the fight for independence. You may want to ask the questions to your child as if he or she were competing on a televised game show.

"IS THAT YOUR FINAL ANSWER?"

The Revolutionary War gave American English many words or slogans. For example, the delegate John Hancock wrote his name so large at the bottom of the Declaration of Independence that his signature became very famous over the years. In fact, we now use the term *John Hancock* to mean "a person's signature." Choose the correct answer to each of the following questions about expressions that grew out of this period in American history.

1. When a boss calls someone a Benedict Arnold, what is he or she saying about that person?
   a. The person is the fastest worker.
   b. The person is a traitor.
   c. The person is a hero.
2. "No taxation without representation" is a catchy way of saying
   a. "We won't pay taxes unless we can have a say in government."
   b. "We won't pay taxes unless the king orders paintings or other representations of us."
   c. "The king doesn't have to pay taxes unless he wants to represent himself."
3. *Redcoat* was the term used to refer to
   a. French soldiers who helped the Americans during the Revolutionary War
   b. American soldiers during the Revolutionary War
   c. British soldiers during the Revolutionary War
4. The "shot heard round the world" was
   a. the first shot fired in the Revolutionary War
   b. the shot that told Paul Revere to start his midnight ride
   c. the shot Cornwallis fired in the air before he surrendered
5. Whom does the following description best fit?

   "First in war, first in peace,
     First in the hearts of his countrymen"

   a. John Peter Zenger
   b. George Washington
   c. Thomas Jefferson

Answers appear in the back, preceding the index.

? The Big Questions

The following questions encourage your child to think critically rather than simply recall facts. If necessary, review the specific information from the preceding pages that will help your child make the necessary inferences to come up with reasonable answers.

1. This chapter tells about a famous court trial concerning freedom of speech. Since Americans have this freedom, why do authorities punish a person who falsely yells "Fire!" in a crowded theater?
2. Some people in the thirteen colonies did not want to break away from Britain. Why might they have stayed loyal to King George III?
3. During the American Revolution, the British soldiers had better supplies and training than the American soldiers. How, then, did the Americans win?
4. How do you think King George III would have treated the colonists if Britain, not America, had won the Revolutionary War?

Suggested Answers

1. *While Americans have freedom of speech, they cannot make false claims—especially, claims that may harm other people—without punishment of one kind or another.*
2. *Colonists in Boston were having trouble with George III, but colonists in other colonies may not yet have bad experiences with him. Some colonists or their families had been British subjects for a long time and might find change hard to accept. Other colonists, such as the Quakers, were against all warfare.*
3. *Some reasons the colonists won: the colonists got the Native Americans on their side; they learned battle techniques from the Native Americans; they knew the land better than the British; they were passionate about their cause; individuals from Europe helped out; women helped; the French and Spanish joined the war on the American side.*
4. *George III considered the American rebels traitors and might have hanged or shot them; he may have taken away whatever lawmaking powers the colonists had had; he might have continued to impose taxes on the colonists.*

Skills Practice

The following activities give your child practice in applying the skills basic to social studies. For some of the activities, your child may need to review the information in the preceding pages.

A. INTERPRETING SAYINGS FROM POOR RICHARD'S ALMANACK

The following activity will allow your child to look closely at language and to appreciate Ben Franklin's wit.

Tell in your own words what Poor Richard, the character made up by Ben Franklin, meant by each of the following sayings.

1. Fish and visitors stink after three days.
2. No gains without pains.
3. Love your neighbor; yet don't pull down your hedge.
4. Early to bed, early to rise, makes a man healthy, wealthy, and wise.
5. Haste makes waste.

Answers

1. *A dead fish can go bad and smell awful after being around for a few days; people who visit you and stay too long can "go bad," too—by getting in your way, for example.*

2. *You have to work hard and suffer a bit in order to make progress.*
3. *Be friendly but not overfriendly.*
4. *Going to bed early is good for one's health; getting up early gives one time to work for wisdom and wealth.*
5. *If you rush through a job, you may make a mess and have nothing to show for your effort.*

Evaluating Your Child's Skills: **In order to complete this activity successfully, your**

child has to use both abstract and concrete thinking. If he or she has trouble, help by giving the *beginning* of the answer.

B. IDENTIFYING POINT OF VIEW

Read to your child the following excerpt from a letter written in 1776 by William Franklin, the governor of New Jersey. Then ask the questions following the passage.

Depend upon it, you can never place yourselves in a happier situation than in your dependence on Great Britain. Independence has not even a chance of being gained, without the loss of the lives and properties of many thousands of honest people of this country—yet *these*, it seems, are as nothing in the eyes of the patriots! But remember, Gentlemen, that I now tell you, that should they by chance achieve their purpose yet their government will not be lasting.

Questions

1. Which of the statements in the letter are statements of fact, and which are statements of opinion?
2. Was the writer of these words on the side of the colonists or the side of the British? What did he think of people on the other side?

Answers

1. *All the sentences are statements of opinion.*
2. *The writer was on the side of the British. He seems to have thought that the Patriots were uncaring risk takers who couldn't face "facts."*

Evaluating Your Child's Skills: **In order to complete this activity successfully, your child needs to know that we can prove facts but not opinions. The other skill your child needs is reading between the lines, since the writer never comes right out and says whose side he is on.**

C. WRITING A LETTER OF INVITATION

Your child can participate in planning a gathering of family and friends.

The next time your family plans to get together with friends and relatives to celebrate an American holiday, think about writing and sending the invitations—in the form of a letter. You can focus your letter on one of the following topics or make one up yourself:

- Why I'm Glad the Colonists Won the Revolutionary War
- Why I'm Proud to Be an American Citizen
- Why I'm Glad I Came to the United States to Live

Don't forget to give your guests all the information they need: when the party will take place, where it will be, whether to respond to the invitation, what to bring.

Top of the Class

Children interested in delving more deeply into the topics covered in this chapter can choose one or more of the following activities. They may do the activities for their own satisfaction or report on what they have done to show that they have been seriously considering the American Revolution.

BOOKS TO READ AND CRITIQUE

Make one of the following novels available to your child. The stories are told in the first person by fictional teenaged American boys who lived before or during the Revolutionary War. After your child has finished the book, you can suggest that he or she may want to share thoughts about it with his or her teacher or class.

Forbes, Esther. *Johnny Tremain.* Houghton, 1943. This book won the prestigious Newbery Award in 1944. Characters in the novel include Paul Revere and Sam Adams.

Collier, Christopher, and James Lincoln Collier. *My Brother Sam Is Dead.* Four Winds, 1974. This title was a Newbery Honor Book. Tim feels caught between his brother's and his father's differing views of the war.

REPRODUCING A FLAG

For this activity, your child will need access to a print or electronic encyclopedia and either crafts materials or a drawing program on a computer. The activity goes beyond the legendary, but unproven, story about Betsy Ross and the first American flag.

Before the war, colonists created flags for the colonies. Some flags showed that a colony wanted freedom from England, some showed that a colony wanted a relationship with England, and some showed that a colony wanted both. Then, when the Revolution broke out, soldiers carried a number of different flags created for the new union of states.

Read about the flags during the colonial period and the war. Then try to produce one of the flags you read about. Bring your artwork to class, and be prepared to tell what each design or object on the flag stood for. You will find, for example, that some flags had stripes and stars; other flags had snakes, pine trees, and words.

CODING A SECRET MESSAGE

Teach your child the following method for sending a secret written message to a friend or classmate. This method, adapted from a Web site of the University of Michigan, www.clements.umich.edu/spies/methods -code.html, allowed the spy Benedict Arnold to communicate with a British officer. Your child can then challenge others in class to figure out the secret method and break the code.

1. You and the person receiving the message must each have a copy of the exact same book.
2. Make up your message.
3. In the book, find the word you want to write in the letter.
4. Instead of writing the word, write the page number, the line number, and the number of the word, counting over from the left. For example, if you want to write the word *surprise* and you both have the 1999 hardcover edition of J. K. Rowling's *Harry Potter and the Prisoner of Azkaban* (Scholastic Trade), you would write 116.8.6, which is one place where the word *surprise* comes up.

CHAPTER 5
The Birth of a New Nation
1781–1820

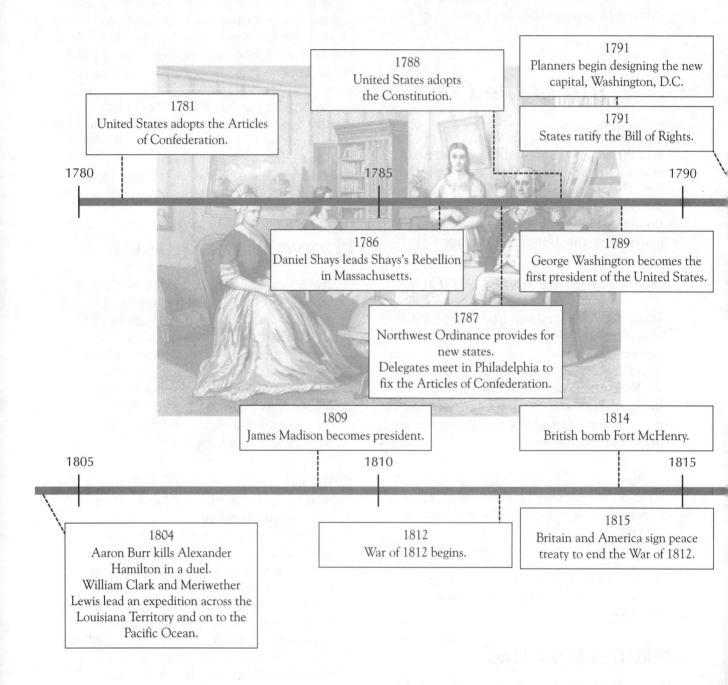

1788
United States adopts the Constitution.

1791
Planners begin designing the new capital, Washington, D.C.

1781
United States adopts the Articles of Confederation.

1791
States ratify the Bill of Rights.

1780

1785

1790

1786
Daniel Shays leads Shays's Rebellion in Massachusetts.

1789
George Washington becomes the first president of the United States.

1787
Northwest Ordinance provides for new states.
Delegates meet in Philadelphia to fix the Articles of Confederation.

1809
James Madison becomes president.

1814
British bomb Fort McHenry.

1805

1810

1815

1804
Aaron Burr kills Alexander Hamilton in a duel.
William Clark and Meriwether Lewis lead an expedition across the Louisiana Territory and on to the Pacific Ocean.

1812
War of 1812 begins.

1815
Britain and America sign peace treaty to end the War of 1812.

This timeline provides an overview of significant events from the country's early years. In the following pages, a narrative goes into greater detail about these events and discusses their significance.

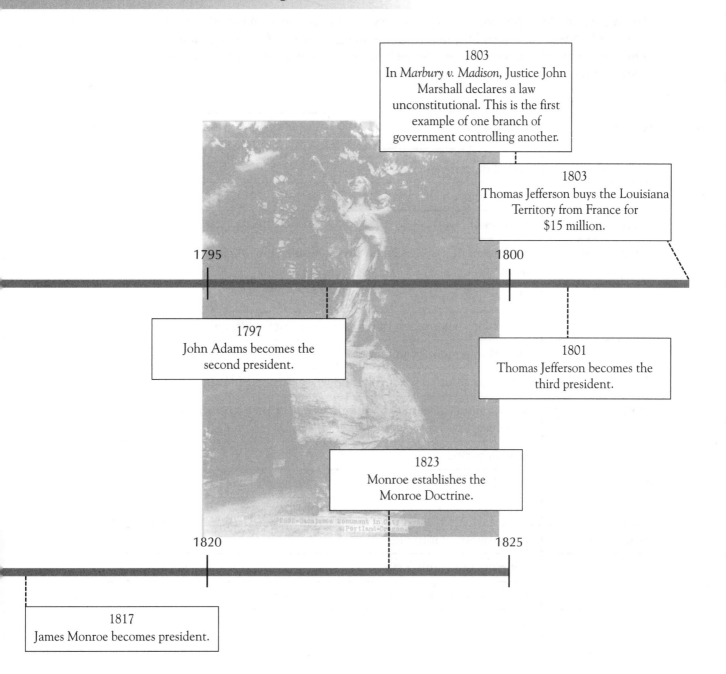

1803
In *Marbury v. Madison*, Justice John Marshall declares a law unconstitutional. This is the first example of one branch of government controlling another.

1803
Thomas Jefferson buys the Louisiana Territory from France for $15 million.

1795

1800

1797
John Adams becomes the second president.

1801
Thomas Jefferson becomes the third president.

1823
Monroe establishes the Monroe Doctrine.

1820

1825

1817
James Monroe becomes president.

Word Power

Word	Definition
abolished	ended officially
accessible	easy to reach or to talk to
alternative	another choice
compromise	settlement of a disagreement by each side agreeing to give up part of its demands
constitution	plan of government
debates	discussions where each of two sides presents a different point of view
doctrine	official statement by a nation
duel	fight, according to strict rules, between two people using swords or guns
economy	way a country uses natural resources and money to produce goods and services
era	time or period
expired	ended
guaranteed	promised
inauguration	act of swearing into office
neutral	not supporting either side
politicians	people who run for or hold government offices
unanimously	with every single person in agreement
unconstitutional	not in keeping with the basic laws of the Constitution of the United States
unstable	unreliable
veteran	person who has served in the armed forces
veto	vote against or overturn

What Your Child Needs to Know

The Americans had won their fight for independence from Britain. Now their challenge was to create a working government. After the trouble they had faced with a king and with the British Parliament, Americans did not want a central government with too much power. Instead, most people wanted each individual state to have much of the power needed to govern itself.

THE ARTICLES OF CONFEDERATION, 1781 TO 1789

The first document that spelled out how the new government would work was the Articles of Confederation. This document was a kind of constitution that the United States adopted in 1781. The Articles of Confederation granted certain powers to **Congress,** or the central government. Congress could declare war and peace, control relations with foreign countries, keep an army and navy, and issue and borrow money. It could not collect taxes or regulate trade. All powers not specifically granted to Congress were given to the states. The states could coin their own money, collect taxes, and make laws. Each state had one vote in Congress regardless of its size and population. The Articles of Confederation did not provide for an executive—a president, prime minister, or monarch. In effect, the states had more power than the central government.

Why were the Articles of Confederation abandoned in 1787 when the Constitutional Convention met in Philadelphia? For one thing, although the central government had the power to maintain an army and navy, it could not collect taxes in order to pay for a military force. Second, no central court system existed to protect individuals' rights. Third, the money system was too complicated. States as well as the central government printed their own money, and as a result much of the money was worthless. Then states began placing heavy tariffs, or taxes, on other states' goods. They also began taxing farmers' lands and seized farms when the farmers couldn't pay.

In 1786, a farmer and Revolutionary War <u>veteran</u> named **Daniel Shays** led hundreds of other Massachusetts farmers in a violent protest, which was later called **Shays's Rebellion.** He and the other farmers were outraged by his state's unfair system of taxation and land seizure. Like many veterans, Shays had not received payment from the Continental Army. Shays's Rebellion highlighted the problems of a weak central government. Leaders felt that it was time to make changes.

The Northwest Ordinance, 1787

One bright moment during this mostly unsuccessful experiment in government took place when Congress passed the Northwest Ordinance in 1787. Rich lands lay in the **Northwest Territory,** the area where Indiana, Ohio, Wisconsin, Michigan, and Illinois are today. Some of the larger states such as Virginia and Massachusetts wanted to keep these lands for themselves. However, the Northwest Ordinance provided a way for these territories to become independent states. The ordinance <u>guaranteed</u> settlers the same rights as any American citizen; it outlawed slavery and set aside lands in each settlement for a public school. The ordinance also allowed a territory to apply for statehood when its population reached sixty thousand. This law, in other words, laid out the route to statehood used by most territories during the eighteenth, nineteenth, and twentieth centuries.

THE CONSTITUTIONAL CONVENTION, 1787

In May 1787, fifty-five delegates from all of the states except for Rhode Island met in Philadelphia for the Grand Convention. The delegates elected George Washington president of the convention. Washington asked for total secrecy about the convention's activities: he wanted the delegates to be able to discuss the issues without the pressure of public opinion.

The goal of the meeting was to revise the Articles of Confederation, but some of the delegates believed that it would be better to create a completely new document. Indeed, this meeting, renamed the Constitutional Convention, was the first step toward producing the **Constitution of the United States,** the document that to this day is the supreme law of the land.

The Virginia Plan

James Madison was one of the delegates who did not support revising the Articles of Confederation. He had arrived at the meeting early in order to write a working document called the Virginia Plan, which proposed a structure for the new government. This became the starting point for the <u>debates</u> of the Constitutional Convention.

Madison's plan proposed a **federal** government, a system in which a national government and the states share power. The federal government would have the rights to declare war, coin money, make treaties, run the post office, and resolve conflicts between the states. States would have the right to set up local governments and public schools. Both state and national governments would have the right to pass laws and collect taxes.

Madison's federal plan included three branches: a **legislative** branch to make laws and raise money; an **executive** branch to carry out the laws; and a **judicial** branch to determine the meaning of laws.

Central to Madison's plan was the idea of **checks and balances,** a system by which each branch could control the actions of the others. For example, while the legislative branch could pass laws, the executive branch could <u>veto</u> them, and the judicial branch could declare them <u>unconstitutional</u>.

Madison presented his plan, and there were hundreds of votes on the details of the document, including on questions such as who could serve in the government and for how long their terms would last. But the basic structure of Madison's plan remained, even after many discussions and arguments, as explained in the following text.

The New Jersey Plan and the Great Compromise

Work on the Constitution broke down for a while when delegates began discussing the structure of the legislative branch. Madison had proposed an assembly made up of representatives from each state—with each state's number of representatives based on population. Therefore, states with greater populations would have more representatives than those with lesser populations.

Not surprisingly, the smaller states turned down this proposal. Concerned that the larger states would band together and ignore them, the smaller states presented an <u>alternative</u> to Madison's document, called the New Jersey Plan. The plan proposed an assembly in which each state had the same number of representatives. This time larger states such as Virginia and Massachusetts rejected the idea, and it looked as if the Constitutional Convention would have to end with no document to show for it.

Then **Roger Sherman,** a delegate from Connecticut, proposed what has come to be known as the Great <u>Compromise</u>. Sherman proposed a **bicameral** system—a legislature made up of not one but two chambers. One chamber would have an equal number of representatives from each state (today's Senate) while the other would have the number of representatives from each state determined by the state's population (today's House of Representatives). Delegates for large and small states accepted the compromise, and work on the Constitution continued.

Delegates made other compromises in the interests of creating a document that everyone could support. Some delegates deeply believed that slavery should be <u>abolished</u>. But the southern states, which relied heavily on slave labor, refused to agree to such a plan. Instead, they promised to end the slave trade by 1808. While this promise was a minor victory for those against slavery, it did not help the thousands of slaves already in the United States. Neither did it move the nation toward the ending of slavery. There were already enough slaves in the United States to make importing new slaves unnecessary. Simply by having children, the slaves themselves would provide slaves for the future.

The issue of how to count slaves led to a sort of compromise, too. The southern states didn't want to grant slaves their freedom, but they did want to take advantage of their numbers when it came to representation in the government. Delegates agreed that each slave should be counted as three-fifths of a person when counting the population. Viewed from where we are today, counting any individual as "three-fifths of a person" seems shocking. However, many slave owners had not considered their slaves to be human at all, so those delegates who opposed slavery considered counting a slave as even a fraction of an individual to be a small step forward.

Delegates also compromised when they discussed how citizens would elect the president. One group, called the **Federalists,** believed that ordinary people could not handle the responsibility of voting directly for the president. The other group, called the Anti-Federalists, wanted each citizen to vote directly for the president. So delegates compromised: they agreed that citizens would vote for an **electoral college,** a group of people who would in turn vote for the president.

Ratification of the Constitution, 1788

The delegates finally signed the Constitution on September 17, 1787. The next challenge was ratification, or approval. The Constitution could not become the supreme law of the land until two-thirds of the states—nine of them—had ratified it.

Many delegates worked actively to support the Constitution. James Madison, **Alexander Hamilton,** and **John Jay** wrote a series of essays that were later published together as the *Federalist Papers.* These explained the strengths of the Constitution. By the summer of 1788, all of the states except North Carolina and Rhode Island had ratified the Constitution.

AMENDMENTS AND THE BILL OF RIGHTS, 1791

A few delegates had refused to sign the Constitution. They realized that it lacked an essential component: a guarantee of individual rights. Without this guarantee, they argued, there was nothing to prevent the government from taking away people's freedoms.

At the same time, the architects of the Constitution realized that the needs of the country would change as time passed. So they built into the Constitution a means for making **amendments,** or changes, to the document. In order for an amend-

ment to take effect, two-thirds of both the House and the Senate and then three-quarters of the states must ratify it. Changing the Constitution is a long, difficult process: of the thousands of amendments proposed since 1788, Congress and the states have passed only twenty-seven to this day.

During the Constitutional Convention, John Hancock of Massachusetts made a promise to delegates worried about individual rights. He promised them that after they ratified the Constitution the delegates could develop amendments to provide for individual rights.

James Madison wrote the first ten amendments and called them the Bill of Rights. Ratified in 1791, the Bill of Rights protects such rights as the freedom of speech, the freedom of worship, and the freedom to bear arms. (The complete text of the Constitution appears at the back of this book, before the index.)

PRESIDENT GEORGE WASHINGTON, 1789 TO 1797

In 1789, the electoral college <u>unanimously</u> elected George Washington as the country's first presi-

Constitution of the United States

dent, with John Adams as his vice president. Washington rode on horseback to his new country's capital, New York City, for his <u>inauguration</u> at Federal Hall.

Washington chose a group of advisers, called the **cabinet,** to guide him in leading the country. Henry Knox, an old friend from the Revolutionary War, became secretary of war; Alexander Hamilton became secretary of the treasury, in charge of directing the country's finances; Thomas Jefferson became secretary of state, in charge of maintaining good relations with foreign countries; and **Edmund Randolph** was the attorney general, who was supposed to make sure the law of the land—the Constitution—was carried out.

Political Parties

During this time, the first political parties began to develop, as the members of Washington's cabinet disagreed about which direction the country should take. Hamilton and Adams led the Federalists, who favored a strong central government and believed that the country's success lay in building factories and trading with other countries. Jefferson led the **Democratic-Republicans,** which was also the party of James Madison and James Monroe. They favored a weaker central government and strong state governments. They saw America as a group of farmers who were self-sufficient—that is, able to take care of their own needs. Washington had difficulty at times managing such differences of opinion within the cabinet. Each side believed that if the other side's opinions won out, the country would be doomed.

PRESIDENT JOHN ADAMS, 1797 TO 1801

After two terms in office, Washington stepped down, and citizens elected John Adams to replace him. A Federalist, Adams wanted to keep power in the hands of only the wealthiest citizens: when the delegates were writing the Constitution, he did not want "the masses" of people to vote directly for the president. Although he was a **radical,** one who believed in extreme political change, during the Revolutionary War period, Adams was far more **conservative**—that is, opposed to radical change—during his presidency.

As president, Adams signed the very unpopular **Alien** and **Sedition Acts.** The Alien Acts made it difficult for foreigners to enter the country, and the Sedition Acts made it illegal to criticize the government. The Sedition Acts were so unpopular, in fact, that a few states passed **resolves,** or declarations, saying that they were unconstitutional. But didn't the system of checks and balances in the Constitution say that only the judicial branch could decide whether or not a law was constitutional?

The Alien and Sedition Acts eventually <u>expired</u>, but the question about their constitutionality continued to bother the nation. What should happen when the president signed a "bad" law? Could a state government refuse to accept it? Finally, in 1803, a Supreme Court justice named **John Marshall** clarified that only the Supreme Court, not a state, has the right to declare a federal law unconstitutional and to throw it out.

A NEW CAPITAL

John Adams was the first American president to live in the country's new capital, **Washington, D.C.** Planning for the new capital had begun back in 1791. Every state wanted the capital to be one of its cities, but the planners decided to establish a separate district for the capital. They chose a site in what was then the middle of the country and called it the **District of Columbia,** in honor of Christopher Columbus. After George Washington's death in 1799, citizens voted to name the city *Washington* in his honor.

Architect **Pierre L'Enfant** (pee AIR lahn FAHN) created an overall design for the city, and other architects designed such buildings as the White House and the Capitol. **Benjamin Banneker** also played an important part in the city's development. An African American and former slave, Banneker was an inventor, a writer, the publisher of a popular almanac, and a surveyor. He surveyed, or measured, much of the land that had been set aside for the capital.

PRESIDENT THOMAS JEFFERSON, 1801 TO 1809

After Adams had just one term in office, his rival from the Democratic-Republicans, Thomas Jefferson, defeated him in the 1800 election. Jefferson viewed the job of president quite differently from Adams. Unlike Adams, Jefferson wanted to be <u>accessible</u> to the common people. Instead of riding around town in the presidential carriage, he rode on horseback, and he opened the White House every day to anyone who wanted to visit.

The Louisiana Purchase, 1803

One of Jefferson's most important acts was to buy a vast piece of land from France in 1803. Jefferson dreamed of extending the United States from coast to coast; he was also concerned about European countries claiming land near American borders. In particular, Jefferson worried about the port of New Orleans at the end of the Mississippi River. The French owned this port, so they had the right to close it to American ships. Such an act could hurt the American <u>economy</u>. Jefferson directed Secretary of State Madison to see if the United States could buy New Orleans from France.

France, in the meantime, had a few other things on its mind. In 1789, the French had had their own revolution and replaced their king and queen with a series of <u>unstable</u> governments. Soon a general named **Napoleon Bonaparte** (BOH nuh *pahrt*) had taken charge and had begun a series of wars in Europe in an effort to claim most of that continent for France. These wars were extremely expensive, and Bonaparte needed more money. So when Madison offered to buy New Orleans, Bonaparte's representative offered all of Louisiana, a territory that stretched from New Orleans, up the Mississippi, and out to the Rockies. Jefferson bought it for $15 million, about four cents per acre. In doing so, he doubled the size of the United States. (Chapter 6 tells about settlement of these lands by white people and the effect of this on Native Americans.)

Burr versus Hamilton, 1804

Alexander Hamilton and Thomas Jefferson opposed each other's views of government. Hamilton, a self-made man, believed in a strong central government run by the wealthy; he distrusted the common people. Jefferson, on the other hand, was born to wealth but believed that ordinary people should have the opportunity to run their country with a minimum of government.

Back in 1791, Hamilton had supported establishing a strong central bank and had persuaded the president and Congress to go along with him in spite of Jefferson's thinking that the government did not have the power to set up a central bank.

Even though Jefferson and Hamilton were bitter rivals, Hamilton in 1804 had supported Jefferson for a second term as president instead of **Aaron Burr,** the opponent. Hamilton had felt that Burr was not fit for the job. Just after the election, the losing candidate, Burr, challenged Hamilton to a <u>duel</u>. No one is exactly sure what happened during the duel, but it ended in Hamilton's death. Many mourned, for Hamilton had made many important contributions to his new country.

The Lewis and Clark Expedition, 1804 to 1806

In 1804, Jefferson decided to find out more about his purchase from France. He directed his personal secretary, **Meriwether Lewis,** to organize an expedition of men to explore the Louisiana Territory. Lewis asked an old army friend named **William Clark** to join him, and they put together a group of forty-two men called the **Corps of Discovery.**

Their goal was not only to map the territory to the west. Jefferson had also directed them to take note of the plants and wildlife that they found and to make friendly contact with the Native American tribes living there.

The Corps of Discovery left St. Louis on May 14, 1804. The group traveled along the Missouri River to the Rockies, which they crossed with help from **Sacajawea** (*sah* cuh jah WEE uh), the Native American wife of a French fur trapper. This remarkable woman served as a guide. On the trip, she gave birth. She continued the trip with the baby strapped to her back.

The corps traveled along the Snake and Columbia rivers, arriving at the Pacific coast on November 15, 1805. After spending the winter on the west coast, the group left for Missouri the following spring and arrived back in St. Louis in October 1806. Their trip had taken twenty-eight months, and they had traveled more than seventy-five hundred miles.

Lewis and Clark's trip was a success as well as a major turning point in America's history. They created accurate maps of the area, they collected use-

Sacajawea Monument in City Park, Portland, Oregon; statue by Alice Cooper, c. 1912

ful information about local plants and animals, and they made friendly contact with Native American tribes. In doing so, they opened the door for westward expansion. First, a few hunters and trappers ventured into the Louisiana Territory. By the middle of the nineteenth century, thousands of settlers were eager to come to this rich new land.

JAMES MADISON AND THE WAR OF 1812

The Democratic-Republican James Madison followed Jefferson as president in 1809, and he served two terms until 1817. The War of 1812, a three-year war with Britain, marked his presidency.

Causes of the War

Napoleon had sold the Louisiana Territory to the United States because he needed money for his wars in Europe. One of these wars was against Britain. Both Britain and France wanted the United States to take sides, but America, led by Madison, tried to stay <u>neutral</u>. This policy became more and more difficult to carry out.

The British began stopping American ships and forcing the sailors who were or had been British to work for the British navy. The British also continued to occupy armed forts in the United States— forts that they were supposed to have left after the Revolutionary War. Further, Madison was being hounded by the **War Hawks,** a group of American <u>politicians</u> who wanted to seize Canada from the British and Florida from the Spaniards. Finally, in 1812, the United States declared war on Britain.

Major Events of the War

The British and the Americans fought each other on both sea and land. With warships such as the **U.S.S. Constitution** (nicknamed *Old Ironsides*), the Americans held their own against the British, who had the strongest navy in the world. In 1813, when the British tried to attack the United States from the Canadian border, Commander **Oliver Perry** led a successful battle against them on Lake Erie. It was during this battle that Perry said words that would become famous: "We have met the enemy, and they are ours."

In 1814, the British marched on Washington, D.C. First Lady **Dolley Madison** escaped from the White House only a few days before the British arrived; as she left, she took with her some important papers and possessions, including a famous portrait of George Washington. The British arrived in the capital to find the White House empty, but they proceeded to set it and other buildings on fire.

From there, the British moved on to the Chesapeake Bay, in Baltimore, Maryland, to bomb **Fort McHenry.** The bombing lasted twenty-five hours, and during this time Americans watched nervously to see if their flag was still flying over the fort. One of these people was poet **Francis Scott Key,** who later wrote a poem about the famous battle. He set the poem to music, and it became our national anthem, "The Star-Spangled Banner."

Britain and the United States signed a peace treaty in December of 1814. Unfortunately, news traveled slowly, and military leaders in the South did not find out until too late. In January 1815, troops fought in the Battle of New Orleans, in which two thousand British soldiers and fifty American soldiers died. It was a battle that did not have to happen—and yet it made the American general in charge, **Andrew Jackson,** a national hero.

It is hard to say who won the War of 1812. The British kept Canada, but they also left the United States for good. Britain had come to realize that the Americans were powerful enough to defend themselves, and the United States gained international respect. A final result of the war was that the Federalist Party, many of whose members had opposed the war, lost whatever power it had left. Another party would soon take its place.

Tecumseh

Madison's term was also marked by conflict with the Native American tribes of the Ohio Valley. A Shawnee chief named **Tecumseh** (tuh CUM suh) attempted to bring many Native American tribes together to drive the Americans off their land. At first, he successfully united many of the tribes. But in 1811, General **William Henry Harrison** led an attack on Tecumseh's forces and destroyed them. Tecumseh was killed by American troops in 1813, and the league he dreamed of never came to be.

PRESIDENT JAMES MONROE, 1817 TO 1825

Another Democratic-Republican, James Monroe, followed Madison, and his presidency has been called the **Era of Good Feelings.** The economy was healthy, the country was at peace, and most people felt hopeful about America's future. During this period, the United States pressured Spain into giving up Florida, guaranteeing America's control of the east coast from north to south.

The Monroe Doctrine, 1823

Monroe believed strongly that Americans should spend their time making their country grow strong. He also observed that, to the south, many Latin American countries had begun to establish independence from their European "mother countries," just as the United States had done.

In 1823, Monroe announced the Monroe <u>Doctrine</u>, which stated that European countries were no longer allowed to establish colonies or meddle in the business of North or South American countries. In return, the United States promised to stay out of other countries' business with existing colonies. The United States held to this policy through the rest of the nineteenth century and into the twentieth.

 # Implications

> To answer the question, "Why does all this matter?" or "What does it mean?," share the following insights with your child.

Today, many people take our Constitution and our system of government for granted. But the most important lesson from this chapter lies in appreciating how our country's founders struggled to create a workable system of government almost from scratch. The idea of *government by the consent of the governed* and the idea of a bill of rights go back to developments in England in the 1200s. The new Americans took these two principles further than anyone else up to the eighteenth century. For one thing, the American Bill of Rights was broader than England's and could not be **repealed,** or canceled (as could the English one). Second, the whole idea of an *elected* head of state was new.

After the American Constitution was in place, other countries soon began using it as a model in rebuilding their own governments. Today, America's form of government—representative democracy—can be found in most parts of the world.

Furthermore, when Madison and the other architects of the Constitution put checks and balances into the new system, they did an important thing. They made the new government "tyrant-proof": they made it difficult for one person to come along and take control. Some people today complain that it takes a long time for the government to accomplish anything, but remember that, even though our checks and balances slow things down, they usually also keep our government fair and stable.

Another event mentioned in this chapter is extremely important. In 1801, Thomas Jefferson defeated his rival, John Adams, in the presidential election. Jefferson took over the job *peacefully*. Many times in history and in the modern world, we read about people from different political parties fighting for control of a government and becoming violent because they disagree so strongly. The French Revolution, for example, became very bloody because people were so hungry for power. But when Adams handed the reins of government to Jefferson, he set the tone for future elections and changes in power: though individuals might disagree, the government would continue.

Finally, Lewis and Clark's expedition to the West set the stage for a whole new wave of American settlers, to be discussed in Chapter 6.

 # Fact Checker

Here are fill-in-the-blank questions for children to answer, using facts they have learned about the early years of the United States of America.

Fill in the blanks in each sentence.

1. The second president of the United States was _____ _____.
2. Aaron Burr killed _____ _____ in a duel.
3. The third president of the United States was _____ _____.
4. The land that Thomas Jefferson bought from France for $15 million is known as the _____ _____.

Answers appear in the back, preceding the index.

? The Big Questions

The following questions encourage your child to think critically rather than simply recall facts. If necessary, review the specific information from the preceding pages that will help your child make the necessary inferences to come up with reasonable answers.

1. The Sedition Act is no longer in effect. The right of a United States citizen to criticize the government is protected by the First Amendment to the Constitution, which guarantees freedom of speech. However, citizens are, to this day, *not* allowed to speak publicly in favor of overthrowing the government. Do you think this is a violation of freedom of speech? Do you agree or disagree that this type of speech should be considered against the law?

2. Alexander Hamilton thought that the presidency and Senate terms should last for life. What would be the disadvantages of such a system? Would there be any advantages? If so, what would they be?

3. Our present two-party system emerged during the presidency of George Washington with the Federalist and the Democratic-Republican parties. Why do you think this two-party system has lasted so long? What is the advantage of a two-party system over a system in which three or more parties compete?

Suggested Answers

1. *Your child may think that any restriction is a violation of freedom of speech. He or she may also mention that, after all, the American colonists spoke—and acted—in favor of overthrowing the British government. On the other hand, he or she may think that our government, which protects our freedom of speech along with all our other rights, has a responsibility to protect itself.*

2. A disadvantage of a lifetime term for presidents and senators: without the knowledge that they must carry out the will of the majority of the people in order to be reelected, political figures could become too powerful. An advantage of lifetime term: presidents and senators would not be beholden to people and organizations that finance their campaigns.

3. With two major parties (and therefore two major presidential candidates), it is more likely that one candidate will win a clear majority of the vote. If there were three or more major parties, the vote would be split into more and smaller segments. The more parties and candidates participating in an election, the less clearly can the will of the people be represented.

 # Skills Practice

The following activities give your child practice in applying the skills basic to social studies. For some of the activities, your child may need to review the information in the preceding pages.

A.   ORGANIZING INFORMATION

The following activity will allow your child to use the graphic organizer known as a Venn diagram to organize information he or she has learned from this chapter.

In the circle on the left, write two powers that the Constitution reserves for the states. In the circle on the right, write at least two powers that the Constitution gives to the federal government. In the middle, where the two circles intersect, write two powers that the state governments and the federal government share.

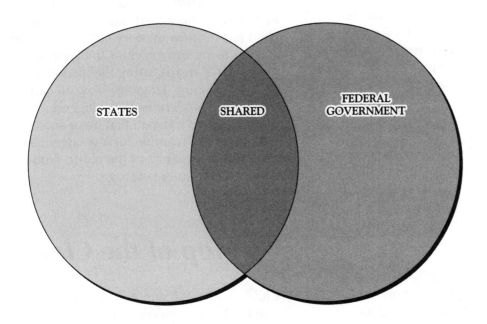

Answers

States: set up local governments, run public schools

Federal: declare war, coin money, make treaties, run the post office, resolve conflicts between the states

Shared: pass laws, collect taxes

> ***Evaluating Your Child's Skills:*** **In order to complete this activity successfully, your child has to recall or find facts from the chapter and organize those facts in a meaningful way. Point out that using graphic organizers such as Venn diagrams makes facts easier to understand and remember.**

B.   DISTINGUISHING FACT FROM OPINION

> **The following activity asks your child to apply reasoning skills to the information he or she has learned from this chapter.**

Decide whether each of the following statements is fact or opinion.

1. The delegates to the Constitutional Convention agreed that citizens would vote for an electoral college rather than vote directly for the president.
2. It is better for citizens to vote directly for the president than to vote for an electoral college.
3. John Adams wanted to keep power in the hands of the wealthiest citizens.
4. Thomas Jefferson was a greater president than John Adams.
5. Aaron Burr killed Alexander Hamilton in a duel.
6. The War of 1812 was already over when the Battle of New Orleans was fought.

Answers

1. fact;   2. opinion;   3. fact;   4. opinion; 5. fact;   6. fact

> ***Evaluating Your Child's Skills:*** **In order to complete this activity successfully, your child needs to be able to identify a state-ment as a fact or an opinion. If necessary, point out that a fact can be checked to find out whether it is true or false. An opinion is neither true nor false; it is an individual's idea about something. People may hold different opinions, but they should be able to back them up with facts or sound reasoning.**

C.   INTERPRETING PRIMARY SOURCES

> **This activity asks your child to look at an important document written more than 200 years ago and show that he or she understands it by "translating" it into modern English.**

The Constitution of the United States appears in this book before the index. Read the Preamble. Then, on a separate sheet of paper, write the Preamble in your own words. If necessary, use a dictionary to look up unfamiliar words.

Answers

Accept any reasonable wording. The "translation" should include the concepts of justice, peace, defense, the good of the people, and freedom. It should also include the idea that the framers wanted to pass the Constitution on to posterity, or future generations.

> ***Evaluating Your Child's Skills:*** **In order to complete this activity successfully, your child has to show mastery of language skills such as using context clues to figure out meanings of words, using the dictionary, and "translating" language from an earlier period into modern English. Suggest that your child imagine that he or she is rewriting the Preamble for a younger child who cannot understand the old-fashioned eighteenth-century language.**

 Top of the Class

> **Children interested in delving more deeply into the topics covered in this chapter can**

choose one or more of the following activities. They may do the activities for their own satisfaction or report on what they have done to show that they have been seriously considering the early history of our nation.

DEBATE ABOUT THE ELECTORAL COLLEGE

The following activity will help your child apply concepts in this chapter to recent history.

Consider the following two facts about the electoral college:

1. The members of the original electoral college could vote for whichever candidates they chose. Now, the electors are informally but firmly committed to voting for a particular candidate. Therefore, when citizens cast their vote for electors, they are really voting for the candidates whom the electors support.
2. Because the number of electors assigned to each state is based on that state's population, the electoral college system can result in a candidate's losing the popular vote but winning the election. The 2000 presidential race between George W. Bush and Al Gore was an example. Gore got more popular votes, but Bush won the electoral vote because he carried more of the larger states.

Now think about the electoral college. Do you think the system should be changed so that citizens simply vote directly for candidates? Or do you think the system should remain as it is? Form your opinion based on facts and back it up with convincing arguments.

PARTIES THEN AND NOW

This activity asks your child to compare the original political parties with those of today. After thinking and/or reading about the issues raised here, your child may wish to raise these issues for class discussion.

The two original political parties in the United States were the Federalists and the Anti-Federalists, or Democratic-Republicans.

- Members of the Federalist Party—which included James Madison, Alexander Hamilton, John Jay, and John Adams—believed in a strong central government. They supported trade and business and wanted to keep power in the hands of the wealthiest citizens.
- Members of the Democratic-Republican Party, which included Thomas Jefferson and James Monroe, were concerned with protecting the rights of the individual states (they did not want the larger states to have more representatives in Congress than the smaller states) and the rights of individual citizens (they insisted on adding the Bill of Rights to the Constitution). They supported farmers and the common man over the wealthy and those involved in trade.

Research today's two major parties—the Republicans and the Democrats. Find out what someone means when he or she uses the labels *conservative* and *liberal.* Then think about which of the original parties is more like today's Democrats and which is more like today's Republicans. Which would be called more liberal or conservative in today's terms?

You may find that each of today's parties incorporates ideas from both the original parties, so it may be impossible to make a one-to-one comparison.

RECOMMENDED READING

The biography of Alexander Hamilton listed here traces the dramatic story of Hamilton's life from his birth in the British West Indies to the fatal duel with Aaron Burr. Your child might want to use the book as the basis for an oral report in class.

Whitelaw, Nancy. *More Perfect Union: The Story of Alexander Hamilton.* Morgan Reynolds (*Notable Americans* series), 1997.

CHAPTER 6
Westward Expansion
1803–1900

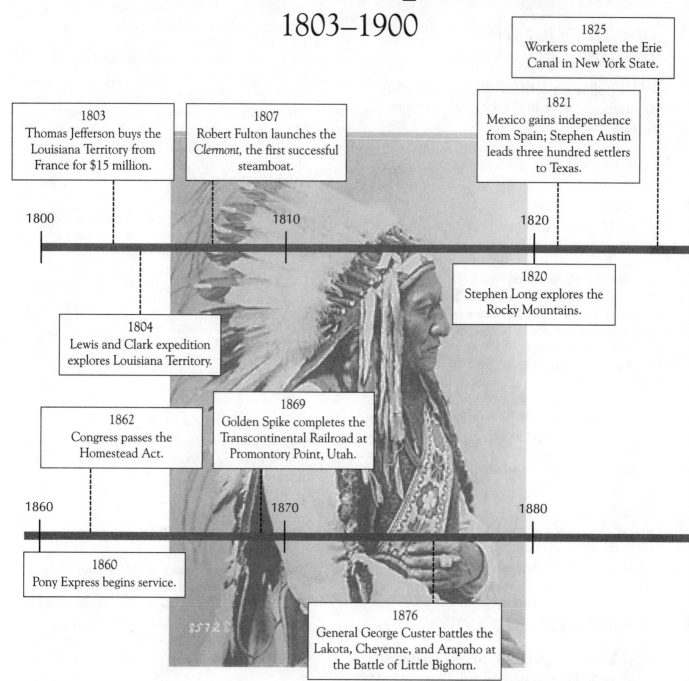

1825
Workers complete the Erie Canal in New York State.

1821
Mexico gains independence from Spain; Stephen Austin leads three hundred settlers to Texas.

1803
Thomas Jefferson buys the Louisiana Territory from France for $15 million.

1807
Robert Fulton launches the *Clermont,* the first successful steamboat.

1800

1810

1820

1820
Stephen Long explores the Rocky Mountains.

1804
Lewis and Clark expedition explores Louisiana Territory.

1862
Congress passes the Homestead Act.

1869
Golden Spike completes the Transcontinental Railroad at Promontory Point, Utah.

1860

1870

1880

1860
Pony Express begins service.

1876
General George Custer battles the Lakota, Cheyenne, and Arapaho at the Battle of Little Bighorn.

This timeline provides an overview of westward expansion in the United States. The following pages detail and explain the importance of how the United States expanded its boundaries during the nineteenth century.

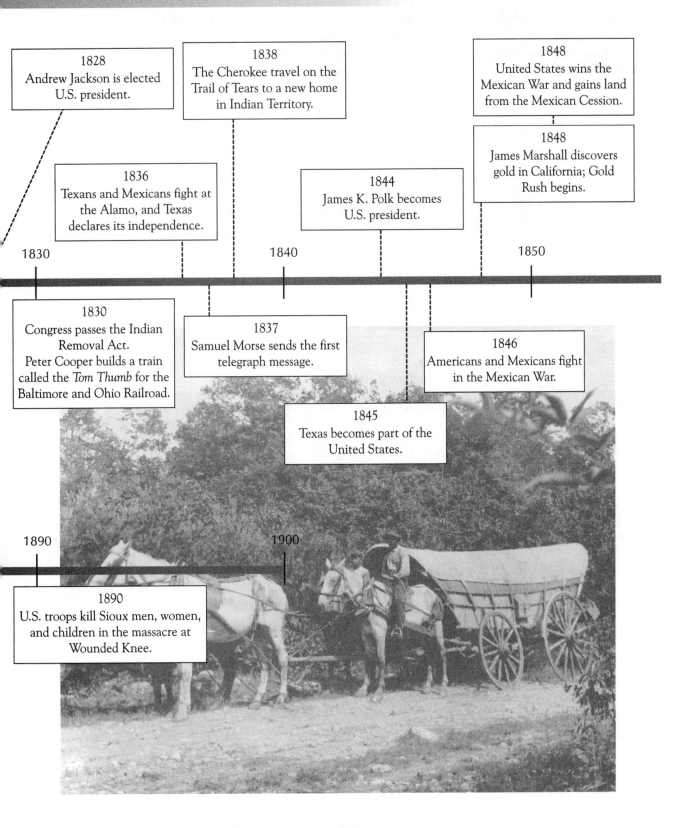

1828
Andrew Jackson is elected U.S. president.

1838
The Cherokee travel on the Trail of Tears to a new home in Indian Territory.

1848
United States wins the Mexican War and gains land from the Mexican Cession.

1848
James Marshall discovers gold in California; Gold Rush begins.

1836
Texans and Mexicans fight at the Alamo, and Texas declares its independence.

1844
James K. Polk becomes U.S. president.

1830

1840

1850

1830
Congress passes the Indian Removal Act.
Peter Cooper builds a train called the *Tom Thumb* for the Baltimore and Ohio Railroad.

1837
Samuel Morse sends the first telegraph message.

1846
Americans and Mexicans fight in the Mexican War.

1845
Texas becomes part of the United States.

1890

1900

1890
U.S. troops kill Sioux men, women, and children in the massacre at Wounded Knee.

Word Power

The words on the following chart are underscored in the section called "What Your Child Needs to Know." Explain their meanings to your child as needed when they come up in reading or discussion. Keep this list handy for you and your child.

Word	Definition
aggression	threatening behavior
census	official count of a country's population
dictator	ruler who takes power and rules unjustly
economic	related to money
frontier	far edge of a country, where few people live; land beyond the settled areas
inflated	higher than is reasonable or fair
livestock	farm animals
pioneers	people who are the first in a new and unknown area
technological	related to progress in the use of machinery, computers, and automation
traditional	handed down by tradition or custom
transcontinental	from one edge of the continent to the other
unjust	unfair
westward	traveling in the direction of west

What Your Child Needs to Know

You may choose to use the following text in several different ways, depending on your child's strengths and preferences. You might read the passage aloud; you might read it to yourself and then paraphrase it for your child; or you might ask your child to read the material along with you or on his or her own.

America was growing rapidly. In 1790, <u>census</u> takers counted just under 4 million Americans. Only ten years later, in 1800, they counted 5.3 million Americans. More people meant the need for more land.

But where to go? Most of the good land east of the Mississippi was already settled. Based on what Lewis and Clark had reported from their 1804 expedition through the Louisiana Territory (see Chapter 5), many people didn't think that this land was fertile enough to farm successfully. In fact, when **Stephen Long,** another explorer, visited the Louisiana Territory in 1820, he referred to the area as the Great American Desert.

In the early 1800s, the U.S. government left the Louisiana Territory to the Native American tribes, many of whom the government had already displaced and resettled several times in the course of making and breaking treaties. The coming years would see more treaties broken and more ill treatment of Native Americans.

TRAILBLAZERS AND MOUNTAIN MEN, 1760 TO 1850S

Settlers generally didn't consider moving to the Louisiana Territory and the west coast in the early part of the nineteenth century, but some Americans were still eager to see these lands for themselves. **Daniel Boone** was among the first American <u>pioneers</u> to head to the <u>frontier</u> in the late 1700s. A trapper and trader, Boone discovered the **Cumberland Gap** in the mountains near where today's Kentucky, Tennessee, and Virginia meet. In 1775, he blazed the complete Wilderness Road through the gap and into what is now central Kentucky. In the early 1800s, other brave men opened additional trails west—for example, the **Santa Fe Trail** and the **Oregon Trail** (both beginning in Missouri). Previously, Native Americans had created sections of these trails.

Hunters and trappers also headed west. Called mountain men, their goal was to live in the wild and make their fortunes. These adventurous risk takers often spent months, or even years, alone in the woods. They caught beavers, skinned them, and saved the pelts, which they would later sell to be made into beaver hats in Europe. Once a year, many of these mountain men gathered to trade goods, sell pelts, and exchange tall tales.

Then the craze for beaver hats in Europe passed and with it the need for the mountain men. Most of these men of the wilderness were no longer able to make their livings as hunters or trappers. Instead, they worked as guides for the many other pioneers who were to come.

TRANSPORTATION AND COMMUNICATION, 1807 TO 1860

<u>Westward</u> expansion proceeded slowly at first because transportation was limited. In America's early days, most roads were made of dirt. These roads were hard and dusty in dry weather and muddy and dangerous when they were wet. **Corduroy roads,** which were paved with wooden logs placed closely together, were a slight improvement. (The surface of these roads looked like corduroy fabric.) But these roads were bumpy, and they rotted quickly. Other roads were paved with rocks—not good for a smooth ride, either.

Then, in 1811, the government began building the **National Road,** which stretched from Maryland to Illinois. This improved road saved travel time considerably; a trip from Baltimore, Maryland, to St. Louis, Missouri, now took four days instead of four weeks.

Steamboats, 1807

Robert Fulton was a painter who became fascinated with engineering. In 1807, he successfully harnessed energy from steam to power the engine of a boat. He launched his steamboat, the *Cler-*

mont, on the Hudson River, and it chugged 150 miles from Albany, New York, down to New York City in thirty-two hours (**barges,** or flat-bottomed boats, required several days for that trip). Steamboats soon became a popular way to transport both goods and people. By 1860, there were over a thousand steamboats plying the Mississippi River.

The Erie Canal, 1817 to 1825

Some people solved their transportation problems by creating **canals,** or human-built waterways, to connect rivers and lakes. Mule-drawn barges traveled more quickly than wagons on bumpy roads, and passengers discovered that gliding along a canal was far more comfortable.

In 1817, New York Governor **DeWitt Clinton** proposed a plan to connect Lake Erie, in the Great Lakes region, with New York City. Many people thought the idea was absurd and made fun of it. They called the canal Clinton's Ditch. But Clinton found enough investors to pay for his project, and by 1825, the Erie Canal was ready for heavy traffic.

The Erie Canal was a huge success. Goods that used to take three weeks and cost $100 a ton to transport by water and land from Buffalo (on Lake Erie) to New York City now could move on the lake, through the canal, and down the river in about one week for only $10 a ton.

Steam Locomotives, 1850

In 1830, a businessman named **Peter Cooper** designed a small steam-driven locomotive, which he named *Tom Thumb.* He attached several train cars and raced the locomotive against a horse-drawn carriage. The horse won, but Cooper proved to Americans that steam engines could do the job. By 1860, more than thirty thousand miles of track had been laid. However, most of the track remained east of the Mississippi River. People still had to figure out how to lay railroad track through the Rocky Mountains and all the way west. (Later pages in this chapter tell about that accomplishment.)

The Pony Express and the Telegraph, 1860 to 1861

Americans also came up with better ways to communicate. During the first half of the nineteenth century, letters traveled slowly; they often took

weeks or months to reach their destinations. But in 1860, the Pony Express galloped into the picture. With new horses every ten miles and new riders every seventy miles, this relay service carried mail between St. Joseph, Missouri, and Sacramento, California, in only eight days—a miracle of speed back then!

After only eighteen months, the Pony Express went out of business. It could not charge enough for its service to make a profit. Besides, a new invention had taken its place. In 1837, **Samuel F. B. Morse** invented the **telegraph,** a system that transferred messages electrically over a wire between a transmitter and a receiver. The coded messages consisted of signs called dots and dashes. In 1861, the first transcontinental telegraph lines went up, and people could send messages across the country in minutes.

INDIAN REMOVAL, 1830 TO 1840

American settlers, hungry for additional land, began eyeing more Native American territory. Yes, the United States had signed treaties recognizing that this land belonged to the Native Americans who had been living on it for hundreds of years. Many Americans, however, felt that it was their own right to use this land.

In 1828, Andrew Jackson became president. Many people thought of Jackson as the people's president; he was the first president who had not been born to one of the wealthy and important families from Virginia or Massachusetts. Jackson's election was also the first in which citizens did not have to be landowners in order to vote, but they did have to be white and male.

Jackson strongly supported the right of white Americans to move and settle where they wished. When Congress passed the **Indian Removal Act** in 1830, he signed it. This law gave the U.S. government the right to claim Indian lands and to make the Native Americans move to an area called *Indian Territory,* where Oklahoma is today.

The Indian Removal Act focused mainly on the valuable, fertile lands of the Southeast. During the winters of 1831 and 1832, the **Choctaw** of Mississippi and the **Creek** and **Chickasaw** of Alabama and Louisiana were forced to move to Indian Territory. Under the leadership of a warrior named

Osceola (*ah* see OH lah), the **Seminole** of Florida fought back when the government came to remove them. They won some victories, but U.S. troops eventually captured Osceola and made many Seminoles leave their homes.

The Cherokee and the Trail of Tears, 1838

The Cherokee people lived in northern Georgia. From the early days of European settlement, the Cherokee had lived side by side with white settlers and had taken on parts of the European-American lifestyle and culture. For example, Cherokee families lived in snug wooden houses; Cherokee women dressed in long, European-style dresses; Cherokee leaders had even written and adopted a constitution based on the Constitution of the United States.

A Cherokee named **Sequoyah** (suh KWOI yuh) had noticed that white settlers used a written language. He thought his people should have a written language, too; he felt that they needed to communicate with each other and write their own treaties. Sequoyah spent twelve years creating a Cherokee writing system with eighty-six symbols. Soon there was a newspaper called the *Cherokee Phoenix*, and Cherokee children were learning to read and write in their own tongue.

Someone discovered gold on Cherokee lands, and American leaders applied the Indian Removal Act. Cherokee chief **John Ross** tried to stay on his homeland and took his case to the U.S. Supreme Court. Justice John Marshall actually ruled in favor of the Cherokee and stated that the United States had no right to force people from their homes. However, President Jackson supported the white settlers, and relocation continued.

During the winter of 1838, U.S. troops drove the Cherokee from their homes and forced them to walk more than eight hundred miles to what is now Oklahoma. The Cherokee called their route the Trail of Tears: during the journey, four thousand of the fifteen thousand Cherokee died from cold, hunger, and disease.

TEXAS, 1821 TO 1845

Meanwhile, other white settlers headed farther west. After years of fighting, Mexico had finally de-clared independence from Spain in 1821. When the new Mexican government found it difficult to get people to colonize the part of Mexico called Texas, it offered land to Americans at cheap prices. In return, American settlers were supposed to become Mexican citizens, learn Spanish, and worship in the Roman Catholic Church.

Many American people took the offer. Land in Texas was rich and fertile, perfect for growing cotton, the valuable cash crop that had replaced tobacco on most southern plantations. In 1821, **Stephen Austin** led a group of three hundred American settlers to Texas. (Today, Texas's capital, Austin, is named for him.) Many more followed. By the early 1830s, somewhere between twenty thousand and thirty thousand Americans had settled in Texas.

There were problems. First, the American settlers refused to learn Spanish or become Catholics. Second, many were keeping slaves, even though slavery was illegal in Mexico. And, third, the settlers wanted more independence. In 1833, Stephen Austin traveled to the capital of Mexico to ask that Texas become its own state, but Austin wound up in jail.

Mexico's <u>dictator</u>, **Antonio López de Santa Anna,** brought troops to take control of Texas. But he ran into **Sam Houston** (HYOO stuhn), the leader of an army raised by Texans. Houston had already organized a government, and Texans were ready to fight to hold onto their land and to gain independence from Mexico. (The large city of Houston, Texas, is named for the Texans' leader.)

The Alamo, 1836

In February 1836, a group of Texan settlers gathered at a fort called the Alamo to protect Texas from Santa Anna. Sources differ in reporting how many men, women, and children were inside—anywhere from 187 to 257. But historians do know that former congressman **Davy Crockett** and trapper **Jim Bowie** were part of the group.

On February 23, Santa Anna's troops attacked. For thirteen days, the Texans held them off, but on March 6, the Mexicans took the fort. The Mexicans executed almost everyone inside; they let a few women and children carry a threat to Houston. The Alamo's defenders never knew that the

Republic of Texas had declared independence from Mexico on March 2.

The cry "Remember the Alamo" inspired the Texan patriots during the battles that followed. Indeed, on April 21, Houston led a surprise attack on Santa Anna and his troops at the **Battle of San Jacinto** (*san* juh SEEN toh). By the end of it, the Texans had captured Santa Anna himself; in exchange for his freedom, Santa Anna promised Texans he would no longer fight their independence.

Joining the Nation, 1845

Soon after, Texan president Houston asked U.S. president Jackson if Texas could become part of the United States. Though Texas would be a valuable addition, Jackson was reluctant. He was concerned that making Mexico a state would cause problems between the United States and Mexico. In addition, if Texas joined the United States, it would count as a slave state and upset the balance between free states and slave states as established in the Missouri Compromise of 1820. (That agreement comes up in Chapter 7.) Texas did not become part of the United States until 1845, when **James K. Polk** was president.

THE MEXICAN WAR, 1846 TO 1848

Jackson was right. When Texas joined the United States, problems with Mexico did surface. Polk (president from 1844 to 1848) declared that the Mexican-American border should follow the river called in Spanish the **Rio Grande** (REE oh GRAHN day). Mexico disagreed: it wanted the border to be farther north, at the **Nueces** (nyu AY sus) **River.** Both countries placed troops along the Rio Grande, and when Mexican soldiers attacked, Polk declared war.

Many Americans felt that this war was <u>unjust</u>. They viewed it as a war of <u>aggression</u> in which the United States was taking land that did not belong to it.

Battles continued—and not only in Texas. Battles raged on Mexican territory in California and in the area that is now the Southwest of the United States. One of the heroes to come out of the war was **Zachary Taylor;** his fame would lead to his election as the eleventh president in 1848.

At last, American troops fought the final battle of the Mexican War in Mexico City at **Chapultepec,** the castle fort that guarded the entrance to the capital. Americans led by General **Winfield Scott** attacked the walls, and those inside the fort surrendered. In 1848, the **Treaty of Guadalupe Hidalgo** (GWAH duh *loo* pay hih DAL goh) ended the war. Mexico agreed to recognize the Rio Grande as the border between Texas and Mexico and also agreed to sell California and other territory to the United States for $15 million. (This land, called the **Mexican Cession,** is now Nevada, Utah, Arizona, and parts of Colorado and New Mexico.)

Fulfilling Manifest Destiny

With the settlement to the Mexican War, America was on its way to fulfilling its manifest destiny. This phrase named the idea that the United States had the right to expand its borders all the way from the Atlantic Ocean to the Pacific Ocean. Many Americans approved of the idea of manifest destiny. In fact, many had voted for President Polk because of his promise to claim for the United States any remaining land between the oceans.

In 1846, the United States had signed a treaty with Britain to work out claims to the Oregon Territory in the Northwest. The two countries agreed to divide the territory along the forty-ninth parallel of latitude. Britain's part is now western Canada; in the United States, the Oregon Territory became Oregon, Washington, Idaho, and parts of Montana and Wyoming.

Finally, in 1853, the United States purchased for $10 million one more strip of land from Mexico, along the southern borders of New Mexico and Arizona. With this treaty, called the **Gadsden Purchase,** the United States created the continental borders it still has today. It fulfilled its manifest destiny—the plan to create one land from coast to coast united by one government.

PIONEERS, 1840 TO 1880

With improved roads, better transportation, and an invitation from the U.S. government to settle the land, thousands of Americans headed west. Most traveled overland, along the **Cumberland Road** in Kentucky, then on the Santa Fe Trail or the Oregon Trail. Some branched off onto the

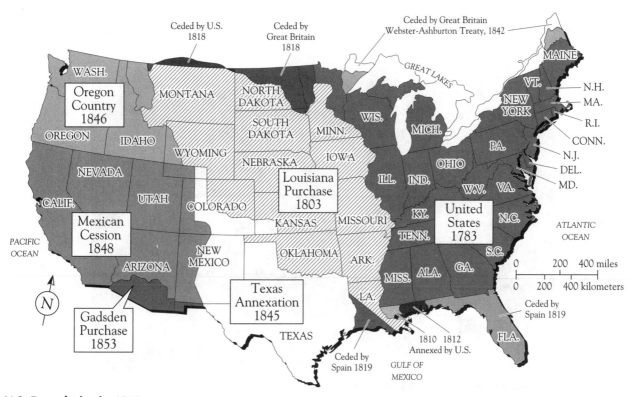

U.S. Boundaries in 1850s

Mormon Trail, explained later in this chapter, and others continued to the **California Trail.**

The pioneers faced long and difficult journeys. Most families set out in the early spring and hoped to reach their destinations before the snows came. They traveled in horse-drawn **Conestoga wagons,** sturdy wagons with broad wheels and large canvas coverings stretched over wooden hoops. Families packed their most important possessions inside the wagons and used what little room remained for the smallest children and sick family members. Trailing along behind the wagon might be the family cow, to be used for milk and, if there were an emergency, for meat.

Most families traveled in **wagon trains,** guided by former mountain men. These were groups of thirty to sixty wagons that rolled west together. On a good day, most wagon trains could expect to cover about fifteen miles.

Wagon trains risked attack from Native American tribes trying to defend their lands. The hot summer weather posed another problem, particularly on days when guides found no water. Pioneers also brought diseases such as cholera with them, and many people became sick and died along the way.

The settlers who did make it had a lot to get used to. Those who decided to start new homes in what we now call the Midwest found treeless plains that provided no wood for houses. Pioneers often built their first homes out of **sod,** or densely packed earth. Men cut the sod out of the earth in brick shapes and built simple, one-room shelters. These early homes provided poor protection from the rains: the houses often leaked and became muddy.

The first pioneers on the plains also had to get used to loneliness and to taking care of themselves. Often, the nearest neighbor was miles away. Each family worked hard to grow or make everything it needed.

There were pleasures also. Early pioneers enjoyed gathering together and did so as often as they could, particularly to share the work of difficult jobs. Families might gather during harvest times or for a quilting bee, or party. These were the pioneers' main opportunities to socialize and share news.

The land of the plains, once described as a desert, soon became fertile farmland because of the

Conestoga wagon drawn by four mules, 1900

pioneers' hard work and a few key <u>technological</u> advances. The invention of the steel plow allowed farmers to cut into the hard-packed soil more easily. Barbed wire, with its spikes, helped farmers to enclose their farms and keep track of <u>livestock</u>. People built windmills to harness the power of the prairie winds in drawing water up from deep within the earth to irrigate the fields. Soon the Midwest was the breadbasket of America; it shipped crops back to the east coast by means of the railroads (discussed further later in this chapter).

MORMON SETTLEMENT, 1847

Many people came west for <u>economic</u> opportunity. Some were also looking for religious freedom. One such group was the **Mormons,** members of the Church of Jesus Christ of Latter-Day Saints. This Bible-based religion was started in 1830 by **Joseph Smith.** The Mormons founded a city in Illinois, called **Nauvoo,** and it became busy and prosperous.

Many people did not want the Mormons to be successful. In 1847, a group of men came to Nauvoo; they burned the city and killed Smith. A man named **Brigham** (BRI guhm) **Young** took over, and he led the Mormons west on a road that came to be called the Mormon Trail. They stopped in the lands of the **Ute** (YOOT), now Utah, along the shore of the Great Salt Lake. They founded **Salt Lake City,** and their settlement grew quickly. It soon became an important stopping point for other settlers traveling west.

The Gold Rush, 1848

An important discovery at **Sutter's Mill** near Sacramento, California, also made its mark on the settlement of the West. On January 24, 1848, **James Marshall** discovered gold.

The Gold Rush began, and thousands of people came to California; these miners called themselves **Forty-Niners** because they arrived in 1849. The population soared. San Francisco went from eight hundred people in 1847 to twenty-five thousand in 1849.

These hopeful settlers expected to get rich mining gold, but usually the only people who truly made money during the Gold Rush were the merchants who sold supplies to the miners. Prices were <u>inflated</u> because goods were limited and demand was high. Many miners spent all their earnings just for basic necessities.

The mining itself was difficult. Most miners **panned** for gold. Panning involved rinsing pans of sand to see if a few flakes of gold might sift to the bottom as larger chunks of rock washed away.

The Homestead Act, 1862

Abraham Lincoln, the sixteenth president, passed the Homestead Act in 1862 to encourage the continued settlement of the West. In exchange for 160 acres of land, a **homesteader** would pay a small fee and promise to live on the land and farm it for five years. After that time, the homesteader would own the land. It was an offer that many Americans accepted.

The Transcontinental Railroad, 1862 to 1869

President Lincoln knew that another way to encourage settlement of the West would be to build a transcontinental railroad. (Most of the track laid before the 1860s was east of the Mississippi River.) In 1862, Congress passed the **Pacific Railroad Act.** The Union Pacific Company would lay track westward from Omaha, Nebraska; the Central Pacific Company would lay track eastward from Sacramento, California. The two teams would meet in the middle.

Over the next seven years, thousands of Chinese and Irish immigrants built more than seventeen hundred miles of track. It was backbreaking work for low pay in dangerous conditions. At last, on May 10, 1869, crowds gathered at **Promontory Point, Utah,** to celebrate the joining of the two tracks. A worker drove in the **Golden Spike,** and the transcontinental railroad was completed. Now travelers could zoom along the tracks at twenty-five miles an hour and travel from coast to coast in about a week.

Cattle Drives and Cowboys, 1860 to 1880

The transcontinental railroad reached from east to west, but in its early days it did not branch south. This situation posed a problem for Texas ranchers, who raised cattle to sell to both coasts. The challenge was to move the cattle more than a thousand miles north to the railroad. Cowboys were the so-

lution. They drove the cattle north from San Antonio, Texas, to Abilene Kansas, on the **Chisholm Trail.** Riding for hours every day, guiding the cattle forward, often singing to keep them calm so that they wouldn't stampede, the cowboys did hard, thankless work.

The period of the cowboys was from about 1860 to 1880. Once the railroad reached Texas, the days of the cattle drives were over.

THE PLAINS WARS

As Americans moved farther west, Native American tribes continued to lose their lands and witnessed the destruction of their culture and traditions.

The tribes of the plains relied on the buffalo for everything: shelter, food, and tools. Across tribal lands, the transcontinental railroad brought thousands of people; in the process, white settlers slaughtered or were otherwise responsible for killing off most of the buffalo. Once there had been millions of buffalo roaming the plains; by 1890, there were fewer than a thousand. As a result, plains tribes could no longer survive in the traditional ways.

The white settlers tried to take the little land that the tribes had left. Once again, the U.S. government did not honor previous treaties and, instead, tried to place the tribes on **reservations,** small areas of land set apart for Native American groups. Many tribes fought back.

In 1874, the **Lakota** (lah KOH tuh), the **Sioux** (SOO), and the **Arapaho** (uh RAP uh *hoh*) came together to protect tribal lands surrounding the Black Hills in what is now South Dakota. But a group of American miners found gold, and the U.S. government offered to buy the land from the Native Americans for $6 million. The tribes refused.

In response, General **George Custer** tried to take the land. He led six hundred U.S. troops into battle. The Native Americans, led by chiefs **Sitting Bull** and **Crazy Horse,** had more than two thousand warriors. They killed Custer and more than two hundred of his men. This battle became known as **Custer's Last Stand.** It was the last Native American victory.

The U.S. government intended to claim lands in the West and did not hesitate to use force. In the next decade when U.S. troops and Native American

Sitting Bull (Tatonka-I-Yatanka), a Hunkpapa Sioux

warriors fought, the Americans usually won. In 1890, at **Wounded Knee,** also in South Dakota, more than two hundred Sioux men, women, and children died at the hands of American troops, even after having surrendered peacefully the night before. With the massacre at Wounded Knee, the U.S. government felt it had succeeded in making the area "safe" for American settlers. The tragic cost was the near-destruction of Native American culture.

 # Implications

To answer the question, "Why does all this matter?" or "What does it mean?," share the following insights with your child.

When we think about how Americans settled the West, we must realize how much happened in one hundred years. The central part of our country had remained wild and mostly untouched for thousands of years. But between 1800 and 1900, this area, once living space and hunting territory for Native Americans, became homesteads and farms. As a result, thousands of people were able to live the American dream of making a fresh start in a new land. And Americans had achieved their goal of making their country stretch from coast to coast.

Developments in technology made settling the West possible. When we think of technology today, we usually think of computers and other electronics. But technology is any tool that solves a problem. When people invented barbed wire and steel plows, they were solving important problems so that they could live in a new land. And today, scientists continue to develop new technologies to make it possible for people to live successfully in yet other new environments—the moon, for example. Chapter 8 tells more about how technological advances changed the way the whole world thought about work.

Based on the ways Americans transformed the land, many people think of the nineteenth century as a century of progress. But here is one final question we all must think about: what is the cost of progress?

It is true that nineteenth-century Americans traveled faster and more efficiently, invented tools to make farming easier, and built new towns and cities. But what about the other side? For the people who lived here before the Europeans arrived, life changed forever in the nineteenth century and definitely not in ways they would have chosen for themselves.

This chapter has not told about everything that happened in America during the 1800s. Chapter 7 considers one of the most tragic times in American history. It was a period that almost ripped the country apart.

Fact Checker

To check that your child knows or can find the basic facts in this chapter, here are questions about its major concepts. Your child should circle his or her answer: *T* for "true" or *F* for "false."

TRUE OR FALSE?

1. T F   Robert Fulton built *Tiny Tim*, the first successful steam locomotive in America.

2. T F   The Texans, including Davy Crockett, won the Battle of the Alamo.

3. T F   The road that the Cherokee traveled from Georgia to Indian Territory was called the Trail of Tears.

4. T F   Custer's Last Stand refers to a battle that General George Custer won.

5. T F   The Gold Rush in 1848 and 1849 took place in New Mexico.

6. T F   Sequoyah produced a writing system for the Cherokee.

7. T F   The border between Texas and Mexico is the Rio Grande.

8. T F   Native Americans were responsible for wiping out most of the buffalo.

9. T F   The Mormons settled permanently in Illinois.

10. T F   Two Native American leaders were Sitting Bull and Crazy Horse.

Answers appear in the back, preceding the index.

? The Big Questions

The following questions encourage your child to think critically rather than simply recall facts. If necessary, review the specific information from the preceding pages that will help your child make the necessary inferences to come up with reasonable answers.

1. If in the 1800s you had lived in the United States near the Atlantic Ocean, what would have made you want to stay there? What would have made you want to head west as a pioneer?
2. Americans in the 1800s called Fulton's plans for a steamboat a folly, or foolishness, and Clinton's canal, in its early stages, a ditch. At least one American said that trying to create a transcontinental railroad was like "trying to build a railroad to the moon." What do you learn about Americans from these opinions?
3. This chapter says that when European settlers and their descendants killed the buffalo, the plains tribes had to give up their traditional ways and lost some of their culture. What does it mean to lose your culture? What would you miss if you had to give up your traditional ways today?

4. What do you think Fulton, Cooper, Morse, and the men who built the transcontinental railroad would say if they came back and saw the transportation and communication systems of twenty-first-century America?

Suggested Answers

1. *Reasons for staying on the east coast might include fear of the unknown, connections to nearby friends and family, and a comfortable lifestyle. Reasons for heading west might include sense of adventure and more economic and social opportunities.*
2. *The opinions show that some Americans thought the plans were absurd or that these Americans didn't have too much faith in their countrymen. In spite of these opinions, the inventors and dreamers knew how to persist until they accomplished the seemingly impossible.*
3. *Losing a culture involves giving up the customs, beliefs, art forms, and lifestyles that a group of people developed and practiced over time. American youths forced to give up traditions today might miss established celebrations and other interactions with friends and relatives as well as certain foods, clothes, music, language, and other cultural markers.*
4. *They might express any or all of the following sentiments: amazement at progress, inability to understand the speeds at which we seem to want to travel and communicate, and pride in the work they did and on which later generations built.*

Skills Practice

The following activities give your child practice in applying the skills basic to social studies. For some of the activities, your child may need to review the information in the preceding pages.

A.   READING A LINE GRAPH

Follow up on the census figures, given in the chapter, for 1790 and 1800 by showing your child the line graph and asking him or her the questions following the graph.

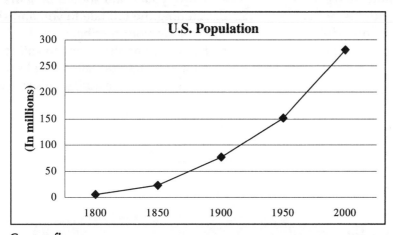

Census figures

1. Between 1900 and 1950, did the population increase by more than it did between 1900 and 1850?
2. Between which two dates on the graph did the country grow by the greatest number of people?

Answers

1. *Yes*
2. *Between 1950 and 2000*

Evaluating Your Child's Skills: **In order to complete this activity successfully, your child has to estimate the population at each point on the graph. If your child has difficulty, help him or her by pointing out that the left-hand side of the graph gives population figures in increases of 50 million. If a dot is halfway between two horizontals, it represents about 25 million people more than the lower horizontal.**

See next page for more skills practice.

B. TELLING A TALL TALE

This chapter says that tall tales were popular among the mountain men. Explain that a tall tale tells an impossible, far-fetched story as if it were true. Usually, the reader or listener finds the story humorous or silly. Read the following summary of a tall tale to your child, or read aloud a tall tale from a book about one of the following American frontier characters: Paul Bunyan, Davy Crockett, John Darling, Mike Fink, Pecos Bill, or Sluefoot Sue.

After you read to your child, suggest that he or she put the tale into his or her own words and tell it to someone else. Your child should notice whether his or her audience thinks the tale is silly or humorous—or not.

Evaluating Your Child's Skills: In order to complete this activity successfully, your child must work on observation skills. If your child has trouble with the stages of this assignment, guide him or her through it as follows:

- First, he or she must listen as you read. Encourage your child to ask for repetition or clarification if necessary. You may want him or her to take notes as you read.
- Then your child needs to spend some time reflecting on what he or she has heard, perhaps reviewing notes.
- Third, your child should do a dry run of retelling the tall tale to you and should consider your feedback.
- Finally, he or she needs to solicit a new audience, tell the tale, and observe and comment on the audience's reaction.

Bridger and the Obsidian Cliff

Jim Bridger was a real mountain man who told tall tales about his travels out west. One of his tales was about the Obsidian Cliff in Yellowstone. Even though obsidian is a natural, dark glass, you can see through it.

Bridger, it seems, was out hunting when he saw a huge elk and fired at it. The elk was not wounded and didn't even seem to hear the shot. Bridger took three more shots with the same result. Then he ran toward the elk and suddenly crashed into a wall of dark, transparent glass. A whole mountain of glass separated Bridger from the elk. And the glass acted like a telescope. So the elk had appeared really close to Bridger when, in fact, it was at least twenty-five miles away.

C.   WORKING WITH SYMBOLS

Explain to your child that a symbol is an object that represents or stands for something else. As a child-friendly example, mention the Statue of Liberty, which, for many people, is a symbol of freedom. Ask your child to talk about one of the following symbols from the chapter. What might it symbolize?

1. The building called the Alamo, which still stands in the Texas city called San Antonio
2. The tears in the name *Trail of Tears*, which the Cherokee walked along from Georgia to Oklahoma
3. The Golden Spike hammered into the railroad track at Promontory Point, Utah, in 1869

Evaluating Your Child's Skills: In order to complete this activity successfully, your child needs to know facts about history and to explain how the object in #1, #2, or #3 connects with those facts. If your child needs help seeing the symbolism, ask him or her questions such as the following.

Alamo: What happened in the Alamo? How might Texans feel if it were torn down?

Tears: Why do people shed tears? What might people feel when they cry?

Spike: When do we give gifts of gold? What does gold mean to you?

 # Top of the Class

Children interested in delving more deeply into the topics covered in this chapter can choose one or more of the following activities. They may do the activities for their own satisfaction or report on what they have done to show that they have been seriously considering westward expansion.

REVIEWING A MOVIE

Rent one of the classic Westerns telling of Americans on the frontier. After your child views the film, ask how it reinforces ideas from this chapter and how it misrepresents ideas. Encourage your child to tell his or her teacher and class about the movie. Here are suggestions.

Red River, 1948, directed by Howard Hawks. Cattle drives and the Chisholm Trail.

High Noon, 1952, directed by Stanley Kramer. A marshal against the bad guys.

Shane, 1953, directed by George Stevens. A stranger helps a homesteading family.

CHAPTER 7

The Slavery Debate, Civil War, and Reconstruction

1820–1877

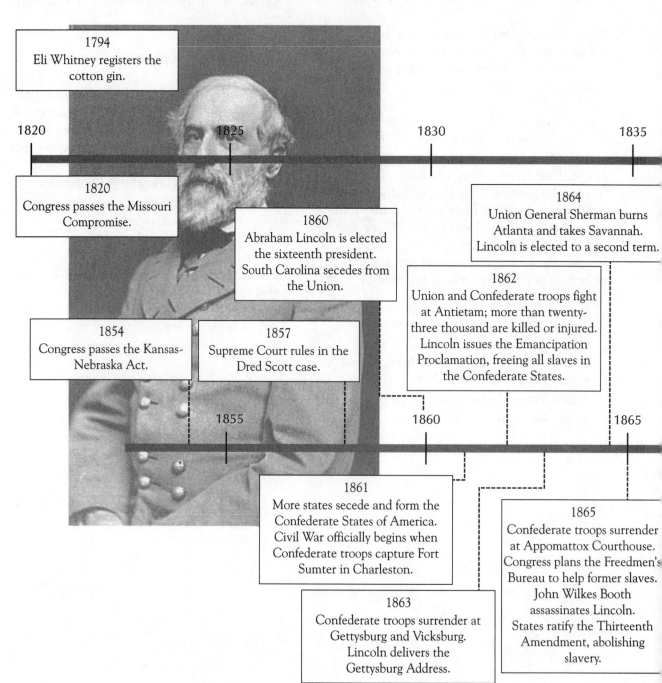

1794
Eli Whitney registers the cotton gin.

1820   1825   1830   1835

1820
Congress passes the Missouri Compromise.

1860
Abraham Lincoln is elected the sixteenth president. South Carolina secedes from the Union.

1864
Union General Sherman burns Atlanta and takes Savannah. Lincoln is elected to a second term.

1862
Union and Confederate troops fight at Antietam; more than twenty-three thousand are killed or injured. Lincoln issues the Emancipation Proclamation, freeing all slaves in the Confederate States.

1854
Congress passes the Kansas-Nebraska Act.

1857
Supreme Court rules in the Dred Scott case.

1855   1860   1865

1861
More states secede and form the Confederate States of America. Civil War officially begins when Confederate troops capture Fort Sumter in Charleston.

1865
Confederate troops surrender at Appomattox Courthouse. Congress plans the Freedmen's Bureau to help former slaves. John Wilkes Booth assassinates Lincoln. States ratify the Thirteenth Amendment, abolishing slavery.

1863
Confederate troops surrender at Gettysburg and Vicksburg. Lincoln delivers the Gettysburg Address.

This timeline provides an overview of the important events of the Civil War and Reconstruction periods. In the following pages, a narrative describes the course of the Civil War and its later effects.

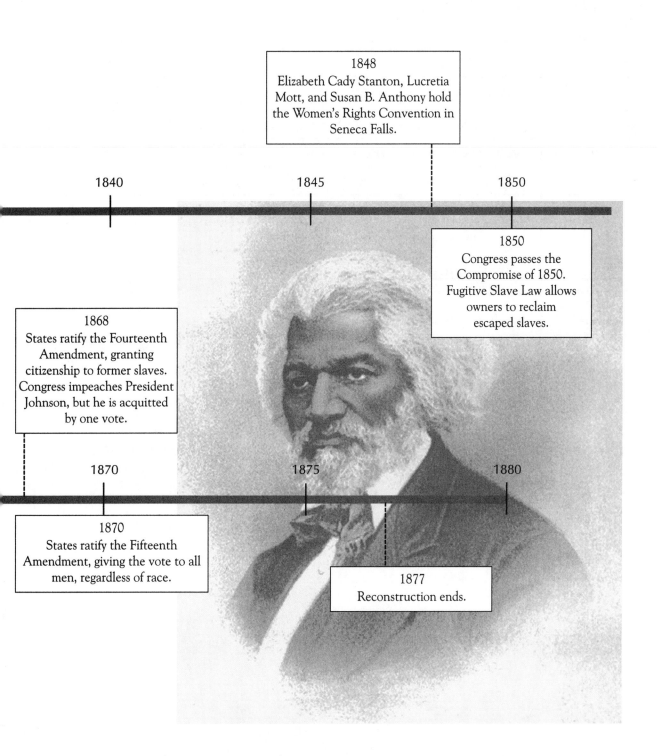

1848
Elizabeth Cady Stanton, Lucretia Mott, and Susan B. Anthony hold the Women's Rights Convention in Seneca Falls.

1840

1845

1850

1850
Congress passes the Compromise of 1850. Fugitive Slave Law allows owners to reclaim escaped slaves.

1868
States ratify the Fourteenth Amendment, granting citizenship to former slaves. Congress impeaches President Johnson, but he is acquitted by one vote.

1870

1875

1880

1870
States ratify the Fifteenth Amendment, giving the vote to all men, regardless of race.

1877
Reconstruction ends.

Word Power

Word	Definition
abolition	elimination or ending of something—in this case, slavery
assassinated	shot and killed; usually used when referring to political leaders
emancipation	state of being made free
fugitive	referring to someone who is running away from authorities
inequalities	treatment in an unequal and unfair way
override	pass a law or ruling over the objection of
pardon	officially forgive
proclamation	official announcement
prosperous	wealthy and successful

What Your Child Needs to Know

You may choose to use the following text in several different ways, depending on your child's strengths and preferences. You might read the passage aloud; you might read it to yourself and then paraphrase it for your child; or you might ask your child to read the material along with you or on his or her own.

AMERICAN SLAVERY IN THE 1800s

The U.S. overseas slave trade had ended by law in 1808, and by the 1830s, <u>abolition</u> of slavery in the North was mostly complete. But many children were born into slavery in the South, and people continued to buy and sell slaves within states and across state lines.

From its colonial days on, the South had relied on slave labor. Even some of the best-known supporters of liberty and equality—Thomas Jefferson and James Madison, for example—owned slaves. They said they disapproved of slavery but called it a "necessary evil" and believed that slavery would die out gradually on its own.

At first, their prediction seemed correct because tobacco growers overworked the land and produced smaller crops. As a result, owning slaves cost too much, and wealthy farmers considered freeing their slaves for economic reasons.

This situation changed in 1793, when **Eli Whitney** invented a machine called the **cotton gin,** which quickly and cheaply separates raw cotton fibers from seeds. (*Gin* is short for *engine.* Some researchers credit **Catharine Greene** with inventing the gin but, as a woman, not being able to register it.) The invention made growing and harvesting cotton highly profitable. Many plantations switched from tobacco to cotton, and plantation owners continued to rely on slave labor to work the fields.

Life was difficult for American slaves. They worked endless hours in the fields or in their masters' homes, lived in crude quarters, and basically had no control over their own lives. Owners split up slave families by selling parents to one plantation and children to another. Owners also forbade slaves to learn to read and write.

Some slaves managed to escape north to freedom on the **Underground Railroad**—the name given to a route of safe houses where escaping slaves could find food and shelter as they headed north to freedom. Each safe house was called a **station,** and the people who guided the slaves to freedom were called **conductors.**

While some slaves escaped to freedom, others rebelled right where they were. In 1831, **Nat Turner** led a revolt in Southampton County, Virginia. He and other slaves killed almost sixty men, women, and children from slave-owning families. He was eventually captured and hanged, but his rebellion frightened many slave owners.

ABOLITIONISTS FIGHT FOR FREEDOM

Many Americans—men and women, black and white—were **abolitionists,** people who fought to abolish, or end, slavery. One of the best known was **Frederick Douglass.** Born a slave in Maryland in

Portrait of Frederick Douglass, c. 1870

1817, Douglass received reading lessons from his owner's wife until the owner found out and stopped them. Later Douglass traded food with poor white boys in exchange for writing lessons. In 1838, he escaped to the North and became a popular and brilliant speaker against slavery. Douglass published his life story and founded the first black abolitionist newspaper, *The North Star.*

William Lloyd Garrison, a white man, was a friend of Douglass's. He founded the American Anti-Slavery Society in 1833 and published another abolitionist newspaper called *The Liberator.*

In 1852, **Harriet Beecher Stowe,** a white woman, wrote *Uncle Tom's Cabin,* a novel about the evils of slavery. It sold more than three hundred thousand copies in its first year and played an important part in publicizing the antislavery movement.

Harriet Tubman was a conductor on the Underground Railroad. After escaping from a plantation in 1849, she returned to the South many times to lead more than three hundred other slaves north to freedom.

Angelina Grimké and **Sarah Grimké** were white southerners who opposed slavery. They decided to leave their father's plantation and move north so that they could safely speak out against slavery. In the North, they spoke publicly for the abolitionist cause.

Some abolitionists believed that bloodshed was the only way to achieve freedom for slaves. In 1859, **John Brown,** a white man who came from a New England family, organized an attack at **Harpers Ferry,** Virginia. He planned to distribute guns to slaves and lead a revolt. Douglass tried but failed to stop Brown, whom some people considered unstable and suicidal. Brown was captured, tried, and hanged. Still, many southerners feared Brown and worried that other northerners would intrude in their affairs.

Women's Rights

Related to the antislavery movement, the women's rights movement gained attention in the mid-nineteenth century. Abolitionists such as **Lucretia Mott** and **Elizabeth Cady Stanton** questioned a government and customs that prevented women from having the same rights as men. At the time, women could not vote or own property; they were considered the property of their fathers or husbands and were not allowed to make independent decisions.

In 1848, Stanton, Mott, and **Susan B. Anthony** organized a convention in **Seneca Falls,** New York, to discuss women's rights. More than 240 women attended, and they adopted the **Bill of Women's Rights,** setting the stage for the full-scale women's movement that was to come.

THE ROAD TO WAR

Slavery highlighted the issue of **states' rights.** Where did the power to allow or abolish slavery in each state reside—at the state level or at the national level? When the country had been founded, individual states made their own decisions about whether or not to allow slavery. When America acquired the Louisiana Territory in 1803, the question arose again.

The South wanted the new territory to allow slavery so that slave states would have more votes and control the Senate. The North, on the other hand, wanted the territory to be free states. Northerners working in factories opposed slavery because free slave labor would threaten the jobs of poor, working immigrants. (Some northerners and some southerners also believed that slavery was morally wrong.)

The Missouri Compromise

When Missouri, within the Louisiana Territory, applied for statehood, Senator **Henry Clay,** the "Great Compromiser," crafted the Missouri Compromise of 1820. According to this plan, Missouri was admitted as a slave state, and Maine was admitted as a free state to maintain the voting balance in the Senate. From then on, the compromise said, all states north of Missouri's southern border would be free and all those south of the border would be slave states. Clay's compromise satisfied most people and preserved the Union—for a time. (By the early 1800s, many Americans had begun to use the term *union* when referring to the United States. During the Civil War itself, the North was called the Union, and the South was called the Confederacy.)

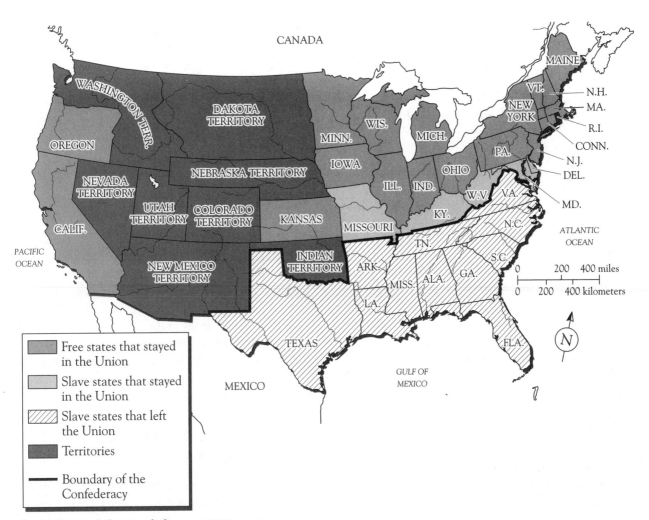

The Union and the Confederacy, 1861

The Great Compromise of 1850 and the Fugitive Slave Act

The question reared its head again after the Mexican War (see Chapter 6): should the former Mexican territory become slave states or free states? Once again, Henry Clay came up with a plan, the Great Compromise of 1850. This plan called for making California a free state and allowing the other areas gained from Mexico to decide later for themselves whether to be free states or slave states. Because this plan contradicted the Missouri Compromise, which had marked a clear dividing line between slave and free states, it angered many people.

Another part of the Great Compromise was the Fugitive Slave Act, which made it legal for slave owners to recapture runaway slaves who had es-

caped to the North. (As a result of this law, the Underground Railroad extended its route all the way to Canada, where U.S. slave owners had no right to recapture slaves.) Angry though people were, the Union once again had survived.

The Kansas-Nebraska Act

In 1854, Congress passed the Kansas-Nebraska Act, which allowed the new territories of Kansas and Nebraska to decide for themselves whether or not to allow slavery. This law once again struck down the Missouri Compromise statement that such new territories would ban slavery.

Settlers rushed into Kansas to establish a majority—some were proslavery, and others were **Free Soilers,** who were against slavery. The two sides became violent and fought for several years. Observers called the area **Bleeding Kansas.**

The Dred Scott Decision

In 1857, a slave named **Dred Scott** brought a case to the U.S. Supreme Court. He and his wife had been slaves in Missouri, but they lived for a time with their master in Illinois, which was a free state. Scott argued that he was free because he had lived in a free state.

Chief Justice **Roger Taney** (TAW nee) ruled against Scott. He stated that slaves are property and that property owners have the right to move their property wherever they wish. Because of these facts, Taney argued, Congress could not outlaw slavery in any state. The Dred Scott decision meant, in other words, that the Missouri Compromise was unconstitutional. Going further, Taney announced that blacks had "no rights which any white man was bound to respect."

In response to Taney's decision, the two sides arguing about slavery and states' rights continued to disagree. What would become of Kansas and Nebraska?

LEADERSHIP IN THE SLAVERY DEBATE

After Andrew Jackson came a series of presidents whom most historians consider to have been relatively weak: **Martin Van Buren** (1836–1840); William Henry Harrison, who died a month after taking office (1840); **John Tyler** (1841–1844); James K. Polk (1844–1848); Zachary Taylor, who also died in office (1848–1850); **Millard Fillmore** (1850–1852); **Franklin Pierce** (1852–1856); and **James Buchanan** (1856–1860). With the exception perhaps of Polk, none had a specific vision for the country, and all avoided solving the problem of slavery.

The Senate, meanwhile, heard dramatic speakers on both sides of the debate. **Daniel Webster** from Massachusetts spoke passionately against slavery, while **John Calhoun** from North Carolina recommended slavery. Others, such as Henry Clay from Kentucky and **Stephen Douglas** from Illinois, were more concerned about preserving the Union than about the morality of slavery, but, though

they worked hard to build unity in Congress, the country was slowly tearing itself apart.

New political parties—or, sometimes, old political parties with new names—arose around the question of slavery. A party called the **Democrats** consisted of wealthy southern slave owners. A party called **Republicans** consisted of abolitionists and Free Soilers, who wanted to put forth their views on Kansas and Nebraska. The Republicans gained popularity quickly: in 1854, they won a hundred seats in Congress.

In 1858, **Abraham Lincoln,** a Republican candidate from Illinois ran for the Senate against Stephen Douglas. Lincoln, a lawyer who had grown up poor in the backwoods of Kentucky, was unknown, but he made a name for himself in a series of seven debates with Douglas. While Douglas was in favor of states' rights, Lincoln spoke powerfully in favor of preserving the Union. Lincoln lost the Senate race. He went on to run for president in 1860. That election he won, and he promised to hold the country together at all costs.

WORSENING RELATIONS BETWEEN NORTH AND SOUTH

Lincoln's promise would be difficult to keep. In an early speech, Lincoln had said that "a house divided against itself cannot stand," meaning that the Union had split in two. Indeed, the North and South sometimes seemed like completely different countries. The North had plenty of small farms, but more and more it was becoming industrial, with people going into manufacturing and trade. It had a large population of immigrants. Small farms and large plantations inhabited by farmers and slaves covered the rural South.

Some southern leaders argued that it would be easier to **secede,** or break away, from the Union than remain part of it. The North claimed that states did not have the right to leave the Union.

After Lincoln's election in 1860, South Carolina became convinced that Lincoln would not represent the South's interests. South Carolina seceded in December 1860. In January 1861, six other states followed: Mississippi, Florida, Alabama, Georgia, Louisiana, and Texas. Together they formed the **Confederate States of America.**

THE CIVIL WAR, 1861 TO 1865

When groups within a country take up arms against each other, they are having what is called a *civil war.* On April 12, 1861, the American Civil War officially began when Confederate troops attacked Union-held **Fort Sumter** in Charleston, South Carolina. After thirty-four hours of cannon blasts, Union soldiers surrendered, and the Confederacy declared its first victory of the war.

More states seceded: Arkansas, North Carolina, Virginia, and Tennessee all joined the Confederacy. However, four slave states remained in the Union; these so-called **border states** were Missouri, Kentucky, Maryland, and West Virginia (a new state that had separated from Virginia after disagreeing about slavery).

War Leaders

In the North, President Lincoln asked one of the country's top military leaders, **Robert E. Lee,** to lead the army, but Lee, who was from Virginia, felt that he could not take up arms against his home state. Lee eventually became the commander of the Confederate forces.

Lincoln then chose General Winfield Scott (see Chapter 6) to lead the army. Scott proposed what became known as the **Anaconda Plan.** Like the anaconda snake, which squeezes its prey, Scott planned to "squeeze" the Confederacy by blockading southern seaports, taking control of the Mississippi River to break the South into two parts, and invading the South from east and west.

The North possessed many advantages on entering the war. Northerners outnumbered southerners. The North had 22 million people compared with 9 million free people and 3.5 million slaves in the South. The North had more factories to manufacture weapons and supplies. It had a strong navy as well as twice as much railroad track for transporting troops. And it had more money.

In the South, the Confederate government established its capital at Richmond, Virginia, and elected **Jefferson Davis** as president of the Confederacy. The South felt confident that it would win because most of the best-trained military leaders (including Lee) came from the South and had declared loyalty to the Confederacy; most southern men were expert horsemen and skilled with rifles, unlike the northern soldiers; and much of the war would be taking place on familiar southern soil.

The Battle of Bull Run

Though the first shots were fired in April, the war began in earnest on July 21, 1861, in the **Battle of Bull Run,** at Manassas (muh NA suhss), Virginia. (This battle is also sometimes called **First Manassas.**) A festive atmosphere existed during battle preparations; it seemed that many people did not fully understand what was about to happen. Some people even brought picnics to the site at Bull Run Creek to watch the action.

The battle was fierce, and at first it looked as though the Union would win. But the Confederates held fast; one soldier noticed General T. J. Jackson holding his position "like a stone wall."

Robert E. Lee, 1863, photographed by Julian Vannerson

The general earned the nickname **Stonewall Jackson,** and he led Confederate troops to a victory that day. The spilled blood made it clear to both sides that the war would be neither easy nor quick.

"The First Modern War"

Many historians consider the Civil War to be the first modern war. War was no longer a simple matter of rows of soldiers in hand-to-hand combat. Technological advances led to the creation of more effective—and deadlier—weapons such as the Gatling machine gun, which could fire up to 250 bullets a minute. **Ironclads,** warships covered in sheets of metal, also appeared for the first time. Telegraphs (see Chapter 6) transported messages quickly, and photography (invented in the 1830s) allowed reporters to capture war scenes for newspapers and magazines.

A modern war, Americans learned, was also a brutal war. After Fort Sumter and Bull Run, both North and South settled in for a long fight. Ironically, the advances in technology made for greater injuries and deaths on both sides. Many men also died from infection and disease; in the South, soldiers also suffered from lack of food and supplies.

At the beginning of the war, young men eagerly signed up for the army; many were worried that the war would be over before they had seen any action. Sadly, this was far from the truth. As the war dragged on and the numbers of soldiers killed and wounded grew, fewer people signed up. Eventually, both North and South began **conscription**—that is, requiring male citizens to join the army for a specific amount of time.

The Civil War was doubly heartbreaking because it so often divided families and put relatives on opposing sides. Some battles found brother fighting against brother. Even Lincoln's wife, **Mary Todd Lincoln,** had brothers who fought for the Confederacy, while she supported the northern cause.

Major Battles

The war progressed, but neither side appeared to be gaining ground. In September 1862, troops fought one of the deadliest battles in American history. At **Antietam** (an TEE tuhm), Maryland, a combined total of more than twenty-three thousand men were killed or wounded.

Eventually, the war began to lose support in the North. Lincoln needed to motivate his country and his troops. After Antietam, on September 23, 1862, he issued the **Emancipation Proclamation.** It freed all slaves in the Confederate states. (Note that the Emancipation Proclamation did not free the slaves in the border states.) This document inspired many Americans to focus on the *moral* purpose of the war.

In the winter of 1862, a Union general named **Ulysses S. Grant** led troops against Confederate forces at **Fort Donelson,** Tennessee. When Grant won the battle there, he demanded "unconditional surrender," which gave new meaning to his first two initials and brought him a reputation for being tough in battle. Grant's determined approach won him the respect of soldiers and political leaders; he would eventually take command of the whole Union army.

The turning point for the North finally came in July 1863. From July 1 to July 3, troops fought at **Gettysburg,** Pennsylvania, in an awful battle. The Union won, but both sides lost thousands of troops.

On July 4, Confederate troops surrendered at **Vicksburg,** Mississippi, a town that had been under siege by Union troops for forty-nine days. With the fall of Vicksburg, the Union gained control of the Mississippi River. These two victories rallied the Union.

Not surprisingly, many blacks were eager to fight for the Union. A white man named **Robert Gould Shaw** led the Massachusetts 54th Regiment, one of the first regiments in which all the enlisted men were black. Shaw died in battle at **Fort Wagner** in 1863, along with nearly half of his men. In all, more than 180,000 blacks, including Douglass's sons, served with the Union forces.

With the Union outlook more hopeful, Lincoln attended a memorial service at Gettysburg in November 1863 to dedicate a national cemetery. There he delivered his famous **Gettysburg Address.** Though it was only two minutes long, this important speech reminded Americans that their fighting had a purpose: to ensure that "government of the people, by the people, for the people, shall not perish from this earth."

Grant took over the Union army in March 1864 and began pursuing Confederate troops. Meanwhile, Union general **William Tecumseh Sherman** (named for the Native American leader mentioned in Chapter 5) led a march designed to cut the South in two horizontally and to destroy the Confederacy for good. Sherman practiced what is called **total war:** he destroyed anything that the enemy could possibly use to fight. He proceeded to Atlanta, Georgia, where his troops burned the city on September 2, 1864. Then he led his army on a "march to the sea." Along the three hundred miles from Atlanta to Savannah, Georgia, his troops destroyed property, crops, and homes in a path forty miles wide. Sherman's march was successful in that it achieved its goal of destroying the supplies and the spirit of the South, but his methods left lasting bitterness.

The End of the War

Lincoln was reelected in 1864. From that point on, the war progressed quickly to an end. On April 2, 1865, Union troops captured Richmond, Virginia, the Confederate capital. Finally, on April 9, 1865, Robert E. Lee surrendered to Ulysses S. Grant at **Appomattox** (*ap* uh MAH tuks) **Courthouse,** Virginia.

The war was over. It had caused more than 620,000 deaths: 360,000 Union soldiers and 260,000 Confederate soldiers. In the South, one out of every four white men had died.

Still, people were relieved that the war had ended, but the relief turned to deep shock and sorrow when on April 14, 1865, an actor named **John Wilkes Booth** assassinated President Lincoln during a play at **Ford's Theater** in Washington. Lincoln had proven himself a valuable leader during wartime; sadly, he would not be there to oversee the rebuilding of his country.

RECONSTRUCTION, 1866 TO 1877

Reconstruction, or rebuilding, began. It was not just a matter of restoring southern cities that had burned to the ground; Reconstruction also meant preparing southerners—both black and white—for life without slavery.

Lincoln's goal was to go gently, to bring about change without making southerners feel angry or humiliated. He planned to make it easy for states to rejoin the Union by requiring that only one-tenth of the population declare loyalty to the United States. Then each state would have to approve the Thirteenth Amendment to the Constitution. This amendment abolished slavery.

Before Lincoln died, the federal government had planned the **Freedmen's Bureau** to help former slaves adjust to their new lives. In addition to providing food, clothing, and shelter, the agency would create schools and colleges for blacks.

Reconstruction Amendments

Thirteenth Amendment: Freed the slaves; passed February 1865; ratified December 1865

Fourteenth Amendment: Declared that all persons born in the United States were citizens and entitled to equal protection; passed June 1866; ratified July 1868

Fifteenth Amendment: Gave male African American citizens the right to vote; passed February 1869; ratified March 1870

Andrew Johnson, who became president after Lincoln's death, proceeded to pardon Confederate soldiers and leaders. Within the year, many of them won seats in Congress. People worried that Johnson and the former Confederates were undoing the work of the Civil War. In the South, many state governments began to pass laws called **black codes,** which took away former slaves' rights to own land and go to school.

The **Radical Republicans,** a group in Congress, decided to overturn the black codes by proposing and pushing for the Civil Rights Act of 1866. **Civil rights** are a citizen's entitlement to equal treatment under the law. Johnson vetoed the act, but Congress voted to override the veto. This was the first time in American history that Congress had overridden the president.

Congress went even further, putting itself, not the president, in charge of Reconstruction. It sent troops to the former Confederate states to protect blacks who lived there. Under supervision by Congress, the Reconstruction period saw the election of the first blacks to Congress. **Hiram Revels** and

Blanche K. Bruce took seats in the Senate, and between 1869 and 1876, fourteen blacks joined the House of Representatives. It was a hopeful time for many who believed that equality was close at hand.

Bad feelings between the North and the South remained, however. Some southerners called whites who sided with Republicans **scalawags,** or rascals. They were also bitter about northerners who came south to do business. They called these people **carpetbaggers** because many of them packed their belongings in bags made of carpetlike fabric. These southerners believed that the carpetbaggers came south solely to get rich. While that may have been true for some, many northerners came to the South because they truly wished to help.

The Impeachment of Andrew Johnson

President Johnson was in constant conflict with Congress. Time after time, Johnson tried to stop Congress's attempts to proceed with Reconstruction.

In 1867, Congress passed the Tenure of Office Act, which stated that the president was not allowed to remove a member of his cabinet without Congress's permission. As a test, Johnson removed his secretary of war, **Edwin Stanton.**

The House of Representatives responded by charging Johnson with "high crimes and misdemeanors" and **impeached** him—that is, accused him and sent him to trial to determine whether he should be removed from office. The Senate conducted the trial. Two-thirds of the Senate would have had to find him guilty in order to remove him from office. When it came to the vote, Johnson survived—but by only one vote.

Reconstruction Fails

Many people were not ready for Reconstruction; instead, they worked to take away the hard-won rights of African Americans.

In 1866, some southern men formed the **Ku Klux Klan,** a group of war veterans who, dressed in white hoods and robes, pretended to be the ghosts of Confederate soldiers. They terrorized blacks and carpetbaggers; they burned homes and **lynched,** or hanged, people.

Even though the black codes had been overturned and three new amendments added to the Constitution, state governments found ways to deny blacks their rights. Some states imposed a **poll tax,** which individuals had to pay before they could vote. Former slaves, many of whom were poor, could not afford to pay the tax.

State governments also passed **Jim Crow laws.** Named for a black character in a popular song, these laws made it legal to **segregate** people—that is, to separate people based on their race. For example, these laws allowed for separate areas for blacks and whites in restaurants, hospitals, and schools.

While some blacks of this period became <u>prosperous</u>, most lived in poverty. Many former slaves became **sharecroppers,** individuals who farmed someone else's land in exchange for a part of the crop. Sharecropping was a hard life, and often the share of cotton or other crop that went to a sharecropper was barely enough for survival.

In 1877, **Rutherford B. Hayes,** a Republican, was declared president after a close, confused election. In exchange for the presidency, Republicans in Congress agreed to pull troops out of the South. This pullout meant the end of Reconstruction and, with it, the hopes of many black men and women.

 # Implications

To answer the question, "Why does all this matter?" or "What does it mean?," share the following insights with your child.

Many people think the Civil War was only about the principle of whether a democratic society could or should allow slavery. It is true that the war ended slavery. But, as with so much in history, there was more than one reason for taking sides. The war was about other issues too.

For one thing, it was about preserving the Union. Lincoln entered the war with this idea foremost in his mind. When he spoke in the Gettysburg Address about "a new birth of freedom," he meant that keeping the country in one piece in the 1860s was as important as the colonies' first declaring their freedom in 1776.

The war was also about economic issues. For slave owners, slaves meant property, and property meant money. For workers in the North, slaves were a threat to their jobs. Both sides, in other words, were fighting for their wallets.

The end of the war and the twelve years afterward gave rights—on paper—to blacks. But a hundred years after the colonies had declared their independence from Britain, black Americans still faced many <u>inequalities</u>—and would continue to in the years ahead.

The tragic losses of the Civil War raise many "what if?" questions. So many young men died; in a way, a whole generation of men was lost. What if these men had lived? What contributions would they have made to the world? When a gifted thinker was killed on the battlefield, what advances in science and technology did we lose? Reconstruction could rebuild factories, establish schools, and pass laws, but it couldn't replace people.

 # Fact Checker

To check that your child knows or can find the basic facts in this chapter, have him or her list the following events chronologically on a separate sheet of paper. Your child should place the earliest event at the top of the paper and the last event at the bottom of the paper.

TIMELINE

A. Compromise of 1850
B. Dred Scott decision by the Supreme Court
C. Election of blacks to Congress
D. Fort Sumter, South Carolina, taken over by the Confederacy
E. Fugitive Slave Law approved
F. Gettysburg Address
G. Lee's surrender to Grant at Appomattox Court House, Virginia
H. Lincoln elected to first term
I. Missouri Compromise

Answers appear in the back, preceding the index.

 # The Big Questions

The following questions encourage your child to think critically rather than simply recall facts. If necessary, review the specific information from the preceding pages that will help your child make the necessary inferences to come up with reasonable answers.

1. Northern states had abolished slavery by the 1830s. What arguments did southern states make in defense of continuing to use slave labor?
2. Why did slave masters not let their slaves learn to read and write?
3. The chapter says that at times during the Civil War brother took up arms against brother. How could such conflicts come about?
4. What were the results of the Civil War?

Suggested Answers

1. *Southern states claimed that plantation owners could not afford to produce cotton and other crops without slave labor. Without slaves, they said, the entire economy would fall apart. In addition,*

southern states said it was their right—not the federal government's right—to decide about slavery.

2. One answer to this question is that literacy can be liberating. If slaves were able to read and write, they could communicate better among themselves and with antislavery supporters.

3. Brothers who were born and grew up together in one state could become separated as one or another moved to another state. In the Civil War, one set of states fought another set of states. It's possible that one brother living in a Union state and one in a Confederate state would have had to take up arms against each other.

4. The war resulted in the deaths of 620,000 men and tens of thousands of injuries. Some cities were burned out. States rejoined the Union, so the United States survived as a single country. Blacks acquired some rights through new amendments and laws, but other laws promoted segregation. In reality, blacks continued to face prejudice and poor living conditions.

Skills Practice

The following activities give your child practice in applying the skills basic to social studies. For some of the activities, your child may need to review the information in the preceding pages.

A.   DEFENDING AN OPINION

The following activity will help your child practice research skills as well as see another side of the Civil War.

Here is a statement of opinion:

Women played an important role in the Civil War.

Select two of the women named in the following list, and find information about the role of each leading to, during, or following the Civil War. You may use a textbook, an encyclopedia, or other reference work. Prepare a few sentences giving facts about these women to support the statement of opinion.

Louisa May Alcott

Clara Barton

Kate Cumming

Dorothea Dix

Rose O'Neal Greenhow

Julia Ward Howe

Sally Tompkins

Sojourner Truth

Answers

Your child should build sentences around the following facts:

Louisa May Alcott: *northern woman who was a short-term nurse; wrote letters, later published, about her nursing experiences*

Clara Barton: *gave up job in Patent Office to work as volunteer distributing supplies to wounded soldiers; after the war, tracked down information about more than twenty thousand missing soldiers*

Kate Cumming: *southern woman who collected supplies for and nursed injured soldiers*

Dorothea Dix: *served with Union army as superintendent of women nurses*

Rose O'Neal Greenhow: *Confederate spy*

Julia Ward Howe: *author who composed "Battle Hymn of the Republic"; she wrote for an antislavery paper*

Sally Tompkins: *southern woman who opened a hospital in Richmond for soldiers; commissioned Captain of Calvary*

Sojourner Truth: *former slave; from 1843 worked in abolitionist movement as a speaker; later solicited gifts for black volunteer regiments*

Evaluating Your Child's Skills: **In order to complete this activity successfully, your child has to show persistence in searching more than one reference source if necessary and in paraphrasing what he or she finds in the source.**

B.   EVALUATING MEMORIALS

Remind your child that the cemetery at Gettysburg and Lincoln's Gettysburg Address are memorials—things created to help people continue to remember a person or an event. Then let your child consider the following activity.

Think about a memorial that you have visited in the past or can visit now. It may be a national monument such as the Vietnam wall or the Lincoln Memorial in Washington, D.C., or it may be a statue, monument, or plaque in your hometown. It may even be a building—say, a hospital, a school, or a theater—named in memory of someone.

1. Describe the memorial.
2. Tell whether you like it—and why.
3. Tell how the memorial makes you feel.
4. Decide whether you would recommend that a friend visit the memorial—and why.

Evaluating Your Child's Skills: **In order to complete this activity successfully, your child needs to describe a memorial in objective terms and then comment about it in subjective terms. Encourage your child to replace words such as *big, nice,* and *sad* with specific adjectives.**

C.   CONSIDERING CURRENT EVENTS

Your child can connect nineteenth-century injustice with contemporary developments.

The slaves endured injustice—unfair treatment. Their human rights were violated. Examine a newspaper, magazine, news broadcast, or Internet site to see if you can find an example of injustice somewhere in the world today. Identify an individual or a group of people who are not being treated fairly or respectfully as human beings. Try to explain why this injustice exists.

Evaluating Your Child's Skills: **In order to complete this activity successfully, your child may need prompting. Before he or she starts the task, have a conversation about ethnic clashes and poor labor policies worldwide.**

 Top of the Class

Children interested in delving more deeply into the topics covered in this chapter can choose one or more of the following activities. They may do the activities for their own satisfaction or report on what they have done to show that they have been seriously considering the Civil War.

BOOKS TO READ AND CRITIQUE

Make one of the following books of nonfiction or poetry available to your child. After your child has finished the book, you can suggest that he or she may want to share thoughts about it with his or her teacher or class.

Fradin, Dennis Brindell. *My Family Shall Be Free: The Life of Peter Still.* New York: HarperCollins, 2001. A critic has called this a "multidimensional look at slavery and the pursuit of freedom."

Fradin, Dennis Brindell. *Bound for the North Star: True Stories of Fugitive Slaves.* Boston: Houghton Mifflin, 2000. Reviews report "inspiring history" as well as "horrifying detailed accounts" of slavery.

McGill, Alice, collector. *In the Hollow of Your Hand: Slave Lullabies.* Boston: Houghton Mifflin, 2000. Part of the country's oral tradition, these poems have been called "achingly beautiful."

Rockwell, Anne. *Only Passing Through: The Story of Sojourner Truth.* New York: Knopf, 2000. A picture-book biography of the legendary former slave who went on to travel and speak.

Thomas, Velma Maia. *Lest We Forget: The Passage from Africa to Slavery and Emancipation: A Three-Dimensional Interactive Book with Photographs and Documents from the Black Holocaust Exhibit.* New York: Crown, 1997.

BROWSING OR SEARCHING FOR PHOTOGRAPHS ON THE INTERNET

> Dozens if not hundreds of Civil War sites exist on the Internet. Direct your child to the comprehensive photography collection available from the Library of Congress.

At rs6.loc.gov/ammem/cwarquery.html, you can browse through photographs taken during the Civil War or you can search for pictures of a particular topic—such as hospitals, women, Gettysburg, and so on. Look in particular for photos by Mathew Brady, one of the more famous and respected photographers of the period.

LEARNING FROM A PRIMARY SOURCE

> If you think your child can handle the reading level of the following letter by Robert E. Lee, make it available to him or her.

What does the letter on page 101 tell you about Lee's feelings?

Arlington, Virginia
April 20, 1861

My Dear Sister:

I am grieved at my inability to see you. I have been waiting for a more convenient season, which has brought to many before me deep and lasting regret. Now we are in a state of war which will yield to nothing. The whole South is in a state of revolution, into which Virginia, after a long struggle, has been drawn; and though I recognize no necessity for this state of things, and would have forborne and pleaded to the end for redress of grievances, real or supposed, yet in my own person I had to meet the question whether I should take part against my native State.

With all my devotion to the Union, and the feeling of loyalty and duty of an American citizen, I have not been able to make up my mind to raise my hand against my relatives, my children, my home. I have, therefore, resigned my commission in the Army, and, save in defense of my native State (with the sincere hope that my poor services may never be needed), I hope I may never be called upon to draw my sword.

I know you will blame me, but you must think as kindly as you can, and believe that I have endeavored to do what I thought right. To show you the feeling and struggle it has cost me I send you a copy of my letter of resignation. I have no time for more. May God guard and protect you and yours and shower upon you everlasting blessings, is the prayer of

Your devoted brother
R. E. Lee

CHAPTER 8
Industrialization and Immigration
1850–1920

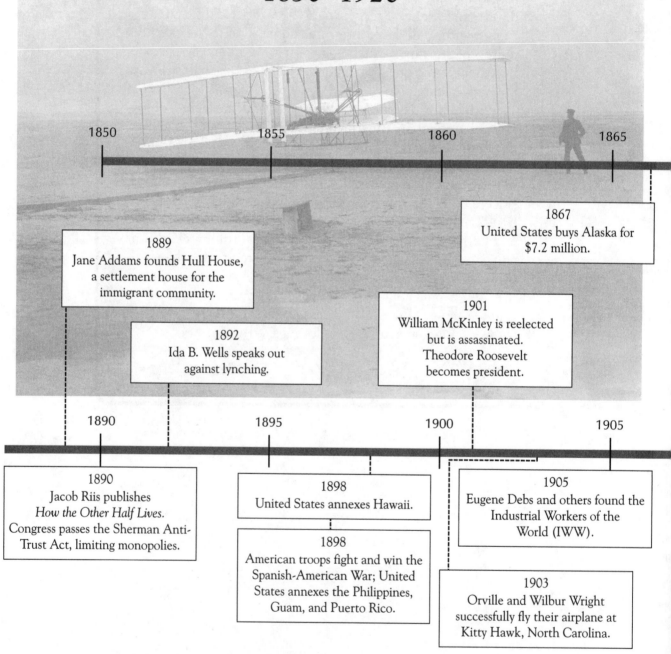

1850   1855   1860   1865

1867
United States buys Alaska for
$7.2 million.

1889
Jane Addams founds Hull House,
a settlement house for the
immigrant community.

1901
William McKinley is reelected
but is assassinated.
Theodore Roosevelt
becomes president.

1892
Ida B. Wells speaks out
against lynching.

1890   1895   1900   1905

1890
Jacob Riis publishes
How the Other Half Lives.
Congress passes the Sherman Anti-
Trust Act, limiting monopolies.

1898
United States annexes Hawaii.

1905
Eugene Debs and others found the
Industrial Workers of the
World (IWW).

1898
American troops fight and win the
Spanish-American War; United
States annexes the Philippines,
Guam, and Puerto Rico.

1903
Orville and Wilbur Wright
successfully fly their airplane at
Kitty Hawk, North Carolina.

This timeline provides an overview of the development of industry and the progress of immigration in the United States. In the following pages, a narrative describes how industrialization and immigration affected the United States.

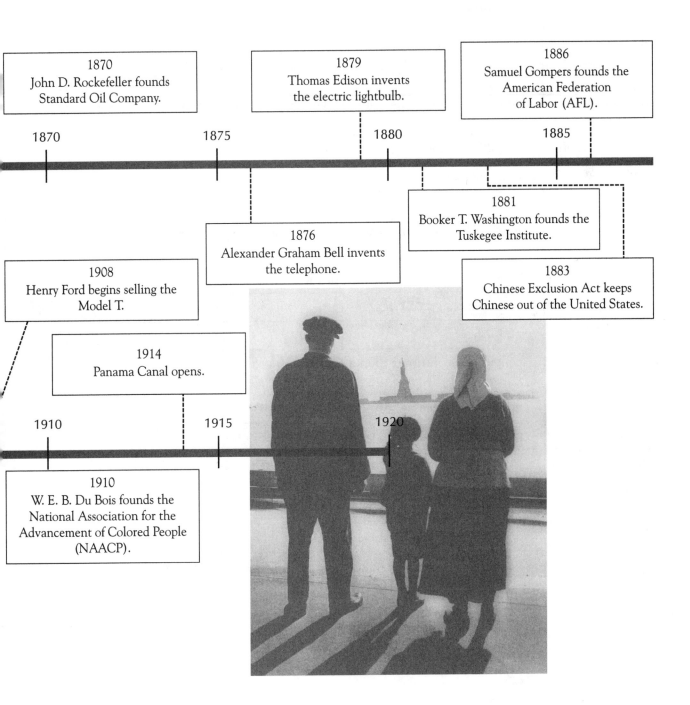

1870
John D. Rockefeller founds Standard Oil Company.

1879
Thomas Edison invents the electric lightbulb.

1886
Samuel Gompers founds the American Federation of Labor (AFL).

1870   1875   1880   1885

1881
Booker T. Washington founds the Tuskegee Institute.

1876
Alexander Graham Bell invents the telephone.

1908
Henry Ford begins selling the Model T.

1883
Chinese Exclusion Act keeps Chinese out of the United States.

1914
Panama Canal opens.

1910   1915   1920

1910
W. E. B. Du Bois founds the National Association for the Advancement of Colored People (NAACP).

Word Power

Word	Definition
barons	wealthy, powerful people
consumers	people who buy goods or services
contract	written agreement that must, by law, be obeyed by those who have signed it
discrimination	prejudice against minority groups
diversity	differences; variety
exposé	written piece that tells the truth about a secret
famine	lack of food; time when people do not have enough to eat
industries	businesses that make products for sale to other people as opposed to families making products only for themselves
injustices	situations that are unfair
innovation	new idea
investors	people who contribute money to a project so they can make a profit on it later
loom	machine for weaving cloth
management	people in charge of a factory or business
negotiation	bargaining back and forth that often ends in a compromise between two parties
radical	extreme
persecution	oppression; unfair punishment
poverty	state of being very poor; state of not having enough money for the necessities of life
textile	cloth

What Your Child Needs to Know

You may choose to use the following text in several different ways, depending on your child's strengths and preferences. You might read the passage aloud; you might read it to yourself and then paraphrase it for your child; or you might ask your child to read the material along with you or on his or her own.

For centuries before the Civil War, people had lived their daily lives in basically the same way. The typical family lived on a farm and raised most of the food they needed on their own land. They wove their own cloth, sewed their own clothes, and made their own furniture. They didn't need much money because they traded with neighbors for most things they needed but did not make themselves.

All of that changed in the second half of the eighteenth century with the **Industrial Revolution.** While the Industrial Revolution did not involve soldiers or battles, it was a real revolution nonetheless. The word *revolution* means "radical change," or "overthrow of the existing order," and once the Industrial Revolution occurred, the world would never be the same. The Age of Machines changed the way people thought about work, money, and just about everything else in their lives.

THE INDUSTRIAL REVOLUTION

The Industrial Revolution began when people started inventing machines that completed jobs faster than humans could. In factories, a **division of labor**—breaking down a job into a series of smaller tasks, each performed over and over again by one person—replaced the age-old way of working in which one skilled artisan made a product from beginning to end. With the new methods, products could be produced more quickly and more cheaply, and factory owners made greater profits. But factory workers did not share in the benefits.

Life in the Mills

The Industrial Revolution began in the 1700s in the textile mills in England. Running on water power, machines spun yarn and wove cloth. As a result, English factories became extremely profitable, and factory owners wanted to keep the machines to themselves. Factories made rules requiring workers to keep information about the machines secret, and the British government even passed laws forbidding factory workers to leave the country. However, in the late 1700s, **Samuel Slater** studied how the spinning machines worked and then escaped to the United States, where he built one from memory.

Textile mills soon sprang up all over New England along fast-flowing rivers that could power the new machines. In 1813, **Francis Cabot Lowell** built the first water-powered loom in the country in Waltham, Massachusetts, near the Charles River. Later, **Lowell,** another mill town, was established near the Merrimack River in Massachusetts and took the inventor's name.

Most of the people who worked in the mills were young women who were fifteen to nineteen years old. For many, it seemed like an excellent opportunity to live independently. But it was a hard life. Most girls worked six days a week, for twelve to fourteen hours each day. Mill jobs were repetitive, boring, and often dangerous. Workers lived in boarding houses run by the mill, and rent was often so expensive that there was rarely any money left over.

The Age of Invention

During the Industrial Revolution, the government issued hundreds of thousands of **patents**—protection assuring an inventor that his or her invention would not be stolen by another person. America became the invention capital of the world. New tools and devices seemed to turn up every day to make people's lives more efficient.

Perhaps the greatest inventor of the period was **Thomas Alva Edison.** Working from his research lab in Menlo Park, New Jersey, Edison and his team invented or improved on many items, such as the phonograph (an early version of a record player), the movie camera, and an advanced typewriter. In 1878, Edison's team changed the world when they perfected a long-lasting electric lightbulb.

Wright brothers' plane at Kitty Hawk

Alexander Graham Bell was an inventor whose work initially focused on helping deaf people to hear. In 1876, his experiments led to the creation of the telephone. He spoke his famous first words by telephone to his assistant in the next room: "Mr. Watson—come here; I want to see you."

In 1872, **Elijah McCoy** invented a labor-saving device called the "oil cup." McCoy designed the cup to be used on railroads and steam engines so that an engineer could oil an engine while the engine was still running.

Many new inventions took advantage of an earlier <u>innovation</u> by Eli Whitney—**interchangeable parts.** When Whitney designed guns for the army, he created standard-sized parts that could be used in any gun, so guns would be easy to assemble and repair. People such as **Henry Ford** followed Whitney's lead. In order to build a car that would be cheap enough for the average American to afford, Ford had to design a car that could be easily assembled from a standard set of parts.

Ford introduced another innovation to factory production: the **assembly line.** Before, workers moved from place to place as they worked in a fac-tory; now, a moving belt transported the product to the worker, who stayed in one place and did the same small job over and over again. Ford's fast assembly-line production method made cars cheaper than ever before. By 1925, the price of a Model T was only $300.

With improved roads, steamboats, railroads, and cars, Americans were truly becoming a society on the move. The only thing left to conquer was the air. On December 17, 1903, brothers **Orville** and **Wilbur Wright** did just that: their airplane flew one hundred feet along the beach in Kitty Hawk, North Carolina.

INDUSTRY AND SOCIETY

Many people describe the period after the Civil War as an age of extremes. On the one hand, a small number of people made a great deal of money by investing in new <u>industries</u>. They lived in luxury and threw grand parties. On the other hand, many other people lived in <u>poverty</u>. They worked long hours and struggled to make barely enough money to shelter and feed their families.

Corporations, Trusts, and Monopolies

Industrialists, or people who make their money from industry, grew rich by creating large, powerful companies. In some cases, the cost of starting a company was so high that no one person could afford it; instead, a group of <u>investors</u> would pool their money to start a **corporation,** or large company owned by a group of people. As the corporation began to make money, each of the investors also received a portion of the profits.

Many corporations during this period became **monopolies:** they bought up competitors' businesses or drove competitors out of business by charging lower prices. Once a business became a monopoly, it had a great advantage. With no competition, the monopoly could charge any price.

Some businesses during this period grouped together to form combinations called **trusts,** which are related to monopolies. In a trust, many or all the businesses in one industry may agree to charge a particular price. (Such an action is now illegal.)

The Robber Barons

Many called the richest industrialists of the day the robber <u>barons</u> because of their tremendous wealth and power and the unfair way they gained their wealth and power. The robber barons were also known by a more flattering term: *captains of industry.* These wealthy industrialists controlled trusts in almost every industry, from **Cornelius Vanderbilt** and his railroads to **Charles Pillsbury** and his flour-milling business.

Andrew Carnegie, the son of poor Scottish immigrants, grew up in Pennsylvania. In 1873, when it became possible to manufacture steel quickly and cheaply, he founded Carnegie Steel. He made a fortune selling steel rails to the railroads. Later in life, Carnegie became a **philanthropist,** giving away most of his fortune to support good causes. He founded libraries across the United States, funded scholarships, and built the famous concert hall in New York City called Carnegie Hall, where people still come to hear the greatest musicians perform.

John D. Rockefeller made his fortune in oil. He established the Standard Oil Company in 1870 and soon bought up all his competitors. Rockefeller created a monopoly by controlling every part of his business, from drilling the oil, to refining it, to making the barrels that held the oil, and even to owning the wagons that delivered the barrels. Many thought Rockefeller was particularly unfair in his dealings with competitors, but he, like Carnegie, also gave away much of his fortune to good causes.

John Pierpont Morgan's monopoly was in banking. He was so wealthy that at one point he loaned the U.S. government $62 million because it didn't have enough gold in the Treasury to pay its debts. His bank, the House of Morgan, controlled many important businesses, such as railroads, telephones, shipping, and telegraph.

The Labor Movement

Some Americans became angry that, while the industrialists grew richer, most people still had to struggle to survive. Workers suffered through fourteen-hour workdays, with no time for meals or breaks. Factories were unhealthy and often dangerous, and factory owners did not have to help workers who were injured on the job. In 1911, 146 women and girls died in a fire at the Triangle Shirtwaist Factory because no one had listened to their requests for fire escapes and unlocked doors. The enormous gap between rich industrialists and poor workers eventually led many workers to demand fairer pay and better working conditions.

People such as **Mary Harris "Mother" Jones** spoke out. Mother Jones was outraged that so many factories hired children to do backbreaking work for low wages. Because of her efforts, Congress and states passed new laws. In Pennsylvania in 1905, a law finally forbade children under age fourteen to work.

Other people organized **unions,** groups of workers who joined together to fight for changes. One of the first unions was the **Knights of Labor,** founded in 1869 by **Uriah Stephens** to represent male workers who cut cloth in clothing factories.

In 1886, a cigar maker named **Samuel Gompers** founded the union called the **American Federation of Labor** (AFL) in Columbus, Ohio. Gompers also developed the technique of **collective bargaining:** <u>negotiation</u> between <u>management</u> and labor for a <u>contract</u> that both sides can agree on. The AFL helped its members by fighting for improvements such as fewer hours in a workday or increased hourly wages.

In 1905, **Eugene Debs** and others founded a labor union called the **International Workers of the World** (IWW). The IWW was a more radical group than the AFL. Many members of IWW were **socialists,** who believed that the government, and not individuals, should control the country's major industries. Instead of collective bargaining, the members of IWW preferred **strikes.** When workers go on strike, they refuse to work until employers meet their demands—for example, an increase in wages.

Unions gave workers a voice for the first time. Wages slowly began to increase, the workday was shortened, and almost every state passed laws regulating working conditions. But management still held the upper hand. Some employers would fire workers for joining unions. Some would threaten to close down a factory completely or hire nonunion workers called **scabs** so that all the workers who joined a union would be unemployed. Sometimes violence broke out between workers and employers. When this happened, the police and the government sided with the employers. The courts jailed and fined union leaders. It would be many years before the country had labor laws that forced management to pay and treat workers fairly.

IMMIGRATION

The Industrial Revolution in America drew immigrants from other countries. From 1820 to 1930, more than 37 million people came from all over the world to live in America. Some, like the Irish, were escaping terrible poverty and <u>famine</u> in their homelands; others, like the Russian Jews, were escaping religious <u>persecution</u> as well.

The first waves of immigrants came to America from northern and western Europe: England, Scotland, Ireland, Scandinavia, and France. Later groups came from southern and eastern Europe: Germany, Poland, Russia, Romania, Italy, and Greece. Families crowded aboard steamships for the two-week trip across the Atlantic to arrive at **Ellis Island** in New York City.

Doctors examined the immigrants on their arrival, and officials questioned them about their willingness to work. It was a frightening time for families, who feared that they would be split up or returned to their home countries.

Once admitted to the country, most immigrants headed for the growing cities of the Northeast, where jobs were easy to find. During this period, America changed from a country of farmers to a land of city dwellers. In 1880, 28 percent of Americans lived in cities and 72 percent lived on farms; by 1910, 45 percent of Americans lived in cities and only 55 percent lived on farms.

Immigrants often moved into neighborhoods where other people from their home countries already lived. In this way, people with a shared language and culture could live together and help each other. But housing was often limited, and living conditions were sometimes primitive. Most people lived in **tenements,** buildings with many tiny apartments. With few windows and no running water, the cramped, dirty quarters often led to the spread of disease. Wooden tenements were also dangerous firetraps. In 1871, the Great Fire of Chicago destroyed eighteen thousand buildings, killed 250 people, and left 90,000 people homeless.

Many immigrants worked long hours in small, airless factories called **sweatshops.** Life was hard

Immigrant family looking at Statue of Liberty from Ellis Island

for them, but even with low pay and difficult living conditions, they were better off than they would have been in their homelands. In addition, their children had the promise of free public education. In this way, many immigrant children moved on to a better way of life.

As the century closed, some people became concerned about the flood of immigrants. People who came to this country as immigrants themselves worried that the newcomers would take away valuable jobs. Congress passed laws limiting people from different parts of the world to enter the United States. For example, the **Chinese Exclusion Act** in 1882 limited Chinese immigration for many years.

Moving West

Not all immigrants stayed in the Northeast. Many went west to work as farmers or miners. The western territories filled with immigrants, and by 1896, Idaho, Wyoming, Utah, and Oklahoma had all become states.

In the 1890s, many African Americans who wanted to escape poverty and <u>discrimination</u> left their homes in the South and headed north and west in the **Great Migration.** For many, factory work was a great improvement over sharecropping (see Chapter 7), and cities such as Chicago saw a huge increase in population.

REFORM

As the gap between rich and poor continued to widen, some people began to call for change. Some of them were writers, called **muckrakers,** who took advantage of the freedom of the press to call attention to <u>injustices</u> in society.

Jacob Riis (REESS) was a Danish immigrant who became a photographer and a journalist. He published a book called *How the Other Half Lives,* which featured photographs of life in the New York slums. His pictures helped many to see how difficult life was for the poor.

In 1903, **Ida Tarbell** wrote about the illegal practices at Rockefeller's Standard Oil Company. In her book *A History of Standard Oil Company,* Tarbell argued that Rockefeller didn't play fair when dealing with competitors, and she encouraged President Roosevelt to make trusts illegal.

Upton Sinclair's book *The Jungle* described unsafe practices in the meatpacking industry. His <u>exposé</u> led Congress to pass the Pure Food and Drug Act in 1906.

In New York, **William Marcy "Boss" Tweed** ran a club called **Tammany Hall,** which illegally traded government favors for citizens' votes and stole money from the government by overcharging for building contracts. The political cartoonist **Thomas Nast** began drawing cartoons criticizing Tweed; when Tweed offered Nast $500,000 to stop drawing him, Nast refused. Eventually, a court of law convicted Tweed and sentenced him to prison, where he died in 1878.

Many reformers during this period focused on the needs of the poor. In Chicago, **Jane Addams** founded **Hull House** in the midst of a poor immigrant neighborhood. As a **settlement house,** Hull House served the community by providing child care, job training, and English classes.

Theodore Roosevelt

Theodore Roosevelt became president in 1901 after the assassination of President **William McKinley.** Roosevelt served as president from 1901 to 1909 and made a name for himself as a progressive reformer.

As time went on, some people realized that monopolies and trusts were unfair to <u>consumers</u> and began to call for changes. It became clear to many Americans that the trusts run by Rockefeller, Morgan, and others were unfair. In 1890, Congress had passed the **Sherman Anti-Trust Act** to place limits on trusts. But nobody had enforced the act until Roosevelt took over. Inspired by muckrakers such as Ida Tarbell, Roosevelt successfully sued a railroad trust called Northern Securities Company in 1902. In the next six years, Roosevelt broke up more than twenty-five trusts.

Roosevelt also supported **conservation,** the practice of preserving natural resources. An avid outdoorsman, Roosevelt worried that America was losing precious open land. He agreed with naturalist **John Muir** (MYUR), who argued that America had a responsibility to preserve its natural treasures. Roosevelt set aside land for national parks, national forests, and wildlife refuges.

African American Reformers

Some reformers fought to improve the lives of African Americans. **Ida B. Wells** spoke out against **lynching** in the South. Groups of white people were taking the law into their own hands and killing people whom they believed to be guilty of crimes. Usually the victims were innocent black men. Wells traveled all over the North and Europe speaking out against lynching, and her persuasive speeches and articles led to antilynching laws.

In 1881, **Booker T. Washington** founded the **Tuskegee** (tus KEE gee) **Institute** in Tuskegee, Alabama. The Institute was a school where African Americans could learn skills such as printing, bricklaying, and teaching. Washington believed that the best way for African Americans to improve their lives was through going to school and getting good jobs. Washington believed that it was more important to strive for economic equality than social equality.

Many agreed with Washington's philosophy, but some passionately disagreed. One of the latter was **W. E. B. Du Bois** (doo BOISS), a thinker and writer who was the first African American to earn a Ph.D. from Harvard University. Du Bois argued that it was most important for African Americans to fight for the social equality that had been promised them in the Constitution. He also felt strongly that African Americans should not forget their own culture and heritage in their struggle to claim equality; America could only get better, he believed, if people accepted and celebrated diversity. In 1910, Du Bois and others founded the National Association for the Advancement of Colored People (NAACP) to fight discrimination.

Populist Reformers

Life became difficult for many farmers after the Civil War. New developments in technology made it easier to grow crops more efficiently, but the greater crop yield drove prices down. As a result, many farmers had trouble paying their bills, and many lost their farms. Some people began to worry that America, which appeared to be controlled by the industrialists, had forgotten the Jeffersonian ideal of a nation of self-sufficient farmers (see Chapter 5).

Farmers formed organizations called **Granges** to protect their rights. The Grange members founded the **Populist Party,** which supported goals such as women's **suffrage,** or right to vote, and the **secret ballot,** or the right to keep one's vote private. The Populists also argued for national control of important industries, such as railroads and telephone, and for the reform of America's money system.

In the past, gold had backed all paper money. Populists thought that if silver and gold backed the paper money, more money would be available to the people. In addition, Populists believed that it wasn't safe to have a single person such as J. P. Morgan supervising the money system. Instead, they argued for supervision by an independent board, or group of people, who would work for the common good rather than for personal interest.

The Populists were a groundbreaking political party; they were the first party to unite blacks and whites. Populist leader **William Jennings Bryan** was a powerful speaker who ran for president unsuccessfully three times. Although the party did not last, its ideals and goals did.

THE SPANISH-AMERICAN WAR

At the end of the nineteenth century, Spain owned Cuba, the Philippines, and Puerto Rico. In 1895, Cuban revolutionaries began to fight for independence, and many Americans supported them.

In 1898, the **U.S.S.** *Maine* sailed to Cuba to provide aid to Americans who were caught in the fighting. On February 15, the *Maine* exploded and sank, killing 260 crew members. No one knew what caused the explosion. Today, experts' examinations of the wreckage suggest that it might have been a problem inside the *Maine*. But in 1898, many Americans who wanted the United States to join the war claimed that Spain had attacked the U.S.S. *Maine*.

Among those who took a pro-war stance were two newspaper owners, **William Randolph Hearst** of the *New York Journal* and **Joseph Pulitzer** of the *New York World*. They both knew that dramatic war stories sold newspapers; so, despite a lack of proof, they blamed Spain for the explosion and called on the United States to join the war. This kind of dramatic, often inaccurate reporting, or yellow journalism, achieved its goal. In April 1898, President McKinley declared war on Spain.

The Spanish-American War lasted five months. On May 1, the U.S. Navy destroyed the Spanish fleet in the Philippines and blockaded the Spanish fleet in Cuba a few weeks later. In July, the Americans defeated the Spanish in the **Battle of San Juan Hill.** Theodore Roosevelt, who was assistant secretary of the Navy at the time, left his post to organize a cavalry troop called the **Rough Riders.** The Rough Riders fought alongside African American cavalry troops, the **Buffalo Soldiers.** The battle made Roosevelt a war hero.

In August, the United States and Spain signed a peace treaty. Cuba won limited independence; the United States paid $20 million for the Philippines and gained Puerto Rico and Guam as American territories.

Growing Imperialism

With its victory in the Spanish-American War, the United States proved itself to be a world power. Like other world powers, it was eager to expand its control in other parts of the world. **Imperialism** is another word for the expansion of a country's power beyond its own boundaries.

Back in 1867, America had purchased **Alaska** from Russia for $7.2 million. Many thought Alaska a useless wasteland and nicknamed it **Seward's Folly** after Secretary of State **William Seward,** but people changed their minds when gold was discovered near Juneau in the 1880s.

A number of Americans had settled on an island in the Pacific called **Hawaii** and developed pineapple and sugar-cane plantations. In 1893, American plantation owners overthrew Hawaiian **Queen Liliuokalani** (lee *lee* woh kuh LAH nee) and established their own government. Hawaii asked to join the United States five years later, in 1898.

America also pursued imperialist goals in leasing from the republic of Panama a narrow strip of land that divides the Atlantic Ocean from the Pacific Ocean. The strip of land is called the **Isthmus** (ISS muhss) **of Panama.** The goal was to create a shorter route from one ocean to the other by building a canal through which ships could pass; this shortcut was preferable to sailing the thirteen thousand miles

around the entire continent of South America. Construction of the Panama Canal began in 1906 but soon stopped because thousands of workers were dying of malaria and yellow fever, diseases spread by mosquitoes. **Dr. William Gorgas,** a physician and the world's leading sanitation expert at the time, finally got the mosquito population under control, and work on the canal picked up again. Workers completed the **Panama Canal** in 1914. In 1999, the United States, which had maintained the canal, turned it over to the republic of Panama.

! Implications

To answer the question, "Why does all this matter?" or "What does it mean?," share the following insights with your child.

The Industrial Revolution changed America from a country of agricultural communities in the countryside to a country of cities with industries. While many criticize the robber barons for being greedy and hungry for power, it is important to keep in mind that they contributed to a surge in economic growth that benefited many—especially a growing middle class. Members of this new middle class were not rich, but they had more money than they needed for survival and the free time in which to spend that money.

The immigrants that flooded into America during the second half of the nineteenth century changed the face of America forever. These hardworking risk takers took American ideals to heart and improved the country as they improved their own lives. Sadly, each new immigrant group suffered from discrimination because the groups that had come before were not always willing to share their gains. Even today, the pattern continues as new immigrant groups from all over the world struggle to make new lives in the United States.

The muckrakers and other reformers of this period highlight the strength of the First Amendment to the Constitution. The First Amendment guarantees all citizens many liberties, including the right to free speech. Today, some people criticize the American press for invading the privacy of public figures;

others argue that such reporting is the price America pays for the right of its citizens to speak freely. As long as Americans fight to preserve this right, the debate will continue.

A final point: During this period, America underwent an important shift from being a mostly isolated country to being a world power with influence in international affairs. America was to play an important role in twentieth-century world politics and in two devastating world wars.

 ## Fact Checker

Here is a puzzle for children to do, using words from the Word Power list for this chapter.

INDUSTRY PUZZLE

Fill in the boxes using the following clues. Each answer is a word from the Word Power list for this chapter.

Across

3. bargaining
5. time when people do not have enough food
8. cloth
9. extreme
11. new idea

Down

1. state of being very poor
2. people who buy things
4. wealthy, powerful people
6. people who contribute money to a project so they can make a profit on it later
7. people in charge of a business
10. machine for weaving cloth

Answers appear in the back, preceding the index.

The Big Questions

The following questions encourage your child to think critically rather than simply recall facts. If necessary, review the specific information from the preceding pages that will help your child make the necessary inferences to come up with reasonable answers.

1. Many people feel that life today moves too quickly. They look back to the preindustrial age as a quieter, more peaceful time when people focused more on family life and life's simple pleasures than on business or careers.

   If you could go back in time, would you prefer to live in the time before the Industrial Revolution, or do you think the inventions and conveniences we have now are worth the greater stress that people have to bear?

2. You read in this chapter that immigrants from all over the world came to the United States in search of a better life. How do you feel about the U.S. immigration policy? Do you think that immigration should be strictly controlled, or do you believe that we should still take seriously these words from the poem inscribed on the base of the Statue of Liberty:

Give me your tired, your poor,
Your huddled masses yearning
    to breathe free,
The wretched refuse of your
    teeming shore.
Send these, the homeless,
    tempest-tost to me,
I lift my lamp beside the golden
    door!

What are the reasons for your opinion on this subject?

Suggested Answers

1. *Your child may answer either way. Accept any answer as long as your child gives sound reasons for his or her feelings on this subject.*
2. *Your child may think that the U.S. government's first responsibility is to American citizens. To allow unlimited immigration could cause overpopulation, unemployment, and an increase in the number of people needing financial aid provided by taxpayers' money. On the other hand, your child may think that severe limits on immigration are a betrayal of the American ideal. He or she may be thinking more "globally," arguing that each country should think of itself more as part of the world than as a separate entity. In that case, he or she would support increasingly free movement of people from one country to another.*

Skills Practice

The following activities give your child practice in applying the skills basic to social studies. For some of the activities, your child may need to review the information in the preceding pages.

A. CONNECTING CAUSES WITH EFFECTS

The following activity asks your child to explain the causes of several events discussed in the chapter.

Each of the following events happened for a reason. That reason is the *cause* of the event. The event is the *effect* of the cause. Tell what caused each event.

1. Products were made more quickly and cheaply than ever before.
2. The labor movement began, and people began to join unions.
3. Many immigrants came to the United States from other countries.
4. Congress passed laws limiting immigration.
5. The United States declared war on Spain in 1898.

Answers

1. New inventions, division of labor, interchangeable parts, the assembly line.
2. Inadequate pay, unfair treatment, and poor living conditions for workers.
3. Famine, poverty, persecution.
4. Competition for jobs.
5. Explosion of the U.S.S. Maine. (People thought Spain had attacked the Maine.)

> **Evaluating Your Child's Skills:** In order to complete this activity successfully, your child will not only need to remember facts from the chapter, but also be able to make causal connections among them. If necessary, review the meaning of the words *cause* and *effect*. Go back into the text with your child to find the cause for each effect in the preceding list.

B. DISTINGUISHING DIFFERENCES

> The following activity asks your child to find differences between people and things discussed in the chapter.

The members of each of the following pairs of people or things are similar in one or more ways but different in at least one way. Name a way in which the members of each pair are different.

1. Corporation/monopoly
2. Samuel Gompers/Eugene V. Debs
3. Tenements/sweatshops
4. Upton Sinclair/Jacob Riis
5. Booker T. Washington/W. E. B. Du Bois

Answers

1. *The word* corporation *usually refers to any large company owned by more than one person; the word* monopoly *implies that a company is able to charge unfair prices for its product because it has eliminated all competing companies that provide the same product.*
2. *Samuel Gompers favored collective bargaining as a way of getting better pay and working conditions for workers; Eugene V. Debs favored the strike.*
3. *A tenement is a building in which people live under crowded and unsanitary conditions; a*
sweatshop is a place where people work under poor conditions.
4. *Upton Sinclair wrote about unsafe practices in the meatpacking industry; Jacob Riis wrote about the terrible living conditions in the slums of New York City.*
5. *Booker T. Washington thought that it was more important for African Americans to gain economic equality; W. E. B. Du Bois thought that social equality was more important.*

> **Evaluating Your Child's Skills:** In order to complete this activity successfully, your child needs to be able to see subtle differences between the items in each pair. If your child has trouble, discuss the ways in which the items in each pair are similar. Then go back into the text to find one way in which they differ.

C. USING SPECIFIC FACTS TO MAKE GENERALIZATIONS

> This activity asks your child to put together facts he or she has learned from this chapter in order to make general statements based on those facts. In other words, more than remembering facts, this activity asks children to understand ideas.

What generalization can you make based on the statements in each numbered item?

1. Thomas Alva Edison perfected the lightbulb; Alexander Graham Bell invented the telephone; the Wright Brothers flew their airplane.
2. A few people were tremendously rich; many people lived in extreme poverty.
3. In the mills, young girls worked six days a week for twelve to fourteen hours each day; their jobs were often dangerous; they had to pay very high rent for the rooms they lived in.
4. Jacob Riis wrote about life in the New York slums; Ida Tarbell wrote about illegal practices at Standard Oil; Upton Sinclair exposed unsafe practices in the meatpacking industry; Thomas Nast drew cartoons that criticized "Boss" Tweed.

Answers

1. *Many new inventions were created during this period.*
2. *There was a huge gap between rich and poor.*
3. *Mill girls were treated unfairly by their employers.*
4. *People called "muckrakers" wanted to improve people's living and working conditions by exposing unfair and unsafe practices to the public.*

> ***Evaluating Your Child's Skills:*** **In order to complete this activity successfully, your child has to be able to move from specific facts to larger general ideas. If he or she needs practice, start by listing specific facts related to your family life that lead to a simple generalization; for example, "Five years ago we lived in Detroit, then we moved to San Francisco, after that we lived in Houston for a short time, and now we live in Philadelphia. What's the general idea? 'Our family has moved around a lot.' "**

 # Top of the Class

> **Children interested in delving more deeply into the topics covered in this chapter can choose one or more of the following activities. They may do the activities for their own satisfaction or report on what they have done to show that they have been seriously considering the period in U.S. history from 1850 to 1920.**

A POINT TO PONDER

> **Encourage your child to think about a more recent revolution in history—the Electronic Revolution. Questions and ideas may come up in discussion that your child may want to raise in class.**

The Industrial Revolution caused life in the United States to change radically. In more recent years, we have experienced another historical revolution. It could be called the Electronic Revolution. Not so long ago, computers were huge objects that took up whole rooms. No one had a computer at home. Now many homes have at least one computer, and everyone in the family—even very young children—knows how to use computers. Have computers changed life for people in the United States? In what ways? Are the changes for better or worse?

ASSEMBLY-LINE PROJECT

> **With a group of classmates, your child can find out and demonstrate to others what it would be like to work on an assembly line in a factory.**

With two or more classmates, you can make a product of your own design—assembly-line style. For example, design a simple car that can be made by putting together several interlocking plastic blocks and attaching wheels. Figure out how the car can be put together by passing it from one classmate to another, each attaching only one part—the same one each time—until the car is completed.

Make several cars this way. Then discuss the difference between putting the car together on your own and working as a member of an assembly line. Which way can you make more cars faster? Which way is more fun? Which way is more boring?

BOOKS TO READ

> **The two titles recommended here tell about the harsh life of mill work for young girls in the nineteenth century. *Lyddie* is for more mature readers, while *The Clock* can be read by average readers in grades 4 through 6.**

Collier, James Lincoln. *The Clock.* Delacorte, 1995.
Paterson, Katherine. *Lyddie.* Dutton, 1991.

RESEARCH: TRANSPORTATION IN THE EARLY 1900S

> **Encourage your child to read up on airplanes and ocean liners from the beginning of the twentieth century.**

Find out what Harriet Quimby, an aviator, accomplished in 1912. Why wasn't her achievement front-page news? What major event stole the headlines?

CHAPTER 9
War and U.S. Leadership
1914–1953

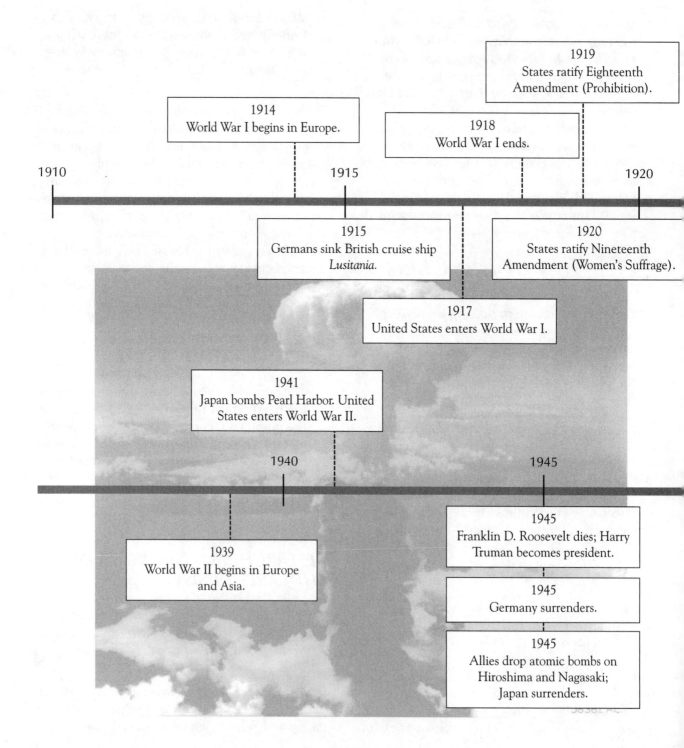

1919
States ratify Eighteenth
Amendment (Prohibition).

1914
World War I begins in Europe.

1918
World War I ends.

1910

1915

1920

1915
Germans sink British cruise ship
Lusitania.

1920
States ratify Nineteenth
Amendment (Women's Suffrage).

1917
United States enters World War I.

1941
Japan bombs Pearl Harbor. United
States enters World War II.

1940

1945

1945
Franklin D. Roosevelt dies; Harry
Truman becomes president.

1939
World War II begins in Europe
and Asia.

1945
Germany surrenders.

1945
Allies drop atomic bombs on
Hiroshima and Nagasaki;
Japan surrenders.

This timeline provides an overview of the involvement of the United States in World Wars I and II. In the following pages, a narrative describes how life in America changed in the first half of the twentieth century.

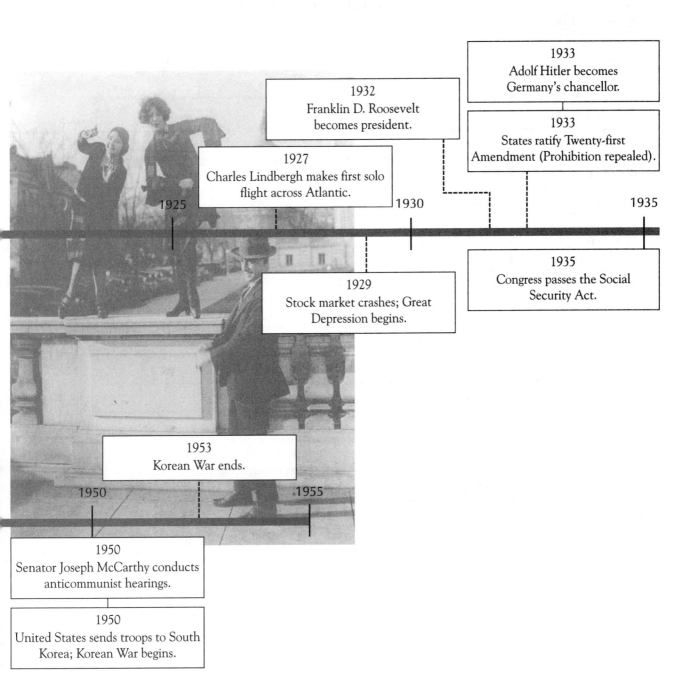

1933
Adolf Hitler becomes Germany's chancellor.

1932
Franklin D. Roosevelt becomes president.

1933
States ratify Twenty-first Amendment (Prohibition repealed).

1927
Charles Lindbergh makes first solo flight across Atlantic.

1925

1930

1935

1929
Stock market crashes; Great Depression begins.

1935
Congress passes the Social Security Act.

1953
Korean War ends.

1950

1955

1950
Senator Joseph McCarthy conducts anticommunist hearings.

1950
United States sends troops to South Korea; Korean War begins.

Word Power

The words on the following chart are underscored in the section called "What Your Child Needs to Know." Explain their meanings to your child as needed when they come up in reading or discussion. Keep this list handy for you and your child to use.

Word	Definition
alcoholic beverages	drinks containing alcohol (beer, whiskey, wine, and so on)
assassin	killer
celebrity	famous person
denounced	criticized harshly
drought	long period of time with no rain
escalating	growing or increasing
exterminate	kill off
fanatical	extreme to the point of being irrational
heir	person who will inherit something
hydroelectric	using water power to generate electricity
infamy	disgrace, reputation for being evil
migrant	traveling from place to place
mortgages	bank loans used to buy property; loans that usually are paid back over time in monthly installments, or payments

What Your Child Needs to Know

> **You may choose to use the following text in several different ways, depending on your child's strengths and preferences. You might read the passage aloud; you might read it to yourself and then paraphrase it for your child; or you might ask your child to read the material along with you or on his or her own.**

By 1914, the United States had become a wealthy, influential nation. Despite this, most Americans believed that the United States should hold to a policy of **isolationism,** focusing on its own affairs rather than those of other nations. But the events of the next few years would force America to change that policy.

WORLD WAR I, 1914 TO 1918

Some countries in Western Europe had developed major industries and created large empires, and they wanted to extend their borders even farther. For example, Germany had taken lands that once belonged to France, and France wanted to take these lands back. In order to protect themselves from countries they feared, the main powers in Europe signed treaties of **alliance,** or loyalty, promising to defend each other if any one of them was attacked. Germany, Austria-Hungary, and the Ottoman Empire formed the **Triple Alliance** to protect its members from attack by France or Russia. The members of the Triple Alliance became known as the **Central Powers.** Russia, Great Britain, and France made an alliance called the **Triple Entente** (arn TARNT), which became known as the **Allies.** Other smaller alliances among countries were made as well, some of them in secret.

These alliances divided Europe and created an atmosphere so tense that even a relatively unimportant event could set off a war. That event took place on June 28, 1914, in **Sarajevo** (*sar* uh YAH *voh*), the capital of the Austrian province of Bosnia. Crowds had come to see the visiting Archduke Franz Ferdinand, <u>heir</u> to the throne of Austria-Hungary. Suddenly, an <u>assassin</u> shot and killed Franz Ferdinand. The assassin was a young Bosnian student who had lived in Serbia, a small country bordering Austria-Hungary. Austria-Hungary responded by attacking Serbia, and the complicated system of alliances, such as one between Serbia and Russia, brought many other countries into conflict. That was the start of **World War I.**

A New Kind of Warfare

Soldiers fighting in World War I saw a new kind of battle, more brutal and deadly than ever before. The warring forces used new methods of warfare, such as aircraft, bombs, tanks, hand grenades, machine guns, and submarines. Soldiers wore masks to protect themselves from poisonous gas.

Soldiers fought in **trenches**—long narrow ditches fenced off with barbed wire. Between the two sides' trenches was an area called **no man's land.** Soldiers who entered this area and attempted to advance on the enemy could easily be shot down by machine-gun fire. Much of the war took place in trenches along the **western front,** a strip of land stretching six hundred miles from the English Channel to the border of Switzerland.

The United States Enters the War

Most Americans wanted to stay out of the war. Woodrow Wilson, who became president in 1913, even campaigned on the promise to keep America neutral. Others felt that America should come to the aid of the Allies.

In Germany, **Kaiser Wilhelm** (KEYE zuhr WIL helm) **II,** was an absolute ruler, but France and Great Britain had democratic governments similar to that of the United States. Many felt that the United States should help Great Britain because of the shared language and cultural traditions. Many thought it was also America's duty to help France, which had come to the aid of the United States in the Revolutionary War.

Then German submarines, called **U-boats,** began sinking Allied ships. On May 7, 1915, a U-boat sank the British cruise ship *Lusitania* and killed twelve hundred passengers; more than one hundred of them were American citizens. In the next two years, Germany sank eight unarmed

American trading ships, and American support for the Allied cause grew.

In January 1917, the British found out and reported to the United States that Germany had proposed an alliance with Mexico, our neighbors to the south. The proposal suggested that, in case Germany went to war with the United States, Mexico should side with Germany. In return, Germany would help Mexico to take back some land it had previously lost to the United States.

This proposal, called the **Zimmerman note,** brought the war too close to home. On April 2, 1917, after still more sinkings of U.S. ships by German submarines, President Wilson read a message to Congress, saying, "The world must be made safe for democracy." On April 6, almost three years after the war in Europe had begun, the United States declared war on Germany.

American troops and supplies were just what the Allies needed in order to win. By the fall of 1918, the Central Powers weakened and were ready to surrender. President Wilson proposed a peace plan, and on November 11, 1918, **Armistice Day** (what we now call *Veterans' Day*), the war ended. Across the world, 10 million people had died and 20 million were wounded. Of these casualties, 323,000 were Americans.

A Harsh Peace

Having grown up in the South during Reconstruction, Wilson understood how difficult it would be for Germany to rebuild after the war. But France and Great Britain, who had suffered much more than the United States, wanted to punish Germany. As a result, the terms of the **Treaty of Versailles** (vur SEYE), which ended the war, were harsh. The treaty demanded that Germany take full responsibility for the war and pay $33 million in damages. The German army was reduced, and Germany was forbidden to have submarines or aircraft. Many historians believe that the Treaty of Versailles laid the groundwork for World War II by humiliating the Germans and making economic recovery impossible.

The League of Nations

One part of Wilson's peace plan that was put into action called for the creation of the League of Nations, an international organization, similar to today's United Nations, to help countries to resolve disagreements peacefully. But the League of Nations was unsuccessful. Because it did not tax its members, it had no money to run its programs. Further, Congress, in an effort to return to isolationism, prevented the United States from joining. All in all, the League of Nations could not stop countries from taking lands from other countries.

THE ROARING TWENTIES

With the end of the Great War, Americans wanted to enjoy their peace—and they did, with a vengeance. Historians call this period the Roaring Twenties because Americans made a lot of money, spent a lot of money, and focused on having fun.

Many Americans got rich by investing in the stock market. A **stock** is a share in a company. If the value of the company increases, so does the value of the stock. In the 1920s, most stocks sharply increased in price, and many people used all of their savings to buy stocks and hoped to sell them when prices rose even more. As more and more people invested their money, stock prices rose far above their actual value. This would lead to trouble later on.

Americans had more free time as the labor movement fought successfully for the eight-hour workday. They used this time to enjoy the technological advances of the period. People bought cars and new electric appliances to make their lives easier. They listened to the radio or went to the movies. In 1927, many flocked to see *The Jazz Singer,* the first "talkie," or movie with sound. And many enjoyed drinking <u>alcoholic beverages</u>.

In 1919, states ratified the Eighteenth Amendment, which called for **Prohibition,** making it illegal to produce or sell alcoholic beverages. This had a profound effect on Americans' lives during the 1920s. The people who supported **temperance** (a movement banning alcohol) hoped that Prohibition would lead to a more moral society.

Prohibition had just the opposite effect. For many, it made drinking alcohol seem all the more glamorous and exciting. Illegal clubs, called **speakeasies,** sprang up where people went to drink and socialize. **Bootleggers** profited by making illegal alcohol, and gangsters got rich selling it. It became obvious that Prohibition was doing more harm than good by pro-

Rep. T. S. McMillan of Charleston, South Carolina, with flappers . . . dancing the Charleston, c. 1920

moting a national atmosphere of lawlessness. In 1933, fourteen years after Prohibition went into effect, the Twenty-first Amendment repealed, or canceled, the Eighteenth.

African American culture flourished during this period, which featured writers and poets such as **Langston Hughes** and **Zora Neale Hurston** and jazz musicians such as **Duke Ellington** and **Louis Armstrong.** This rebirth of African American culture is called the **Harlem Renaissance** because so much of it took place in Harlem, a mostly African American neighborhood in New York City.

The 1920s also saw a new phenomenon: the media celebrity. For the first time, newspapers and radios could reach huge numbers of people, and sensational stories made individuals famous overnight. In 1927, **Charles Lindbergh** became world famous when he made the first solo flight across the Atlantic Ocean. **Amelia Earhart** also gained celebrity status when in 1928 she became the first woman to pilot a craft across the Atlantic.

It was an exciting time with money, entertainment, and novelty all around. But it was not a wonderful time for all Americans. Minority groups experienced discrimination as some people argued that the only "true" Americans were white Protestants whose ancestors came from Western Europe. In the South, the Ku Klux Klan became more powerful. African Americans continued to face Jim Crow laws, and lynchings continued. In Congress, politicians passed laws limiting immigration.

Women's Suffrage

American women continued to fight for **suffrage,** or the right to vote, during this period. The movement had begun with the 1848 convention at Seneca Falls, and it gained momentum in 1872 after passage of the Fifteenth Amendment, which gave African American men the right to vote. Some territories and states actually granted women suffrage early on, beginning with Wyoming in 1869 and followed by Colorado, Idaho, and Utah. But the fight for a Constitutional amendment that would apply to the whole nation continued. Leaders such as Susan B. Anthony, Elizabeth Cady Stanton, and **Carrie Chapman Catt** led the way, with speeches, marches, and **hunger strikes.**

A women's suffrage amendment came before Congress in 1878 and every year for the next forty years. Finally, in 1919, Congress passed the **Nineteenth Amendment,** giving women the right to vote. States ratified the amendment in 1920.

THE GREAT DEPRESSION

The Roaring Twenties came to a screeching halt on **Black Friday,** October 29, 1929. On that day the stock market crashed. The values of stocks, which had been so high, tumbled. People who had invested their life's savings in the stock market lost everything. People were unable to pay their debts, and more than five thousand banks failed. Thousands of other businesses failed, too, and put millions of people out of work. The Great Depression had begun.

The stock market crash wasn't the only cause of the Depression. American farmers had been having trouble, too. Prices for their crops remained so low that farmers had difficulty making a profit. Many farmers who had mortgages on their property couldn't make their payments, and they lost their farms to the banks from which they had borrowed money.

Things got even worse in the mid-1930s, when years of <u>drought</u> turned the Midwest into a **Dust Bowl.** For decades, farmers had overused the land and exhausted the soil, so after a long period of time with no rain, the dry topsoil blew away in huge dust storms. Many homeless farmers headed west to California as <u>migrant</u> farm workers.

By the mid-1930s, 12 million Americans were unemployed—one out of four people was out of work. There was no welfare system to help jobless or homeless people get back on their feet. President **Herbert Hoover** became increasingly unpopular. Many people moved into **Hoovervilles,** urban **shantytowns** where families lived in tiny shacks made of cardboard or tin. The country's outlook grew increasingly dismal. Hoover's policy was to let the problem resolve itself on its own, but people soon realized that this wasn't going to work.

In the 1933 presidential election, Hoover lost to Democrat **Franklin Delano Roosevelt,** a cousin of former president Theodore Roosevelt. Like his cousin, FDR had energy and enthusiasm, and people welcomed his optimistic promise of a **New Deal** for the country. Roosevelt disagreed with Hoover's hands-off policy. In fact, FDR believed that the most effective strategy would involve strong and far-reaching government action.

In order to rebuild America's economy, Roosevelt passed laws and created government agencies designed to get people back to work:

- The **Civilian Conservation Corps (CCC)** employed people to replant forests.
- The **Works Progress Administration (WPA)** put people to work constructing buildings. It hired musicians, writers, and artists to work on government-funded arts projects.
- The **Tennessee Valley Authority (TVA)** brought electricity to poor communities in the Tennessee Valley. People employed by the TVA worked to build dams and create <u>hydroelectric</u> power.
- Another key piece of legislation was the **Social Security Act** of 1935, which provided benefits to the elderly, orphans, and people hurt and disabled in industrial accidents.

Not everyone loved Roosevelt. Some people felt that he was creating a federal government that was too strong and controlling. They worried that America had yet again moved away from the Jeffersonian ideal of minimal government.

THE RISE OF DICTATORS

The Depression affected the entire world. People everywhere were suffering the effects of poverty and unemployment. Some countries turned to **dictators,** leaders with absolute power. People believed these leaders could provide solutions to their problems. Instead, these leaders created harsh **totalitarian** governments supported by strong police forces. By using military forces to bring other countries under their control, these dictators would eventually lead their people into yet another devastating war.

Japan, for example, had been steadily growing stronger. In the 1930s, military leaders took over, and General **Hideki Tojo** came to power. Japanese leaders believed it was Japan's destiny to control all of Asia and started moving toward that goal by invading a region called **Manchuria.**

In Italy, dictator **Benito Mussolini** led the **Fascist** party, whose members supported the idea of a totalitarian government that emphasized the strength of the state over the individual rights of people. In pursuit of its goal to claim natural resources from the African continent, Italy invaded Ethiopia.

Germany also had a totalitarian government. **Adolf Hitler,** leader of Germany's **Nazi** party, was elected chancellor in 1933. Hitler's goal was to bring all of Europe—and eventually, the world—under German control. Like other dictators, Hitler encouraged his people to take a <u>fanatical</u> pride in their country. He argued that a "true" German was a white Protestant Christian with what he called "Aryan" characteristics—blond hair, fair skin, and blue eyes. Other people, according to Hitler, were inferior.

Persecuting Jewish people was central to Hitler's plan. Hitler blamed German Jews for the country's problems and began passing laws to take away their homes and jobs. Germans boycotted Jewish-owned businesses. Jewish citizens had to wear yellow stars on their clothing to identify themselves. Jewish children had to attend separate schools. Eventually, German soldiers forcibly removed Jews from their homes and placed them in restricted neighborhoods called **ghettos.**

Then Hitler began a calculated plan to exterminate the Jewish people. German soldiers packed families onto trains and sent them to **concentration camps,** such as **Auschwitz.** Camp guards treated Jews as slaves, starved them, tortured them, and put them to death in gas chambers. This systematic destruction of the Jews is now called the **Holocaust** (Greek for "destruction by fire"). During the **Third Reich,** the time when Hitler was in power, the Germans killed 6 million Jews—40 percent of the world's Jewish population.

WORLD WAR II, 1939 TO 1945

Ignoring the terms of the Treaty of Versailles, Hitler spent most of the 1930s building up the German army. When he went on the offensive, his armies easily invaded Austria and Czechoslovakia. At first, other countries didn't respond. Some leaders thought that Hitler would be satisfied once he had taken over a few countries. But as Hitler continued to push forward, people began to worry. Finally, when Hitler invaded Poland in 1939, Great Britain and France declared war on Germany. But the United States remained apart from the conflict. To many, the battles across the sea still seemed too far away to worry about.

In Asia, Japan had taken over Manchuria and other parts of China, and the Japanese army was heading for Thailand and the Philippines. Despite concerns about Japan's aggression, the United States still believed that the world could avoid another major conflict.

The Attack on Pearl Harbor

On December 7, 1941, the Japanese launched a surprise attack on American forces stationed at Pearl Harbor, in Hawaii. The Japanese goal was to drive the United States out of Asia. In two hours, Japanese bombers sank most of the American warships and damaged or destroyed all of the American aircraft. Over twenty-four hundred Americans died; President Roosevelt called it "a day that will live in infamy." A few days later, the United States declared war on Japan. Germany and Italy declared war on the United States soon after.

The Axis versus The Allies

The **Axis Powers**—Germany, Japan, and Italy—hoped to expand their borders by conquering other countries. The **Allies**—Great Britain (led by Prime Minister **Winston Churchill**) and the United States—were fighting to protect each country's right to choose its own government. France also entered the war on the Allied side, but Germany invaded France in June 1940, and General **Charles de Gaulle** (CHARL duh GAWL) had to lead the French **Resistance,** a protest movement, from London.

Russia played an unusual part in wartime politics. For centuries, Russia had been ruled by an all-powerful king, called a **czar.** Then in 1917 the **Bolsheviks,** a radical political group, took over the government and renamed the country the **Union of Soviet Socialist Republics** (U.S.S.R.), or the **Soviet Union.** Led by **V. I. Lenin,** the Bolsheviks put a **communist** government in place. In a communist government, the state owns and controls everything, including businesses and property. (In a **capitalist** system, such as the one we have in the United States, individuals own businesses and property.) In the 1920s, **Josef Stalin** took over as the Soviet leader and enforced a harsh police state.

At the beginning of World War II, Stalin signed a treaty of alliance with Hitler, but in 1941, Hitler invaded the Soviet Union; Stalin turned to the Allies. It was indeed odd that Stalin, who led a totalitarian government, was suddenly on the side of the United States and Great Britain. The Allies, however, might not have won the war without Soviet help.

The Allies now had the unique challenge of fighting a war on two fronts, or areas of battle: in the Pacific, against the Japanese, and in Europe and Africa, against Italy and Germany.

The War Effort at Home

America shifted into high gear in support of its troops. Factories produced huge quantities of weapons and supplies to send overseas. As in World War I, many of the factory workers were women, hired to replace the men who were at the front. People also conserved products like scrap metal and rubber for recycling and did without other items, like gasoline or meat.

American patriotism took a tragic turn, however, when it came to Japanese Americans. Some people feared that Japanese Americans, even though they were American citizens, would spy for the Japanese and betray the American cause. In 1942, the U.S. government forced one hundred thousand Japanese Americans to leave their homes and move to **internment camps.** Officials packed families into crowded housing and kept them there until the war ended. Most lost the homes and businesses that they had left behind. Many years later, President George Bush issued an apology for the internment to all Japanese Americans.

A Slow Victory

The war progressed slowly for the Allied forces. Both Japan and Germany seemed unbeatable. In Europe, the tide turned when General **Dwight D. Eisenhower** led an invasion of France. On **D-Day,** June 6, 1944, thousands of Allied troops stormed French beaches at Normandy. In the next months, the Allies pushed the German army back and liberated many Western European countries. Allied troops also liberated the concentration camps, revealing the horrors that the Nazis had inflicted on the Jews. Germany finally surrendered on May 6, 1945.

On the Pacific front, the Allies' luck changed after two successful battles for the islands of **Okinawa** (*oh* kuh NAH wah) and **Iwo Jima** (EE woh JEE muh). Though the Allies were gaining ground, the Japanese still fought fiercely and refused to surrender.

Truman Takes Over

President Roosevelt died in April 1945, and his vice president, Harry S Truman, took over as the new president. The Allies had won the war in Europe, but Truman faced a difficult decision regarding Japan.

A group of scientists led by **J. Robert Oppenheimer** had been working on the **Manhattan Project**—a secret plan to design a deadly new weapon,

the atomic bomb. Only the United States knew how to make an "A-bomb." Truman believed that, though the bomb would be unbelievably destructive, it might save lives in the end by ending the war sooner. On August 6, 1945, a plane called the *Enola Gay* dropped an atomic bomb on the Japanese city of **Hiroshima;** one hundred thousand people died. On August 9, Allies dropped another bomb on **Nagasaki;** another seventy thousand people died. On August 15, Japan surrendered. The war was over. Americans still disagree over whether Truman's decision was right or wrong.

THE COLD WAR

When the fighting ended, Soviet troops occupied most of the countries of Eastern Europe: Albania, Bulgaria, Czechoslovakia, Hungary, Poland, Romania, and Yugoslavia. The Soviet Union also controlled East Germany. Although Stalin had promised to allow free elections in these **satellite countries,** he did not keep his promise. In addi-

Second atomic bombing of Nagasaki, Japan, 1945

tion, he cut off communication, trade, and travel between the satellites and countries to the west. Winston Churchill declared that an **Iron Curtain** of dictatorship had descended over Eastern Europe.

President Truman's policy toward communism was one of **containment**—preventing the further spread of communism without military intervention. Truman supported Secretary of State George C. Marshall's plan. Under the **Marshall Plan,** the United States provided billions of dollars in aid to European countries so that they could recover from the losses of World War II. Truman believed that a speedy economic recovery would give Europeans the strength and energy to maintain democratic governments and resist communism.

The rivalry and distrust between communist and democratic countries was called the Cold War. The Cold War never became an actual "hot" war, but conflicts arose as both sides struggled for control. To keep these conflicts from <u>escalating</u> into a real war, more than fifty countries in 1945 formed the **United Nations.**

In April 1949, the democratic governments of the United States, France, and Great Britain, still fearing Soviet aggression, formed an alliance called the **North Atlantic Treaty Organization,** or **NATO.** The member countries agreed to consider an attack against one of them an attack against all.

Until 1949, the United States had remained the only country that had the knowledge and technology to explode a nuclear weapon. Then, in September of that year, the Soviet Union exploded its first atomic bomb. Now that two world powers had the capacity to launch a nuclear attack, the **arms race** began. The world had witnessed what happened in Hiroshima and Nagasaki and knew that, with the threat of nuclear warfare, it was more important than ever for countries to resolve their differences peacefully. War could mean total destruction.

The Korean War

After World War II, Korea was divided into two countries. North Korea had a communist government, and South Korea, or the Republic of Korea, had a democratic government. In June 1950, North Korea invaded South Korea in an ef-

fort to join the two countries together as a communist nation. The United Nations sent troops led by General **Douglas MacArthur** into South Korea to force the North Koreans out. Most of the troops were Americans. They were successful at first, but then China entered the war on the side of North Korea. In April of 1951, President Truman and General MacArthur disagreed about how to conduct the war. Truman replaced MacArthur with another general—**Matthew B. Ridgway.** MacArthur had wanted to wage an "all-out" war, bombing bases in Manchuria and even using the atomic bomb against the Chinese. Truman was afraid that such actions might lead to a disastrous World War III and to the mass destruction that atomic warfare would cause. Later that year, truce talks began, but fighting continued. The Korean War finally ended with the signing of a peace treaty in July 1953. By that time, Truman was no longer president.

Although most people today view Truman's decision not to escalate the war as a wise one, at the time it was unpopular. Truman decided not to run for another term as president, and on November 4, 1952, Dwight D. Eisenhower became president-elect with Richard M. Nixon as vice president. General Eisenhower had been supreme commander of the Allied armies in Europe during World War II.

Joseph McCarthy

Toward the end of the Korean War, many Americans feared that communists were trying to take over the world, including the U.S. government. Senator Joseph McCarthy played into Americans' fear of communism by launching a communist "witch hunt" in 1950. With no evidence to prove his claims, McCarthy accused many loyal Americans of being communists and brought them to testify before the **House Un-American Activities Committee.** Over the next four years, McCarthy ruined people's reputations and careers by suggesting that they were communist sympathizers and spies. Eventually the government <u>denounced</u> McCarthy, and the term **McCarthyism** has lived on to refer to the persecution of people for their political beliefs without regard for truth or fairness.

Implications

To answer the question, "Why does all this matter?" or "What does it mean?," share the following insights with your child.

The events of this chapter mark the change of the United States from a young, isolated nation to a superpower with great influence in an increasingly connected world community. World War I and World War II had brought the United States to the forefront of international relations; the decisions that American leaders made had a direct impact on world events.

It is important to note how technological developments played a part in this change. Telephones, telegraphs, radio, and newspapers made the transfer of information almost instant. Important events that happened halfway around the world suddenly seemed closer and more important.

With the United Nations, world leaders had acknowledged the interconnectedness of this new world community and the importance of keeping the peace—especially with the threat of nuclear war always in the background.

What part would the United States play in this new world? Chapter 10 describes the triumphs—and the failures—of postwar America.

Fact Checker

Here is a classification activity for children to do, using facts learned from this chapter. If necessary, guide your child back to the chapter to check answers.

This chapter covers three wars in which U.S. troops fought. Each of the people in the following list was involved in one of those wars. Classify the names by putting them in the correct columns. (One name will appear in two columns.)

Archduke Franz Ferdinand
Adolf Hitler
General MacArthur
Woodrow Wilson
Benito Mussolini
J. Robert Oppenheimer

General Ridgway
Joseph Stalin
Hideki Tojo
Harry S Truman
Kaiser Wilhelm II

World War I	World War II	Korean War

Answers appear in the back, preceding the index.

? The Big Questions

The following questions encourage your child to think critically rather than simply recall facts. If necessary, review the specific information from the preceding pages that will help your child make the necessary inferences to come up with reasonable answers.

1. Prohibition did not work. Making alcohol illegal did more harm than good. People drank more than ever, and criminals became rich and powerful by making and selling illegal alcohol. Finally, the Twenty-first Amendment repealed Prohibition.

    Consider the similarities and differences between the drinking problem of the 1920s and the drug problems we face today.
    • Decide whether you support laws against drugs, or whether you believe such laws cause more harm than good.

• Should law enforcement agencies continue to enforce laws against selling drugs?
2. Do you think that dropping atomic bombs on Hiroshima and Nagasaki was justified because, as President Truman argued, the action ended a war that would have taken even more lives than the bombs? Or do you believe that using weapons of mass destruction is never justified?

Suggested Answers

1. *Your child may answer either way. He or she may argue for legalization of drugs because laws against drugs are not very successfully enforced, the illegal drug trade makes criminals wealthy, and drugs are more attractive to people simply because they are illegal. If your child feels that drugs should remain illegal, he or she might back up that opinion by saying that drugs are more addictive and more harmful to more people than alcohol. Your child might argue that we need not repeal the laws against drugs but find a better way to enforce them.*
2. *Your child may answer either way. Make sure he or she backs up opinions with sound reasoning.*

Skills Practice

The following activities give your child practice in applying the skills basic to social studies. For some of the activities, your child may need to review the information in the preceding pages.

A. INTERPRETING PRIMARY SOURCES

The following activity asks your child to explain a famous quotation by FDR.

Franklin Delano Roosevelt's speech when he became president during the Great Depression is famous. Explain what you think he meant by the most famous part of the speech, which is in italics in the following passage.

> This is pre-eminently the time to speak the truth, the whole truth, frankly and boldly. Nor need we shrink from honestly facing conditions in our country today. This great nation will endure as it has endured, will revive and will prosper.
>
> So first of all let me assert my firm belief that *the only thing we have to fear is fear itself*—nameless, unreasoning, unjustified terror which paralyzes needed efforts to convert retreat into advance.

Answer

Roosevelt knew that some people were afraid of letting a president become too powerful, but he was telling the nation that strong leadership and drastic action were necessary to help the nation recover from the Depression. The programs of the New Deal—the "needed efforts"—would make the country prosper again.

> ***Evaluating Your Child's Skills:*** In order to complete this activity successfully, your child will need to use reading skills to figure out or look up the meanings of unfamiliar words in the speech. Then he or she will need to connect information from the chapter with the quoted words.

B. IDENTIFYING EFFECTS OF CAUSES

> This activity asks your child to identify events that were caused by other events.

Each of the events in the following list *caused* another event to occur. From the events named in the box, choose the event that was the *effect* of each event listed.

> Korean War begins.
> United States enters World War I.
> World War I begins in Europe.
> Great Depression begins.
> United States enters World War II.

1. Cause: Japan bombs Pearl Harbor.
   Effect:_____
2. Cause: Germany sinks the *Lusitania* and sends Zimmerman note.
   Effect:_____
3. Cause: Archduke Franz Ferdinand is assassinated.
   Effect:_____
4. Cause: North Korea invades South Korea.
   Effect:_____
5. Cause: Stock market crashes in 1929.
   Effect:_____

Answers

1. U.S. enters World War II.
2. United States enters World War I.
3. World War I begins in Europe.
4. Korean War begins.
5. Great Depression begins.

> ***Evaluating Your Child's Skills:*** In order to complete this activity successfully, your child will have to understand the difference between a cause and an effect and be able to make causal connections between events he or she learned about from this chapter. If your child needs help, try asking the questions in a different way; for example, "What would *not* have happened if North Korea had never invaded South Korea?" or "What might *not* have happened if Japan had not attacked the United States by bombing Pearl Harbor?"

Top of the Class

> Children interested in delving more deeply into the topics covered in this chapter can choose one or more of the following activities. They may do the activities for their own satisfaction or report on what they have done to show that they have been seriously considering the years from 1914 to 1953.

INTERVIEW

> By interviewing a World War II veteran or anyone who lived through the war years, your child can get firsthand information about what it was like to be overseas or at home during World War II.

Consult with your family about people you know who were involved in World War II, either abroad or here in the United States. If possible, arrange to interview that person. With this person's permission, you might tape the interview and present it in class.

Be sure to prepare your questions in advance. What you've learned about World War II from this chapter will help you think of questions. Don't ask any embarrassing questions or questions that are too personal. And always be considerate of your interviewee's feelings.

RESEARCH PROJECT

By doing research in the library or in a good encyclopedia, your child can find an explanation of communism as a philosophy and as a form of government.

Find out more about communism and how it differs from capitalism. Try to find answers to the following questions: What problems of capitalism was communism supposed to solve? What are the problems of a communist system? Which countries have communist governments today? You might want to share what you have learned when your class discusses Stalin and the Iron Curtain.

BOOKS TO READ

The titles recommended here focus on issues raised in this chapter. Your child might wish to share one of these books with classmates by preparing an oral report or by bringing up relevant details from the book in class discussion.

Coerr, Eleanor. *Mieko and the Fifth Treasure.* Putnam, 1993. The story of a Japanese girl who is injured during the atomic bomb attack on Nagasaki.

Rinaldi, Ann. *Keep Smiling Through.* Harcourt, 1996. Life in the United States during World War II as seen through the eyes of a lonely ten-year-old girl.

Stanley, Jerry. *Children of the Dust Bowl: The True Story of the School at Weedpatch Camp.* Crown, 1992.

Uchida, Yoshiko. *Journey Home.* Macmillan, 1978. The life of a Japanese American family after its release from a World War II internment camp.

CHAPTER 10
The Modern United States
1950–Present

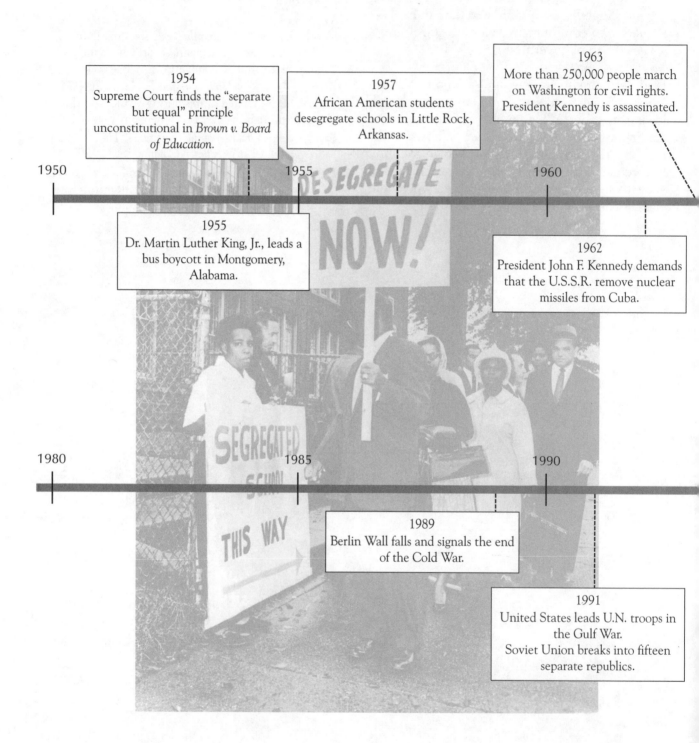

1954
Supreme Court finds the "separate but equal" principle unconstitutional in *Brown v. Board of Education*.

1957
African American students desegregate schools in Little Rock, Arkansas.

1963
More than 250,000 people march on Washington for civil rights. President Kennedy is assassinated.

1955
Dr. Martin Luther King, Jr., leads a bus boycott in Montgomery, Alabama.

1962
President John F. Kennedy demands that the U.S.S.R. remove nuclear missiles from Cuba.

1950   1955   1960

1980   1985   1990

1989
Berlin Wall falls and signals the end of the Cold War.

1991
United States leads U.N. troops in the Gulf War.
Soviet Union breaks into fifteen separate republics.

This timeline provides an overview of the important events in the United States from 1950 to the present. In the following pages, a narrative describes life in America in the second half of the twentieth century and the very beginning of the twenty-first.

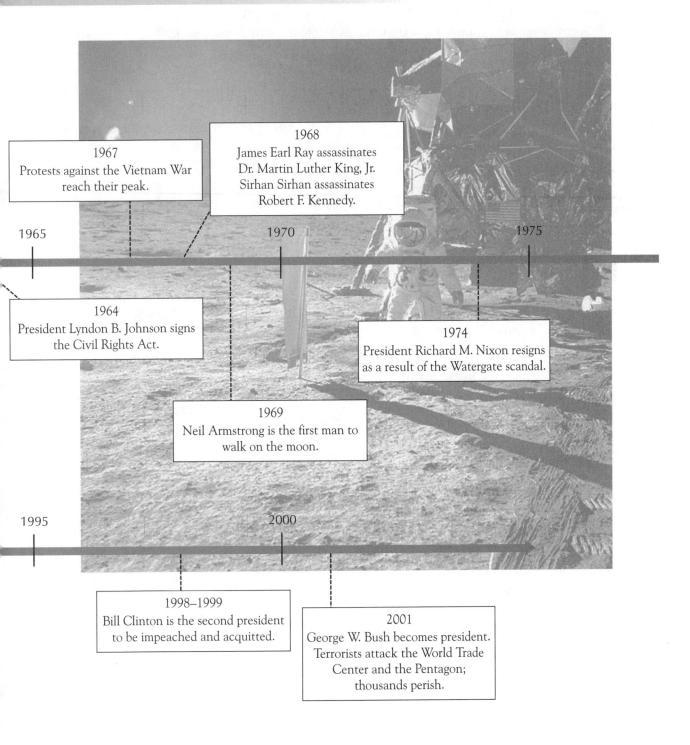

1967
Protests against the Vietnam War reach their peak.

1968
James Earl Ray assassinates Dr. Martin Luther King, Jr. Sirhan Sirhan assassinates Robert F. Kennedy.

1965

1970

1975

1964
President Lyndon B. Johnson signs the Civil Rights Act.

1974
President Richard M. Nixon resigns as a result of the Watergate scandal.

1969
Neil Armstrong is the first man to walk on the moon.

1995

2000

1998–1999
Bill Clinton is the second president to be impeached and acquitted.

2001
George W. Bush becomes president. Terrorists attack the World Trade Center and the Pentagon; thousands perish.

Word Power

Word	*Definition*
administration	group who make up the executive position in a government
bankruptcy	state of not being able to pay debts
conspiracy	secret, illegal plan
controversial	causing people to disagree
disabilities	restrictions on physical activity
discriminated	treated unfairly
guerrilla	referring to a fighter who launches surprise attacks against an official army
minority	referring to a group of people of a particular race, ethnic group, or religion living among a larger group of a different race, ethnic group, or religion
missiles	weapons sent off to strike something at a distance
negotiated	brought to an agreement
prosecutors	lawyers who represent the government
standard of living	necessities, comforts, and luxuries that a person is used to
unethical	not following the rules of right and wrong

What Your Child Needs to Know

You may choose to use the following text in several different ways, depending on your child's strengths and preferences. You might read the passage aloud; you might read it to yourself and then paraphrase it for your child; or you might ask your child to read the material along with you or on his or her own.

The end of World War II marked the beginning of the modern era in the United States. This chapter describes the events that have brought the country to the present day.

THE 1950s

For many, the 1950s were a peaceful, prosperous time. After a period of wars, people were eager for comfort and stability. Many World War II veterans came home, married, and had families. The dramatic increase in births between 1946 and 1964 went by the name **baby boom.**

Families eager to own their own homes flocked to new neighborhoods, called **suburbs,** that rapidly sprang up on the outskirts of cities. Suburbs in turn led to the increased importance of the automobile and freeway systems because families needed an easy way to get around the towns and back and forth to the city.

The American economy boomed, in part because Americans had saved their money during the war years when there was nothing to spend it on. Now they were ready and willing to make purchases. In addition, Congress passed a **GI Bill,** which paid for many war veterans to go to college. As a result, thousands of men got education and learned skills that led to higher-paying jobs and a higher <u>standard of living</u> for their families.

In recent years, it has become common to describe the 1950s as a time when people held so-called traditional American family roles, with a husband who worked outside the home, a wife whose duties as mother and housekeeper took up all her time, and children who were expected to practice and continue the values of the family.

These values were seen on television, which became increasingly important as the decade progressed. Few families had television sets at the beginning of the 1950s; a large number of families had them by the end of the 1950s. Television brought about a huge change in American life. First, it brought Americans into direct contact with world events. In addition, Americans began to turn to TV (as they still do today) for clues on how to dress, talk, eat, and think.

THE CIVIL RIGHTS MOVEMENT

Only part of the population experienced the picture-perfect American life in the 1950s. Many African Americans and other minorities were living in poverty, had poor access to education, and saw no way to improve their lives. In some cities and states, African Americans had lost their voting rights through poll taxes and other laws that <u>discriminated</u> against them. **Segregation,** or separation, of blacks and whites was common.

Segregation had become the law of the land in 1896 with a Supreme Court decision called *Plessy v. Ferguson.* Law enforcement officers arrested Homer Plessy, an African American, for sitting in a "whites only" railroad car. The Supreme Court decided it was legal to maintain "separate but equal" facilities not only for transportation but also for hospitals, restaurants, schools, and other public spaces.

In the segregated states, education for African American children was separate but generally not equal. African American children went to school in crowded, unheated classrooms, with few books or supplies. In the early 1950s, the parents of **Linda Brown** went to court against the state of Kansas. They argued that the school system was denying their daughter the right to a decent education.

The case, called *Brown v. Board of Education,* eventually went to the Supreme Court, where lawyer (and future Supreme Court justice) **Thurgood Marshall** represented the Browns. In 1954, the Supreme Court unanimously reversed the "separate but equal" principle by stating that it was impossible for people to receive equal treatment if they were separated based on the color of their skin.

Now, **desegregation**—doing away with segregation—was the law, but school desegregation progressed slowly. All over the South, schools closed their doors rather than accept African American children. In Little Rock, Arkansas, the governor posted the National Guard outside the high school to prevent nine African American students from entering. In response, President Eisenhower sent more than a thousand paratroopers to uphold the law and protect the children, who were jeered at and spat on as they entered the school.

Dr. Martin Luther King, Jr.

On December 1, 1955, an African American woman named **Rosa Parks** was arrested in Montgomery, Alabama, when she refused to give up her seat on the bus to a white passenger. In response, the black community (and many white people) boycotted the city buses; they refused to ride the buses until the city took its segregation laws off the books. In December 1956, the Supreme Court ordered Montgomery to end segregation on all buses.

The successful bus boycott in Montgomery brought attention to an African American church leader named the Reverend Dr. **Martin Luther King, Jr.** King was a pastor who followed the teachings of nineteenth-century American thinker **Henry David Thoreau** and of **Mohandas Gandhi,** the force behind India's independence from Britain in the 1940s. Thoreau and Gandhi both believed that the most powerful way to fight injustice was **nonviolent resistance.** King believed that more people would be willing to hear the message of peaceful protesters.

After the success in Montgomery, Dr. King led a campaign to end segregation in Birmingham, Alabama. Protesters participated in boycotts, marches, and sit-ins. During a **sit-in,** protesters would position themselves on seats or on the floor of a segregated establishment and refuse to get up. In Birmingham, local police responded with force. When television coverage showed the violent response to the protesters, people all over the country were outraged, and support poured in for the protesters. Eventually, Birmingham agreed to end most kinds of segregation.

On August 28, 1963, King led 250,000 peaceful marchers to the Mall in Washington, D.C., in support of a new civil rights law. It was there that King made his famous "I Have a Dream" speech, in which he said, "I have a dream that my four little children will one day live in a nation where they will not be judged by the color of their skin but by the content of their character."

THE 1960s

Even with the protests of the 1950s, the 1960s, by comparison, were a decade of disturbances. During this period, the civil rights movement continued to gain strength. As the baby boomers reached college age and adulthood, many of them began to question the structure and values of American society.

John F. Kennedy

America began the 1960s with President John F. Kennedy, the first Roman Catholic president and, at forty-three, the youngest man ever elected to the office. He and his wife, Jacqueline, were glamorous and full of energy; they brought with them a sense of hope and enthusiasm. Kennedy's vision, called the **New Frontier,** included programs that

Protest calling for desegregation

addressed the problems of discrimination and poverty. The **Peace Corps,** a Kennedy program that still exists, began to send Americans to underdeveloped countries to teach English and help communities.

The Cold War (see Chapter 9) continued in full force during Kennedy years in the White House. A clear example of the Cold War in action appeared in 1961, when the Soviet Union built the **Berlin Wall,** which separated communist East Berlin from democratic West Berlin.

Tensions increased further when Cuba, led by **Fidel Castro,** established a Soviet-supported communist government. Americans became particularly nervous because Cuba was only ninety miles from the Florida coast. In 1961, the American government trained anticommunist Cuban rebels and sent them to overthrow the government. This plan, known by the name **Bay of Pigs** after the Cuban bay in which the rebels landed, was a complete failure; relations between the two countries worsened.

Then, in 1961, the Soviet Union set up nuclear <u>missiles</u> in Cuba and aimed them at the United States. Kennedy responded by sending American war vessels to bar other ships from entering or leaving Cuba; he demanded the immediate removal of the missiles. People called this tense face-off the **Cuban Missile Crisis.** For thirteen days, the United States and the Soviet Union stood at the edge of nuclear war, and the world waited to see what would happen. Finally, Cuba and the Soviet Union agreed to American demands and removed the missiles.

A year later, Kennedy and his wife visited Dallas. On November 22, 1963, as they drove through town in a motorcade, Kennedy was shot in the head and killed. Police arrested **Lee Harvey Oswald. Jack Ruby** then shot Oswald. Although later investigations claimed Oswald acted independently, many wondered if Oswald might have been part of a larger <u>conspiracy</u>.

Lyndon Baines Johnson

Lyndon Baines Johnson, Kennedy's vice president, finished Kennedy's term and in 1964 won a term of his own.

Johnson's program for the nation focused on poverty; his goal was to create a **Great Society** in which the government would provide education and health care for all Americans. During his presidency, the United States established programs such as **Medicare,** which helps senior citizens with health care costs, and the **Job Corps,** which provides training for work.

These were expensive programs, and as time went on the government ran into trouble paying for them. Some say that the financial problem arose because the government was spending more and more money every year on the war in Vietnam (which is described in more detail later).

Civil rights workers achieved a major goal when Johnson signed the **Civil Rights Act** of 1964, which outlawed segregation in public places, and the **Voting Rights Act** of 1965, which protected African Americans. However, Johnson's dream of a Great Society appeared to be falling apart as various groups became upset with the slow pace of change.

La Causa

As the civil rights movement progressed, other minority groups began to speak out for equal treatment under the law. In 1962, a farm worker named **Cesar Chavez** (say ZAH shah VEZ) founded an organization that became known as the **United Farm Workers** (see "The Labor Movement" in Chapter 8). Chavez had difficulty organizing farm workers at first because they were migrant, moving frequently from job to job. Chavez's movement, called *La Causa,* used boycotts, strikes, and marches to speak out against poor wages and dangerous working conditions for migrant workers.

Malcolm X

Many African Americans became angry that the civil rights movement was progressing so slowly. Some even began to question King's belief in nonviolent resistance.

A group of black Muslims called the **Nation of Islam** supported a more dramatic—and more violent—form of protest. Malcolm X (who took the last name X to replace the family name given years before to his relatives by a slave owner) was one of the Nation of Islam's most powerful speakers. He argued that African Americans should take pride in their culture and history by setting themselves apart, using violence if necessary. Later, Malcolm X changed his views and began talking about a more peaceful approach, but before he could make his message heard, he was assassinated in 1965.

1968

For many, the year 1968 marked the peak of the years of unrest in America. Two major leaders were assassinated: Dr. Martin Luther King, Jr., and Robert Kennedy, John Kennedy's brother and a candidate for president. During that summer, many cities also broke into riots; poor people—many of them African American—became enraged by the crime and poverty in their communities. In 1968, negative views about the Vietnam War also reached a new high.

The War in Vietnam

A <u>controversial</u> conflict in Vietnam in Southeast Asia—a war that was never officially declared a war—marked the 1960s.

For many years, Vietnam had been a colony of France. When the French left in 1954, the country divided in two. North Vietnam established a communist government, and South Vietnam had a democratic government. To many, the situation appeared similar to the one in Korea (see Chapter 9).

People called **hawks** believed it was the United States's responsibility to support the democratic south in a fight against the communist north and to protect the rest of the world from communism. Others, the **doves,** claimed that parts of South Vietnam's government were corrupt and argued that America should not be involved in a struggle without a direct threat to the United States.

At the beginning of the 1960s, Kennedy and Johnson both sent thousands of American advisers to help the South Vietnamese. Then, in 1964, Johnson persuaded Congress to give him the authority to send thousands of troops to Vietnam to fight. Then he sent more and more troops. As the number of dead Americans rose, the war grew increasingly unpopular.

American officials realized too late that they were fighting an unwinnable war. Some historians have compared the efforts of the communist rebels known as the **Viet Cong** to the colonial rebels fighting in the Revolutionary War: they were poor, ill-equipped soldiers fighting against a powerful, well-organized army. But they used <u>guerrilla</u> tactics to defend their land in a way that made them unbeatable.

When **Richard Nixon** was elected president in 1968, he promised Americans "peace with honor." But even as he pulled out troops, he began a bombing campaign that extended into nearby Cambodia.

As the war continued, protests broke out all over the United States, especially in colleges, where students participated in marches and sit-ins. At Kent State University in Ohio, four students died during a protest in which National Guardsmen fired on the crowd.

In 1973, the United States finally signed a peace treaty with North Vietnam to end the fighting, but it wasn't until some years later that the last American troops finally left. During the conflict, more than 2 million people died; of this number, fifty-six thousand were Americans.

The Space Race

While the hot conflict raged in Vietnam, the Cold War continued. Back in 1957, Americans felt shock when the Soviet Union launched *Sputnik,* the first satellite to go into space. Some Americans feared that the Soviets would develop new space technology to attack the United States, so the government funded new programs to beat the Soviet Union in the space race.

In 1961, **Alan Shepard** became the first American to orbit Earth. On July 16, 1969, *Apollo 11* shot into space and headed for the moon with **Edwin E. "Buzz" Aldrin, Jr.,** Neil Armstrong, and **Michael Collins** on board. On July 20, Neil Armstrong was the first person ever to walk on the surface of the moon, saying, "That's one small step for man, one giant leap for mankind."

The space program continued developing new technology to travel farther, faster, and safer. In the 1980s, the **National Aeronautics and Space Administration (NASA)** introduced the space shuttle, a reusable spacecraft that takes off like a rocket and lands like an airplane. The space program, it must be added, has not been without its controversies or crises. People have lost their lives for it.

THE 1970s

The 1970s was a period of continued change and growth for the United States. On the home front,

Apollo 11 **astronaut on the moon, next to a solar wind experiment, 1969 NASA photo**

minority groups continued to fight for equal treatment. Beyond its borders, the United States continued to play an important part in world affairs.

Watergate

In 1972, Republican president Richard Nixon was running for reelection. On June 17, 1972, five men broke into the Democratic National Committee offices, located in the Watergate apartment building in Washington, D.C. Investigators discovered that the men had connections to the Committee to Reelect the President (called CREEP) and had intended to spy on Nixon's Democratic opponent.

Over the next two years, reporters, special prosecutors, and the Senate looked into the president's personal involvement in the break-in and a cover-up of that involvement. Along the way, many Nixon aides and advisers faced removal from office and prison sentences for their roles in breaking the law. By August 1974, Congress was prepared to impeach, or accuse, the president of high crimes. On August 9, 1974, President Nixon resigned from office rather than face impeachment. He was the first American president to do so.

Gerald Ford succeeded Nixon. Nixon had appointed him vice president after his original vice president, **Spiro Agnew,** had resigned because of charges that he had accepted bribes and had not paid his taxes. Ford became the only man ever to become president without having been elected to either presidential or vice presidential office.

Immediately after becoming president, Ford pardoned Nixon, officially forgiving him for any crimes. Some people disagreed with Ford's decision because they felt Nixon should have been punished; others believed Ford's approach was the best way to end the crisis so that the country could move forward.

The Women's Movement

Throughout the 1970s, the civil rights movement expanded to include people from many different ethnic and cultural groups. Senior citizens, Native Americans, and people with disabilities all fought for equal opportunities and equal treatment.

Women were another group who sought equality, in the workplace and under law. In 1963, **Betty Friedan** wrote a book called *The Feminine Mystique* (Norton, 1963), which energized the women's movement. In her book, Friedan argued that some women wanted, but were not allowed, to move beyond the roles of wife and mother. With other **feminists,** people who fought for women's rights, Friedan founded the **National Organization for Women** (**NOW**), devoted to gaining equality for women.

NOW and others believed laws would help their cause, so they began lobbying for an **Equal Rights Amendment (ERA)** that would guarantee women and men equal protection under the law. Both the Senate and the House passed the amendment in 1972, but to this day it has not been ratified by three-fourths of the states.

The 1970s did see a dramatic shift in women's roles—from wife, mother, nurse, or teacher to fairer representation in many professions, including government, medicine, and law.

The United States in World Affairs

The United States continued to play a key role in world affairs. Despite the fact that relations remained uneasy in the Cold War, world leaders took a few small steps toward **détente** (day TAHNT), or relaxation of tension. In 1972, President Nixon visited China and met with Communist leader **Mao Zedong.** In 1978, **Jimmy Carter,** who followed Gerald Ford as president, <u>negotiated</u> an important peace treaty between Israel, led by **Menachem Begin** (muh NAH kuhm BAY gin), and Egypt, led by **Anwar Sadat** (ahn WAHR suh DAHT).

THE 1980s

The 1980s were dominated by Republican leadership: **Ronald Reagan** was president from 1981 to 1989, and his vice president, **George H. Bush,** followed him as president from 1989 to 1993.

Many historians believe that the confusion of the 1960s and 1970s left Americans exhausted; they turned to Reagan and a more conservative political approach in the hopes that it would make the country seem more stable again.

The American economy boomed in the 1980s, in part because Reagan deregulated many big businesses. *Deregulation* means "lifting of rules and restrictions on an industry." Reagan and other Republicans believed that if big businesses were successful, better economic times would "trickle down" to the whole economy.

Reagan also favored a tough approach in Cold War relations. He was strongly anticommunist and even called the Soviet Union an "evil empire." During Reagan's years, building up weapons and defense took a big portion of the budget.

But the Cold War was nearing an end. In the late 1980s, Reagan speeded up détente by meeting with Soviet leader **Mikhail Gorbachev.** Gorbachev, himself, recognized that the communist government was not working; he began a program of **perestroika** (restructuring) and **glasnost** (openness).

In 1989, during George H. Bush's presidency, Germans tore down the Berlin Wall, reuniting the city and all of Germany. Soon after, Poland, Hungary, Czechoslovakia, and Romania overthrew their communist governments. Then, in 1991, the Soviet Union split apart into fifteen separate republics. The Cold War was over.

THE 1990s

On the home front, Bush's years in office marked the slowing down of the American economy. Going back to the Reagan years, consumers as well as the government had spent far more than they received. As a result, during Bush's term, banks failed, airlines went out of business, department stores filed for <u>bankruptcy</u>, and workers faced mass layoffs.

Still, the 1990s saw the United States in a continued position of world influence. Americans during this period also witnessed a dramatic change in culture and lifestyle as technological developments—computers, faxes, cellular phones, and the Internet—changed life forever. The world had been in the Industrial Age since the opening of the first mills in England in the eighteenth century. The world had now entered the **Information Age.**

The Gulf War

In 1990, the Middle Eastern country of Iraq invaded Kuwait, an oil-rich neighbor. In January 1991, the United States led United Nations forces in a war against Iraq. This war, called the Gulf War, took place in Iraq and in the nearby Persian Gulf. Led by generals **Norman Schwarzkopf** and **Colin Powell,** the United Nations soldiers defeated Iraq in six weeks.

Bill Clinton

In 1993, Democrat Bill Clinton moved into the Oval Office; he served two terms. During his time in office, he and Vice President **Al Gore** promoted anticrime measures and greater use of computer technology. The economy became stronger. Like most Democrats, Clinton believed it was important for the government to take an active role in helping people. **Hillary Rodham Clinton,** the president's wife, was an active participant at the beginning of Clinton's presidency. She led a task force set up to create a national health care system. Ultimately, however, such a system was not put in place during the Clinton years.

Clinton also worked actively on foreign affairs. He helped to negotiate agreements between Israelis and Palestinians in an attempt to settle differences that had resulted in four wars since 1948.

The <u>administration</u> suffered through several scandals, or accusations of improper conduct. Some people described Clinton's investments as <u>unethical</u>; some questioned the ways in which

Clinton raised election funds; some disapproved of Clinton's relationship with a White House intern and his denial of it. Many in Congress believed that Clinton had not told the truth about the intern scandal, and in 1998, the House of Representatives impeached Clinton. But the accusers could not prove the charges, and the Senate did not remove the president from office.

THE NEW MILLENNIUM

The 2000 Election

In 2000, the presidential election required many weeks of postelection effort to determine who would take the office come January. At the beginning of 2001, George H. Bush's son **George W. Bush** became president of the United States.

September 11, 2001

Almost eight months into Bush's term, on the morning of September 11, 2001, terrorists hijacked four commercial airliners from U.S. airports. The terrorists flew two of these planes into New York City's World Trade Center towers and crashed a third plane into the Pentagon, headquarters for America's military forces, just outside Washington, D.C. The fourth plane, possibly destined for Washington, crashed in Pennsylvania. In all, more than three thousand people died.

The terrorists who carried out this act left no messages about their purpose or identity. However, the massive worldwide investigation that was immediately launched quickly revealed the terrorists' ties to the Middle East, a region long plagued by turmoil.

For the first time since the Civil War, America suffered wide-scale casualties on its own soil as the result of hostile intent from abroad. President Bush and his administration described the event as the beginning of the first war of the twenty-first century. The United States immediately moved forward to forge alliances with countries around the world to battle terrorism. The battle promised to be long and costly, but the president vowed to wipe out terrorism. As this book goes to press, the world waits to see how the events of September 11, 2001, will affect everyone's future.

! Implications

To answer the question, "Why does all this matter?" or "What does it mean?," share the following insights with your child.

One of the most important lessons from this chapter—and from the whole book—is that Americans' values and opinions change over time and that new laws replace or overturn old laws to reflect those changes. For example, America in its early days allowed slavery, then went on to abolish slavery and to establish "separate but equal" facilities, and now legally ensures civil rights for all—regardless of race, ethnic group, or religion. Values and laws have also begun to change to protect people regardless of gender and sexual preference.

In a similar way, abortion, which used to be illegal in the United States, became legal with the 1972 Supreme Court decision *Roe v. Wade.* Since then and up to today, some Americans believe that the Supreme Court decision was wrong and want to see it overturned, while others believe that the ruling is proper. The future may or may not see changes in abortion laws.

In the coming years, other critical issues will lead to emotional debate and maybe to changes in laws: gun control, election reform, homelessness, terrorism, and the environment. What will happen with these issues depends on whom the American people elect to serve in Congress and the White House.

One reminder in this discussion of change: sometimes laws change *before* human behavior changes. Discrimination is technically illegal in the United States, but day-to-day experiences sometimes show discrimination still in practice. On certain issues, how laws and behavior will come together remains to be seen.

The United States faces challenges presented by an increasingly connected world community. In 1993, the United States signed the **North American Free Trade Agreement (NAFTA)**, which abolished trade restrictions between Mexico, the United States, and Canada. European countries are linked to one another in a similar way. Such agreements will only continue to make the world seem like a small place.

Technology, of course, will also make the world feel smaller and smaller. As computers and the Internet play a bigger part in more people's lives, Americans will have to look closely at how they define their freedoms and their privacy and how they choose to protect them.

The United States has survived a lot in the last half century. Some of the issues of the past fifty years have been with us for a long time—for example, how much the government should touch people's daily lives and how the races get along—and will continue to concern us. What will happen in the next chapter in the story of America? It is up to today's Americans to decide.

 ## Fact Checker

To check that your child knows or can find the basic facts in this chapter, ask him or her to make up one or more questions that would go with each of the following answers.

JEOPARDY

1. *Sputnik*
2. Vietnam
3. Martin Luther King, Jr.
4. Cuban Missile Crisis
5. Watergate
6. Little Rock, Arkansas
7. John F. Kennedy
8. Rosa Parks
9. Cesar Chavez
10. Information Age

Answers appear in the back, preceding the index.

 ## The Big Questions

The following questions encourage your child to think critically rather than simply recall facts. If necessary, review the specific information from the preceding pages that will help your child make the necessary inferences to come up with reasonable answers.

1. When a law passes or the Supreme Court hands down a decision, why doesn't it automatically stay in place forever? How do you explain, for example, that the Supreme Court in 1954, in *Brown v. Board of Education*, could totally change what the court had ruled in 1896, in *Plessy v. Ferguson*?
2. Knowing what you know about the American frontier of the 1900s (Chapter 6), why was *New Frontier* a good name for President Kennedy's programs in the 1960s?

3. Why are *hawks* and *doves* good labels to use for those who are in favor of a particular war and those who are against it?
4. If you were a leader of people who did not like the way the government treated them, would you recommend nonviolent protest, or would you agree to starting a riot? Why?

Suggested Answers

1. *Just as the Constitution allows people to amend it as time passes, so this country has always allowed lawmakers and judges to change laws they feel are outdated or have been misinterpreted. Lawmakers and judges must follow strict guidelines in coming up with new laws and new interpretations of old laws.*
2. Frontier *means "territory that hasn't been explored or settled yet," as in the context of westward expansion and, under Kennedy, of space exploration. But* frontier *can also mean "the limits of knowledge about a subject." Kennedy chose the name* New Frontier *because he wanted to inspire Americans to approach science and social issues*

with the same bravery and dedication that they had applied in conquering the physical frontier in the nineteenth century.

3. Hawks are birds of prey with bills and claws designed to kill and tear other animals. They are, in other words, aggressive or militant. Doves feed mostly on vegetable matter. They tend to be nonaggressive. Their behavior translates into human tendencies toward conciliation and negotiation.

4. Responses should acknowledge advantages and disadvantages of each approach. Nonviolent protests usually protect people and property but don't always bring immediate results. Rioting gets public attention and sometimes brings change in response to people's fears but often at great cost in lives and property.

Skills Practice

The following activities give your child practice in applying the skills basic to social studies. For some of the activities, your child may need to review the information in the preceding pages.

A. WRITING TO A GOVERNMENT REPRESENTATIVE

This chapter mentions individuals who have made their protests heard. The following activity will give your child a chance to be heard beyond family and school.

Write a letter to a holder of a federal, state, or local elected position. The letter should express your opinion about an issue that is important to you and the official. The issue can be as small as a request for more playing fields in the park or as major as a call for a new policy toward another country. Make sure you back up your opinion with facts, examples, or other support. Remember to be brief and polite. (You can use e-mail or regular mail.)

Evaluating Your Child's Skills: In order to complete this activity successfully, your child has to have an issue he or she feels strongly about. If necessary, help him or her through the writing process—getting an idea; listing support; writing a draft; getting feedback from a reader; and then revising, editing, and proofreading the letter—and sending it to the right address.

B. WORKING WITH A PRIMARY SOURCE

Have your child read or listen to the following excerpt from John F. Kennedy's Inaugural Address. Then ask him or her the question that follows the excerpt.

> In the long history of the world, only a few generations have been granted the role of defending freedom in its hour of maximum danger. I do not shrink from this responsibility—I welcome it. I do not believe that any of us would exchange places with any other people or any other generation. The energy, the faith, the devotion which we bring to this endeavor will light our country and all who serve it—and the glow from that fire can truly light the world.
>
> And so, my fellow Americans: ask not what your country can do for you—ask what you can do for your country.

Question

Are President Kennedy's words from 1961 still good advice for Americans at the beginning of the twenty-first century? Why or why not?

Answer

Your child may claim that the United States is not in any danger of losing its freedom from outside sources, but he or she may mention domestic issues that you have discussed together and that are on the line these days—freedom of speech, freedom to bear arms, freedom to choose, right to life, and so on. Your child's response to the relevance of "Ask what you can do for your country" will probably reflect what he or she sees at home and in the community.

> ***Evaluating Your Child's Skills:*** In order to complete this activity successfully, your child may need you to paraphrase the first paragraph and to provide examples of the final sentence in this excerpt.

C.   MAKING A TIMELINE

> Give your child limitations for this graphic arts project. That is, tell him or her whether to create a desktop timeline or a wall-size one.

Go beyond what the chapter tells you about key dates in the space race from its beginnings to today. Use reference sources to find more accomplishments and disappointments in the American space program or in the American *and* the Soviet space programs. Include on the timeline not only dates and words but pictures as well. You can trace, photocopy, or download and print illustrations—or draw some on your own.

> ***Evaluating Your Child's Skills:*** In order to complete this activity successfully, your child needs to use research skills (for locating and selecting the information) and math and visual skills (for laying out the timeline and illustrating the timeline). If your child has trouble with the scope of this skills practice, limit the time period—say, just the 1970s.

Top of the Class

> Children interested in delving more deeply into the topics covered in this chapter can choose one or more of the following activities. They may do the activities for their own satisfaction or report on what they have done to show that they have been seriously considering the period from the 1960s to today.

A TIME CAPSULE

> If your family didn't prepare a time capsule at the beginning of the twenty-first century, this might be a good time for your child to make one.

Take on the project of making and putting away a time capsule of life during this period of American history. Here are some of the questions you will have to consider.

1. What will the time capsule be made out of? Will it be a plastic bag, a metal container, an old backpack, or something else?
2. Will it be a family time capsule or a time capsule of only your life?
3. Will you put in pictures of objects or the objects themselves?
4. Will you include pieces of writing by yourself or others, music, art, tools, software? What else?
5. Once the time capsule is full, where will you put it? Will you bury it on your or a friend's property? Will you stuff it in the back of a closet?
6. How long do you want the capsule to remain untouched? For a hundred years? Fifty? Twenty? Ten? Two?
7. Will you tell anyone else (grown-ups or children) about your time capsule now?

BOOKS TO READ AND CRITIQUE

> Make one of the following books available to your child. After your child has finished

the book, you can suggest that he or she may want to share thoughts about it with his or her teacher or class.

Curtis, Christopher Paul. *The Watsons Go to Birmingham—1963*. Delacorte, 1995. Novel about African American children visiting their grandmother in Alabama at the time of the Birmingham church bombing.

Paterson, Katherine. *Park's Quest*. Viking, 1989. Novel in which a boy searches for the cause of his father's death in Vietnam.

Rediger, Pat. *Great African Americans in Civil Rights*. Crabtree, 1996. Short chapters on civil rights leaders such as Thurgood Marshall, Rosa Parks, and Jesse Jackson.

Wartski, Maureen C. *A Boat to Nowhere*. Signet, 1981. A story about the Vietnamese "boat people."

LANGUAGE SURVEY

Multilingualism will be increasingly important in the America of today and tomorrow. This activity might interest your child in learning another language.

Take a survey of family members, friends, classmates, and neighbors to find out who knows which languages. Set up your questions so that you get information about whether each person can read the language, speak the language, or understand when spoken to in the language. Consider asking people to judge themselves as excellent, good, or not-so-good with the language. You may want to organize your data by age group. Finally, come up with one to three generalizations about the information you collect.

APPENDIX A

Presidents of the United States

No.	President (birth and death dates)	Term(s)	Party	Vice President(s)
1	George Washington (1732–1799)	1789–1797		John Adams
2	John Adams (1735–1826)	1797–1801	Federalist	Thomas Jefferson
3	Thomas Jefferson (1743–1826)	1801–1809	Democratic-Republican	Aaron Burr George Clinton
4	James Madison (1751–1836)	1809–1817	Democratic-Republican	George Clinton Elbridge Gerry
5	James Monroe (1758–1831)	1817–1825	Democratic-Republican	Daniel D. Tompkins
6	John Quincy Adams (1767–1848)	1825–1829	Democratic-Republican	John C. Calhoun
7	Andrew Jackson (1767–1845)	1829–1837	Democratic	John C. Calhoun Martin Van Buren
8	Martin Van Buren (1782–1862)	1837–1841	Democratic	Richard M. Johnson
9	William H. Harrison (1773–1841)	1841	Whig	John Tyler
10	John Tyler (1790–1862)	1841–1845	Whig	None
11	James K. Polk (1795–1849)	1845–1849	Democratic	George M. Dallas
12	Zachary Taylor (1784–1850)	1849–1850	Whig	Millard Fillmore
13	Millard Fillmore (1800–1874)	1850–1853	Whig	None
14	Franklin Pierce (1804–1869)	1853–1857	Democratic	William R. King
15	James Buchanan (1791–1868)	1857–1861	Democratic	John C. Breckinridge

No.	President (birth and death dates)	Term(s)	Party	Vice President(s)
16	Abraham Lincoln (1809–1865)	1861–1865	Republican	Hannibal Hamlin Andrew Johnson
17	Andrew Johnson (1808–1875)	1865–1869	Republican	None
18	Ulysses S. Grant (1822–1885)	1869–1877	Republican	Schuyler Colfax Henry Wilson
19	Rutherford B. Hayes (1822–1893)	1877–1881	Republican	William A. Wheeler
20	James A. Garfield (1831–1881)	1881	Republican	Chester A. Arthur
21	Chester A. Arthur (1830–1886)	1881–1885	Republican	None
22 24	Grover Cleveland (1837–1908)	1885–1889 1893–1897	Democratic	Thomas A. Hendricks Adlai E. Stevenson
23	Benjamin Harrison (1833–1901)	1889–1893	Republican	Levi P. Morton
25	William McKinley (1843–1901)	1897–1901	Republican	Garret Hobart Theodore Roosevelt
26	Theodore Roosevelt (1858–1919)	1901–1909	Republican	Charles W. Fairbanks
27	William H. Taft (1857–1930)	1909–1913	Republican	James S. Sherman
28	Woodrow Wilson (1856–1924)	1913–1921	Democratic	Thomas R. Marshall
29	Warren G. Harding (1865–1923)	1921–1923	Republican	Calvin Coolidge
30	Calvin Coolidge (1872–1933)	1923–1929	Republican	Charles G. Dawes
31	Herbert C. Hoover (1874–1964)	1929–1933	Republican	Charles Curtis
32	Franklin D. Roosevelt (1882–1945)	1933–1945	Democrat	John N. Garner Henry A. Wallace Harry S Truman
33	Harry S Truman (1884–1972)	1945–1953	Democrat	Alben W. Barkley

No.	President (birth and death dates)	Term(s)	Party	Vice President(s)
34	Dwight D. Eisenhower (1890–1969)	1953–1961	Republican	Richard M. Nixon
35	John F. Kennedy (1917–1963)	1961–1963	Democrat	Lyndon B. Johnson
36	Lyndon B. Johnson (1908–1973)	1963–1969	Democrat	Hubert H. Humphrey
37	Richard M. Nixon (1913–1994)	1969–1974	Republican	Spiro T. Agnew Gerald R. Ford
38	Gerald R. Ford (1913–)	1974–1977	Republican	Nelson A. Rockefeller
39	James E. Carter (1924–)	1977–1981	Democrat	Walter F. Mondale
40	Ronald W. Reagan (1911–)	1981–1989	Republican	George H. Bush
41	George H. Bush (1924–)	1989–1993	Republican	J. Danforth Quayle
42	William Jefferson Clinton (1946–)	1993–2001	Democrat	Albert Gore, Jr.
43	George W. Bush (1946–)	2001–	Republican	Richard B. Cheney

APPENDIX B

Constitution of the United States of America

Preamble (1789)

We the people of the United States, in order to form a more perfect Union, establish justice, insure domestic tranquility, provide for the common defence, promote the general welfare, and secure the blessings of liberty to ourselves and our posterity, do ordain and establish this Constitution for the United States of America.

Article I

Section 1

All legislative powers herein granted shall be vested in a Congress of the United States, which shall consist of a Senate and House of Representatives.

Section 2

The House of Representatives shall be composed of members chosen every second year by the people of the several States, and the electors in each State shall have the qualifications requisite for electors of the most numerous branch of the State Legislature.

No Person shall be a Representative who shall not have attained to the age of twenty-five years, and been seven years a citizen of the United States, and who shall not, when elected, be an inhabitant of that State in which he shall be chosen.

(Representatives and direct taxes shall be apportioned among the several States which may be included within this Union, according to their respective numbers, which shall be determined by adding to the whole number of free persons, including those bound to service for a term of years, and excluding Indians not taxed, three fifths of all other persons.) The actual enumeration shall be made within three years after the first meeting of the Congress of the United States, and within every subsequent term of ten years, in such manner as they shall by law direct. The number of Representatives shall not exceed one for every thirty thousand, but each State shall have at least one Representative; and until such enumeration shall be made, the State of New Hampshire shall be entitled to choose three, Massachusetts eight, Rhode-Island and Providence Plantations one, Connecticut five, New York six, New Jersey four, Pennsylvania eight, Delaware one, Maryland six, Virginia ten, North Carolina five, South Carolina five, and Georgia three.

When vacancies happen in the representation from any State, the Executive Authority thereof shall issue writs of election to fill such vacancies.

The House of Representatives shall choose their Speaker and other officers; and shall have the sole power of impeachment.

Section 3

The Senate of the United States shall be composed of two Senators from each State, chosen by the Legislature thereof, for six years; and each Senator shall have one vote.

Immediately after they shall be assembled in consequence of the first election, they shall be divided as equally as may be into three classes. The seats of the Senators of the first class shall be vacated at the expiration of the second year, of the second class at the expiration of the fourth year, and of the third class at the expiration of the sixth year, so that one-third may be chosen every second year; and if vacancies happen by resignation, or otherwise, during the recess of the Legislature of any State, the Executive thereof may make temporary appointments (until the next meeting of the Legislature, which shall then fill such vacancies).

No person shall be a Senator who shall not have attained to the age of thirty years, and been nine years a citizen of the United States, and who shall not, when elected, be an inhabitant of that State for which he shall be chosen.

The Vice President of the United States shall be President of the Senate, but shall have no vote, unless they be equally divided.

The Senate shall choose their other officers, and also a President pro tempore, in the absence of the Vice President, or when he shall exercise the office of President of the United States.

The Senate shall have the sole power to try all impeachments. When sitting for that purpose, they shall be on oath or affirmation. When the President of the United States is tried, the Chief Justice shall preside: and no person shall be convicted without the concurrence of two thirds of the members present.

Judgment in cases of impeachment shall not extend further than to removal from office, and disqualification to hold and enjoy any office of honor, trust, or profit under the United States: but the party convicted shall nevertheless be liable and subject to indictment, trial, judgment and punishment, according to Law.

Section 4

The times, places, and manner of holding elections for Senators and Representatives, shall be prescribed in each State by the Legislature thereof; but the Congress may at any time by law make or alter such regulations, except as to the places of choosing Senators.

The Congress shall assemble at least once in every year, and such meeting shall be on the first Monday in December, unless they shall by law appoint a different day.

Section 5

Each House shall be the judge of the elections, returns, and qualifications of its own members, and a majority of each shall constitute a quorum to do business; but a smaller number may adjourn from day to day, and may be authorized to compel the attendance of absent members, in such manner, and under such penalties as each House may provide.

Each House may determine the rules of its proceedings, punish its members for disorderly behavior, and, with the concurrence of two thirds, expel a member.

Each House shall keep a journal of its proceedings, and from time to time publish the same, excepting such parts as may in their judgment require secrecy; and the yeas and nays of the members of either House on any question shall, at the desire of one fifth of those present, be entered on the journal.

Neither House, during the session of Congress, shall, without the consent of the other, adjourn for more than three days, nor to any other place than that in which the two Houses shall be sitting.

Section 6

The Senators and Representatives shall receive a compensation for their services, to be ascertained by law, and paid out of the Treasury of the United States. They shall in all cases, except treason, felony, and breach of the peace, be privileged from arrest during their attendance at the session of their respective Houses, and in going to and returning from the same; and for any speech or debate in either House, they shall not be questioned in any other place.

No Senator or Representative shall, during the time for which he was elected, be appointed to any civil office under the authority of the United States, which shall have been created, or the emoluments whereof shall have been increased during such time; and no person holding any office under the United States shall be a member of either House during his continuance in office.

Section 7

All bills for raising revenue shall originate in the House of Representatives; but the Senate may propose or concur with amendments as on other bills.

Every bill which shall have passed the House of Representatives and the Senate, shall, before it becomes a law, be presented to the President of the United States; if he approve he shall sign it, but if not he shall return it, with his objections to that House in which it shall have originated, who shall enter the objections at large on their journal, and proceed to reconsider it. If after such reconsideration two thirds of that House shall agree to pass the bill, it shall be sent, together with the objections, to the other House, by which it shall likewise be reconsidered, and if approved by two thirds of that House, it shall become a law. But in all such cases the votes of both Houses shall be determined by yeas and nays, and the names of the persons voting for and against the bill shall be entered on the journal of each house, respectively. If any bill shall not be returned by the President within ten days (Sundays excepted) after it shall have been presented to him, the same shall be a law, in like manner as if he had signed it, unless the Congress by their adjournment prevent its return, in which case it shall not be a law.

Every order, resolution, or vote to which the concurrence of the Senate and House of Representatives may be necessary (except on a question of adjournment) shall be presented to the President of the United States; and before the same shall take effect, shall be approved by him, or being disapproved by him, shall be repassed by two thirds of the Senate and House of Representatives, according to the rules and limitations prescribed in the case of a bill.

Section 8

The Congress shall have power to lay and collect taxes, duties, imposts and excises, to pay the debts and provide for the common defense and general welfare of the United States; but all duties, imposts and excises shall be uniform throughout the United States;

To borrow money on the credit of the United States;

To regulate commerce with foreign nations, and among the several States, and with the Indian tribes;

To establish a uniform rule of naturalization, and uniform laws on the subject of bankruptcies throughout the United States;

To coin money, regulate the value thereof, and of foreign coin, and fix the standard of weights and measures;

To provide for the punishment of counterfeiting the securities and current coin of the United States;

To establish post offices and post roads;

To promote the progress of science and useful arts, by securing for limited times to authors and inventors the exclusive right to their respective writings and discoveries;

To constitute tribunals inferior to the Supreme Court;

To define and punish piracies and felonies committed on the high seas, and offences against the law of nations;

To declare war, grant letters of marque and reprisal, and make rules concerning captures on land and water;

To raise and support armies, but no appropriation of money to that use shall be for a longer term than two years;

To provide and maintain a navy;

To make rules for the government and regulation of the land and naval forces;

To provide for calling forth the militia to execute the laws of the Union, suppress insurrections, and repel invasions;

To provide for organizing, arming, and disciplining, the militia, and for governing such part of them as may be employed in the service of the United States, reserving to the States, respectively, the appointment of the officers, and the authority of training the militia according to the discipline prescribed by Congress;

To exercise exclusive legislation in all cases whatsoever, over such district (not exceeding ten miles square) as may, by cession of particular States, and the acceptance of Congress, become the seat of the Government of the United States, and to exercise like authority over all places purchased by the consent of the Legislature of the State in which the same shall be, for the erection of forts, magazines, arsenals, dock-yards, and other needful buildings;—And

To make all laws which shall be necessary and proper for carrying into execution the foregoing powers, and all other powers vested by this Constitution in the Government of the United States, or in any department or officer thereof.

Section 9

The migration or importation of such persons as any of the States now existing shall think proper to admit, shall not be prohibited by the Congress prior to the year one thousand eight hundred and eight, but a tax or duty may be imposed on such importation, not exceeding ten dollars for each person.

The privilege of the writ of habeas corpus shall not be suspended, unless when in cases of rebellion or invasion the public safety may require it.

No bill of attainder or ex post facto law shall be passed.

No capitation, or other direct, tax shall be laid, unless in proportion to the census or enumeration herein before directed to be taken.

No tax or duty shall be laid on articles exported from any State.

No preference shall be given by any regulation of commerce or revenue to the ports of one State over those of another: nor shall vessels bound to, or from, one State, be obliged to enter, clear, or pay duties in another.

No money shall be drawn from the Treasury, but in consequence of appropriations made by law; and a regular statement and account of the receipts and expenditures of all public money shall be published from time to time.

No title of nobility shall be granted by the United States: and no person holding any office of profit or trust under them, shall, without the consent of the Congress, accept of any present, emolument, office, or title, of any kind whatever, from any king, prince, or foreign state.

Section 10

No State shall enter into any treaty, alliance, or confederation; grant letters of marque and reprisal; coin money; emit bills of credit; make any thing but gold and silver coin a tender in payment of debts; pass any bill of attainder, ex post facto law, or law impairing the obligation of contracts, or grant any title of nobility.

No State shall, without the consent of the Congress, lay any imposts or duties on imports or exports, except what may be absolutely necessary for executing its inspection laws; and the net produce of all duties and imposts, laid by any State on imports or exports, shall be for the use of the Treasury of the United States; and all such laws shall be subject to the revision and control of the Congress.

No State shall, without the consent of Congress, lay any duty of tonnage, keep troops, or ships of war in time of peace, enter into any agreement or compact with another state, or with a foreign power, or engage in war, unless actually invaded, or in such imminent danger as will not admit of delay.

Article II

Section 1

The executive power shall be vested in a President of the United States of America. He shall hold his office during the term of four years, and, together with the Vice President, chosen for the same term, be elected, as follows.

Each State shall appoint, in such manner as the Legislature thereof may direct, a number of electors, equal to the whole number of Senators and Representatives to which the State may be entitled in the Congress: but no Senator or Representative, or person holding an office of trust or profit under the United States, shall be appointed an elector.

(The electors shall meet in their respective States, and vote by ballot for two persons, of whom one at least shall not be an inhabitant of the same State with themselves. And they shall make a list of all the persons voted for, and of the number of votes for each; which list they shall sign and certify, and transmit sealed to the seat of the Government of the United States, directed to the President of the Senate. The President of the Senate shall, in the presence of the Senate and House of Representatives, open all the certificates, and the votes shall then be counted. The person having the greatest number of votes shall be the President, if such number be a majority of the whole number of electors appointed; and if there be more than one who have such majority, and have an equal number of votes, then the House of Representatives shall immediately choose by ballot one of them for President; and if no person have a majority, then from the five highest on the list the said House shall in like manner choose the President. But in choosing the President, the votes shall be taken by States, the representation from each State having one vote; A quorum for this purpose shall consist of a member or members from two thirds of the States, and a majority of all the states shall be necessary to a choice. In every case, after the choice of the President, the person having the greatest number of votes of the electors shall be the Vice President. But if there should remain two or more who have equal votes, the Senate should choose from them by ballot the Vice President.)

The Congress may determine the time of choosing the electors, and the day on which they shall give their votes; which day shall be the same throughout the United States.

No person except a natural born citizen, or a citizen of the United States, at the time of the adoption of this Constitution, shall be eligible to the office of President; neither shall any person be eligible to that office who shall not have attained to the age of thirty-five years, and been fourteen years a resident within the United States.

In case of the removal of the President from office, or of his death, resignation, or inability to discharge the powers and duties of the said office, the same shall devolve on the Vice President, and the Congress may by law provide for the case of removal, death, resignation or inability, both of the President and Vice President, declaring what officer shall then act as President, and such officer shall act accordingly, until the disability be removed, or a President shall be elected.

The President shall, at stated times, receive for his services, a compensation, which shall neither be increased nor diminished during the period for which he shall have been elected, and he shall not receive within that period any other emolument from the United States, or any of them.

Before he enter on the execution of his office, he shall take the following oath or affirmation:—"I do solemnly swear (or affirm) that I will faithfully execute the office of President of the United States, and will to the best of my ability, preserve, protect, and defend the Constitution of the United States."

Section 2

The President shall be Commander in Chief of the Army and Navy of the United States, and of the militia of the several States, when called into the actual service of the United States; he may require the opinion, in writing, of the principal officer in each of the executive departments, upon any subject relating to the duties of their respective offices, and he shall have power to grant reprieves and pardons for offences against the United States, except in cases of impeachment.

He shall have power, by and with the advice and consent of the Senate, to make treaties, provided two thirds of the Senators present concur; and he shall nominate, and by and with the advice and consent of the Senate, shall appoint ambassadors, other public ministers, and consuls, judges of the Supreme Court, and all other officers of the United States, whose appointments are not herein otherwise provided for, and which shall be established by law: but the Congress may by law vest the appointment of such inferior officers, as they think proper, in the President alone, in the courts of law, or in the heads of departments.

The President shall have power to fill up all vacancies that may happen during the recess of the Senate, by granting commissions which shall expire at the end of their session.

Section 3

He shall from time to time give to the Congress information of the state of the Union, and recommend to their consideration such measures as he shall judge necessary and expedient; he may, on extraordinary occasions, convene both Houses, or either of them, and in case of disagreement between them, with respect to the time of adjournment, he may adjourn them to such time as he shall think proper; he shall receive ambassadors and other public ministers: he shall take care that the laws be faithfully executed, and shall commission all the officers of the United States.

Section 4

The President, Vice President, and all civil officers of the United States shall be removed from office on impeachment for, and conviction of, treason, bribery, or other high crimes and misdemeanors.

Article III

Section 1

The judicial Power of the United States, shall be vested in one Supreme Court, and in such inferior courts as the Congress may from time to time ordain and establish. The judges, both of the supreme and inferior courts, shall hold their offices during good behavior, and shall, at stated times, receive for their services, a compensation, which shall not be diminished during their continuance in office.

Section 2

The judicial power shall extend to all cases, in law and equity, arising under this Constitution, the laws of the United States, and treaties made, or which shall be made, under their authority; to all cases affecting ambassadors, other public ministers and consuls; to all cases of admiralty and maritime jurisdiction; to controversies to which the United States, shall be a party; to controversies between two or more States; between a State and citizens of another State; between citizens of different States; between citizens of the same State claming lands under grants of different states, and between a State, or the citizens thereof, and foreign states, citizens, or subjects.

In all cases affecting ambassadors, other public ministers and consuls, and those in which a State shall be party, the Supreme Court shall have original jurisdiction. In all the other cases before mentioned, the Supreme Court shall have appellate jurisdiction, both as to law and fact, with such exceptions, and under such regulations, as the Congress shall make.

The trial of all crimes, except in cases of impeachment, shall be by jury; and such trial shall be held in the State where the said crimes shall have been committed; but when not committed within any State, the trial shall be at such place or places as the Congress may by law have directed.

Section 3

Treason against the United States, shall consist only in levying war against them, or, in adhering to their enemies, giving them aid and comfort. No person shall be convicted of treason unless on the testimony of two witnesses to the same overt act, or on confession in open court.

The Congress shall have power to declare the punishment of treason, but no attainder of treason shall work corruption of blood, or forfeiture except during the life of the person attained.

Article IV

Section 1

Full faith and credit shall be given in each State to the public acts, records, and judicial proceedings of every other State. And the Congress may by general laws prescribe the manner in which such acts, records, and proceedings shall be proved, and the effect thereof.

Section 2

The citizens of each State shall be entitled to all privileges and immunities of citizens in the several States.

A person charged in any State with treason, felony, or other crime, who shall flee from justice, and be found in another State, shall on demand of the Executive authority of the State from which he fled, be delivered up, to be removed to the State having jurisdiction of the crime.

No person held to service or labor in one State, under the laws thereof, escaping into another, shall, in consequence of any law or regulation therein, be discharged from such service or labor, but shall be delivered up on claim of the party to whom such service or labor may be due.

Section 3

New States may be admitted by the Congress into this Union; but no new State shall be formed or erected within the jurisdiction of any other State; nor any State be formed by the junction of two or more States, or parts of States, without the consent of the Legislatures of the States concerned as well as of the Congress.

The Congress shall have power to dispose of and make all needful rules and regulations respecting the territory or other property belonging to the United States; and nothing in this Constitution shall be so construed as to prejudice any claims of the United States, or of any particular State.

Section 4

The United States shall guarantee to every State in this Union a Republican form of government, and shall protect each of them against invasion; and on application of the Legislature, or of the Executive (when the Legislature cannot be convened) against domestic violence.

Article V

The Congress, whenever two thirds of both Houses shall deem it necessary, shall propose amendments to this Constitution, or, on the application of the Legislatures of two thirds of the several States shall call a convention for proposing amendments, which, in either case, shall be valid to all intents and purposes, as part of this Constitution, when ratified by the Legislatures of three fourths of the several States, or by conventions in three fourths thereof, as the one or the other mode of ratification may be proposed by the Congress; provided that no amendment which may be made prior to the year one thousand eight hundred and eight shall in any manner affect the first and fourth clauses in the ninth Section of the first Article; and that no State, without its consent, shall be deprived of its equal suffrage in the Senate.

Article VI

All debts contracted and engagements entered into, before the adoption of this Constitution, shall be as valid against the United States under this Constitution, as under the Confederation.

This Constitution, and the laws of the United States which shall be made in pursuance thereof; and all treaties made, or which shall be made, under the authority of the United States, shall be the supreme law of the land; and the judges in every State shall be bound thereby, any thing in the Constitution or laws of any State to the contrary notwithstanding.

The Senators and Representatives before mentioned, and the members of the several State Legislatures, and all executive and judicial officers, both of the United States and of the several States, shall be bound by oath or affirmation, to support this Constitution; but no religious test shall ever be required as a qualification to any office or public trust under the United States.

Article VII

The ratification of the conventions of nine States shall be sufficient for the establishment of this Constitution between the States so ratifying the same.

Done in convention by the unanimous consent of the States present the seventeenth day of September in the year of our Lord one thousand seven hundred and eighty seven and of the independence of the United States of America the Twelfth. In witness whereof we have hereunto subscribed our names.

George Washington
President and Deputy from Virginia

New Hampshire
John Langdon
Nicholas Gilman

Massachusetts
Nathaniel Gorham
Rufus King

Connecticut
Wm. Saml. Johnson
Roger Sherman

New York
Alexander Hamilton

New Jersey
Wil. Livingston
Wm. Paterson

David Brearley
Jona. Dayton

Pennsylvania
B. Franklin
Thomas Mifflin
Robt. Morris
Geo. Clymer
Thos. FitzSimons
Jared Ingersoll
James Wilson
Gouv. Morris

Delaware
Geo. Read
Gunning Bedford Jun.

John Dickinson
Richard Bassett
Jaco. Broom

Maryland
James McHenry
Dan. of St. Thos. Jenifer
Danl. Carroll

Virginia
John Blair
James Madison, Jr.

North Carolina
Wm. Blount
Richd Dobbs Spaight
Hu. Williamson

South Carolina
J. Rutledge
Charles Cotesworth
    Pinckney
Charles Pinckney
Pierce Butler

Georgia
William Few
Abr. Baldwin
Attest: William Jackson,
    Secretary

Amendments to the Constitution of the United States

Amendments I to X are known as the **Bill of Rights**, ratified in 1791.

Amendment I

Congress shall make no law respecting an establishment of religion, or prohibiting the free exercise thereof; or abridging the freedom of speech, or of the press; or the right of the people peaceably to assemble, and to petition the Government for a redress of grievances.

Amendment II

A well regulated militia, being necessary to the security of a free State, the right of the people to keep and bear arms, shall not be infringed.

Amendment III

No soldier shall, in time of peace be quartered in any house, without the consent of the owner, nor in time of war, but in a manner to be prescribed by law.

Amendment IV

The right of the people to be secure in their persons, houses, papers, and effects, against unreasonable searches and seizures, shall not be violated, and no warrants shall issue, but upon probable cause, supported by oath or affirmation, and particularly describing the place to be searched, and the persons or things to be seized.

Amendment V

No person shall be held to answer for a capital, or otherwise infamous crime, unless on a presentment or indictment of a Grand Jury, except in cases arising in the land or naval forces, or in the militia, when in actual service in time of war or public danger; nor shall any person be subject for the same offence to be twice put in jeopardy of life or limb; nor shall be compelled in any criminal case to be a witness, against himself, nor be deprived of life, liberty, or property, without due process of law; nor shall private property be taken for public use, without just compensation.

Amendment VI

In all criminal prosecutions, the accused shall enjoy the right to a speedy and public trial, by an impartial jury of the State and district wherein the crime shall have been committed, which district shall have been previously ascertained by law, and to be informed of the nature and cause of the accusation; to be confronted with the witnesses against him; to have compulsory process for obtaining witnesses in his favor, and to have the assistance of counsel for his defense.

Amendment VII

In suits at common law, where the value in controversy shall exceed twenty dollars, the right of trial by jury shall be preserved, and no fact tried by a jury, shall be otherwise re-examined in any court of the United States, than according to the rules of the common law.

Amendment VIII

Excessive bail shall not be required, nor excessive fines imposed, nor cruel and unusual punishments inflicted.

Amendment IX

The enumeration in the Constitution, of certain rights, shall not be construed to deny or disparage others retained by the people.

Amendment X

The powers not delegated to the United States by the Constitution, nor prohibited by it to the States, are reserved to the States, respectively, or to the people.

Amendment XI

The judicial power of the United States shall not be construed to extend to any suit in law or equity, commenced or prosecuted against one of the United States by citizens of another State, or by citizens or subjects of any foreign state.

Amendment XII

The electors shall meet in their respective states, and vote by ballot for President and Vice President, one of whom, at least, shall not be an inhabitant of the same state with themselves; they shall name in their ballots the person voted for as President, and in distinct ballots the person voted for as Vice President, and they shall make distinct lists of all persons voted for as President, and of all persons voted for as Vice President, and of the number of votes for each, which lists they shall sign and certify, and transmit sealed to the seat of the government of the United States, directed to the President of the Senate; the President of the Senate shall, in the presence of the Senate and House of Representatives, open all the certificates and the votes shall then be counted; the person having the greatest number of votes for President, shall be the President, if such number be a majority of the whole number of electors appointed; and if no person have such majority, then from the persons having the highest numbers not exceeding three on the list of those voted for as President, the House of Representatives shall choose immediately, by ballot, the President. But in choosing the President, the votes shall be taken by states, the representation from each State having one vote; a quorum for this purpose shall consist of a member or members from two thirds of the states, and a majority of all the states shall be necessary to a choice. And if the House of Representatives shall not choose a President whenever the right of choice shall devolve upon them, before the fourth day of March next following, then the Vice President shall act as President, as in the case of the death or other constitutional disability of the President. The person having the greatest number of votes as Vice President, shall be the Vice President, if such number be a majority of the whole number of electors appointed, and if no person have a majority, then from the two highest numbers on the list, the Senate shall choose the Vice President; a quorum for the purpose shall consist of two thirds of the whole number of Senators, and a majority of the whole number shall be necessary to a choice. But no person constitutionally ineligible to the office of President shall be eligible to that of Vice President of the United States.

Amendment XIII

Section 1

Neither slavery nor involuntary servitude, except as a punishment for crime whereof the party shall have been duly convicted, shall exist within the United States, or any place subject to their jurisdiction.

Section 2

Congress shall have power to enforce this article by appropriate legislation.

Amendment XIV

Section 1

All persons born or naturalized in the United States, and subject to the jurisdiction thereof, are citizens of the United States and of the State wherein they reside. No State shall make or enforce any law which shall abridge the privileges or immunities of citizens of the United States; nor shall any State deprive any person of life, liberty, or property, without due process of law; nor deny to any person within its jurisdiction the equal protection of the laws.

Section 2

Representatives shall be apportioned among the several States according to their respective numbers, counting the whole number of persons in each State, excluding Indians not taxed. But when the right to vote at any election for the choice of electors for President and Vice President of the United States, Representatives in Congress, the executive and judicial officers of a State, or the members of the Legislature thereof, is denied to any of the male inhabitants of such State, being twenty-one years of age, and citizens of the United States, or in any way abridged, except for participation in rebellion, or other crime, the basis of representation therein shall be reduced in the proportion which the number of such male citizens shall bear to the whole number of male citizens twenty-one years of age in such State.

Section 3

No person shall be a Senator or Representative in Congress, or elector of President and Vice President, or hold any office, civil or military, under the United States, or under any State, who, having previously taken an oath, as a member of Congress, or as an officer of the United States, or as a member of any State Legislature, or as an executive or judicial officer of any State, to support the Constitution of the United States, shall have engaged in insurrection or rebellion against the same, or given aid or comfort to the enemies thereof. But Congress may, by a vote of two thirds of each House, remove such disability.

Section 4

The validity of the public debt of the United States, authorized by law, including debts incurred for payment of pensions and bounties for services in suppressing insurrection or rebellion, shall not be questioned. But neither the United States nor any State shall assume or pay any debt or obligation incurred in aid of insurrection or rebellion against the United States, or any claim for the loss or emancipation of any slave; but all such debts, obligations, and claims shall be held illegal and void.

Section 5

The Congress shall have power to enforce, by appropriate legislation, the provisions of this article.

Amendment XV

Section 1

The right of citizens of the United States to vote shall not be denied or abridged by the United States or by any State on account of race, color, or previous condition of servitude.

Section 2

The Congress shall have power to enforce this article by appropriate legislation.

Amendment XVI

The Congress shall have power to lay and collect taxes on incomes, from whatever source derived, without apportionment among the several States, and without regard to any census or enumeration.

Amendment XVII

The Senate of the United States shall be composed of two Senators from each State, elected by the people thereof, for six years; and each Senator shall have one vote. The electors in each State shall have the qualifications requisite for electors of the most numerous branch of the State Legislatures.

When vacancies happen in the representation of any State in the Senate, the executive authority of such State shall issue writs of election to fill such vacancies: Provided, that the legislature of any State may empower the executive thereof to make temporary appointment until the people fill the vacancies by election as the legislature may direct.

This amendment shall not be so construed as to affect the election or term of any Senator chosen before it becomes valid as part of the Constitution.

Amendment XVIII

Section 1

After one year from the ratification of this article the manufacture, sale, or transportation of intoxicating liquors within, the importation thereof into, or the exportation thereof from the United States and all territory subject to the jurisdiction thereof for beverage purposes is hereby prohibited.

Section 2

The Congress and the several States shall have concurrent power to enforce this article by appropriate legislation.

Section 3

This article shall be inoperative unless it shall have been ratified as an amendment to the Constitution by the legislatures of the several States, as provided in the Constitution, within seven years from the date of the submission hereof to the States by Congress.

Amendment XIX

The right of citizens of the United States to vote shall not be denied or abridged by the United States or by any State on account of sex.

Congress shall have power to enforce this article by appropriate legislation.

Amendment XX

Section 1

The terms of the President and Vice President shall end at noon on the twentieth day of January, and the terms of Senators and Representatives at noon on the third day of January, of the years in which such terms would have ended if this article had not been ratified; and the terms of their successors shall then begin.

Section 2

The Congress shall assemble at least once in every year, and such meeting shall begin at noon on the third day of January, unless they shall by law appoint a different day.

Section 3

If, at the time fixed for the beginning of the term of the President, the President-elect shall have died, the Vice President-elect shall become President. If a President shall not have been chosen before the time fixed for the beginning of his term, or if the President-elect shall have failed to qualify, then the Vice President shall have qualified; and the Congress may by law provide for the case wherein neither a President-elect nor a Vice President-elect shall have qualified, declaring who shall then act as President, or the manner in which one who is to act shall be selected, and such person shall act accordingly until a President or Vice President shall have qualified.

Section 4

The Congress may by law provide for the case of the death of any of the persons from whom the House of Representatives may choose a President whenever the right of choice shall have devolved upon them, and for the case of the death of any of the persons from whom the Senate may choose a Vice President whenever the right of choice shall have devolved upon them.

Section 5

Sections 1 and 2 shall take effect on the 15th day of October following the ratification of this article.

Section 6

This article shall be inoperative unless it shall have been ratified as an amendment to the Constitution by the legislatures of three fourths of the several States within seven years from the date of its submission.

Amendment XXI

Section 1

The eighteenth article of amendment to the Constitution of the United States is hereby repealed.

Section 2

The transportation or importation into any State, territory, or possession of the United States for delivery or use therein of intoxicating liquors, in violation of the laws thereof, is hereby prohibited.

Section 3

This article shall be inoperative unless it shall have been ratified as an amendment to the Constitution by convention in the several States, as provided in the Constitution, within seven years from the date of the submission thereof to the States by the Congress.

Amendment XXII

Section 1

No person shall be elected to the office of the President more than twice, and no person who has held the office of President, or acted as President, for more than two years of a term to which some other person was elected President shall be elected to the office of the President more than once. But this article shall not apply to any person holding the office of President when this article was proposed by the Congress, and shall not prevent any person who may be holding the office of President, or acting as President, during the term within which this article becomes operative from holding the office of President or acting as President during the remainder of such term.

Section 2

This article shall be inoperative unless it shall have been ratified as an amendment to the Constitution by the legislatures of three fourths of the several States within seven years from the date of its submission to the States by the Congress.

Amendment XXIII

Section 1

The District constituting the seat of Government of the United States shall appoint in such manner as the Congress may direct: A Number of electors of President and Vice President equal to the whole number of Senators and Representatives in Congress to which the District would be entitled if it were a State, but in no event more than the least populous State; they shall be in addition to those appointed by the States, but they shall be considered, for the purposes of the election of President and Vice President, to be electors appointed by a State; and they shall meet in the District and perform such duties as provided by the twelfth article of amendment.

Section 2

The Congress shall have the power to enforce this article by appropriate legislation.

Amendment XXIV

Section 1

The right of citizens of the United States to vote in any primary or other election for President or Vice President, for electors for President or Vice President, or for Senator or Representative in Congress, shall not be denied or abridged by the United States or any State by reasons of failure to pay any poll tax or other tax.

Section 2

The Congress shall have the power to enforce this article by appropriate legislation.

Amendment XXV

Section 1

In case of the removal of the President from office or of his death or resignation, the Vice President shall become President.

Section 2

Whenever there is a vacancy in the office of the Vice President, the President shall nominate a Vice President who shall take office upon confirmation by a majority vote of both Houses of Congress.

Section 3

Whenever the President transmits to the President pro tempore of the Senate and the Speaker of the House of Representatives his written declaration that he is unable to discharge the powers and duties of his office, and until he transmits to them a written declaration to the contrary, such powers and duties shall be discharged by the Vice President as Acting President.

Section 4

Whenever the Vice President and a majority of either the principal officers of the executive departments or of such other body as Congress may by law provide, transmit to the President pro tempore of the Senate and the Speaker of the House of Representatives their written declaration that the President is unable to discharge the powers and duties of his office, the Vice President shall immediately assume the powers and duties of the office as Acting President.

Thereafter, when the President transmits to the President pro tempore of the Senate and the Speaker of the House of Representatives his written declaration that no inability exists, he shall resume the powers and duties of his office unless the Vice President and a majority of either the principal officers of the executive department or of such other body as Congress may by law provide, transmit within four days to the President pro tempore of the Senate and the Speaker of the House of Representatives their written declaration that the President is unable to discharge the powers and duties of his office. Thereupon Congress shall decide the issue, assembling within forty-eight hours for that purpose if not in session. If the Congress, within twenty-one days after receipt of the latter written declaration, or, if Congress is not in session, within twenty-one days after Congress is required to assemble, determines by two thirds vote of both Houses that the President is unable to discharge the powers and duties of his office, the Vice President shall continue to discharge the same as Acting President; otherwise, the President shall resume the powers and duties of his office.

Amendment XXVI

Section 1

The right of citizens of the United States, who are 18 years of age or older, to vote shall not be denied or abridged by the United States or by any state on account of age.

Section 2

The Congress shall have power to enforce this article by appropriate legislation.

Amendment XXVII

No law, varying the compensation for the services of the Senators and Representatives, shall take effect, until an election of Representatives shall have intervened.

APPENDIX C

Declaration of Independence (1776)

When in the Course of human events it becomes necessary for one people to dissolve the political bands which have connected them and to assume among the powers of the earth the separate and equal station to which the Laws of Nature and of Nature's God entitle them, a decent respect to the opinions of mankind requires that they should declare the causes which impel them to the separation.

We hold these truths to be self-evident: that all men are created equal; that they are endowed by their Creator with certain unalienable Rights; that among these are Life, Liberty and the pursuit of Happiness; That to secure these rights, Governments are instituted among Men, deriving their just powers from the consent of the governed; That whenever any Form of Government becomes destructive of these ends, it is the Right of the People to alter or to abolish it, and to institute new Government, laying its foundation on such principles, and organizing its powers in such form, as to them shall seem most likely to effect their Safety and Happiness. Prudence, indeed, will dictate that Governments long established should not be changed for light and transient causes; and accordingly all experience hath shown that mankind are more disposed to suffer while evils are sufferable than to right themselves by abolishing the forms to which they are accustomed. But when a long train of abuses and usurpations, pursuing invariably the same Objects, evinces a design to reduce them under absolute Despotism, it is their right, it is their duty, to throw off such Government, and to provide new Guards for their future security. Such has been the patient sufferance of these Colonies; and such is now the necessity which constrains them to alter their former Systems of Government. The history of the present King of Great Britain is a history of repeated injuries and usurpations, all having in direct object the establishment of an absolute Tyranny over the States. To prove this, let Facts be submitted to a candid world.

He has refused his Assent to Laws the most wholesome and necessary for the public good.

He has forbidden his Governors to pass Laws of immediate and pressing importance, unless suspended in their operation till his Assent should be obtained; and when so suspended, he has utterly neglected to attend to them.

He has refused to pass other Laws for the accommodation of large districts of people, unless these people would relinquish the right of Representation in the Legislature, a right inestimable to them and formidable to tyrants only.

He has called together legislative bodies at places unusual, uncomfortable, and distant from the depositary of their public records, for the sole purpose of fatiguing them into compliance with his measures.

He has dissolved Representative Houses repeatedly, for opposing with manly firmness his invasions on the right of the people.

He has refused for a long time after such dissolutions to cause others to be elected, whereby the Legislative powers, incapable of Annihilation, have returned to the People at large for their exercise, the State remaining in the mean time exposed to all the dangers of invasions from without and convulsions within.

He has endeavored to prevent the population of these States; for that purpose obstructing the Laws for Naturalization of Foreigners, refusing to pass others to encourage their migration hither, and raising the conditions of new Appropriations of Lands.

He has obstructed the Administration of Justice, by refusing his Assent to Laws for establishing Judiciary powers.

He has made Judges dependent on his Will alone for the tenure of their offices, and the amount of their salaries.

He has erected a multitude of New Offices, and sent hither swarms of Officers to harass our people and eat out their substance.

He has kept among us, in times of peace, Standing Armies, without the Consent of our legislatures.

He has affected to render the Military independent of, and superior to, the Civil power.

He has combined with others to subject us to a jurisdiction foreign to our constitution and unacknowledged by our laws; giving his Assent to their Acts of pretended Legislation:

For quartering large bodies of armed troops among us;

For protecting them, by a mock Trial, from punishment for any murders which they should commit on the Inhabitants of these States;

For cutting off our Trade with parts of the world;

For imposing Taxes on us without our Consent;

For depriving us, in many cases, of the benefits of Trial by Jury;

For transporting us beyond Seas to be tried for pretended offenses;

For abolishing the free System of English Laws in a neighboring Province, establishing therein an Arbitrary government, and enlarging its boundaries, so as to render it at once an example and fit instrument for introducing the same absolute rule into these Colonies;

For taking away our Charters, abolishing our most valuable Laws, and altering, fundamentally, the Forms of our Governments;

For suspending our own Legislatures, and declaring themselves invested with Power to legislate for us in all cases whatsoever.

He has abdicated Government here, by declaring us out of his Protection and waging War against us.

He has plundered our seas, ravaged our Coasts, burned our towns, and destroyed the lives of our people.

He is at this time transporting large Armies of foreign Mercenaries to complete the works of death, desolation and tyranny, already begun with circumstances of Cruelty and perfidy scarcely paralleled in the most barbarous ages, and totally unworthy the Head of a civilized nation.

He has constrained our fellow Citizens taken on the high Seas to bear Arms against their Country, to become the executioners of their friends and Brethren, or to fall themselves by their Hands.

He has excited domestic insurrections amongst us, and has endeavored to bring on the inhabitants of our frontiers the merciless Indian Savages whose known rule of warfare is an undistinguished destruction of all ages, sexes, and conditions.

In every stage of these Oppressions We have Petitioned for Redress in the most humble terms. Our repeated Petitions have been answered only by repeated injury. A Prince whose character is thus marked by every act which may define a Tyrant is unfit to be the ruler of a free people.

Nor have We been wanting in attentions to our British Brethren. We have warned them from time to time of attempts by their legislature to extend an unwarrantable jurisdiction over us. We have reminded them of the circumstances of our emigration and settlement here. We have appealed to their native justice and magnanimity, and we have conjured them by the ties of our common kindred to disavow these usurpations, which would inevitably interrupt our connections and correspondence. They too have been deaf to the voice of justice and consanguinity. We must therefore acquiesce in the necessity which denounces our Separation and hold them, as we hold the rest of mankind, Enemies in War, in Peace Friends.

We, therefore, the Representatives of the United States of America in General Congress Assembled, appealing to the Supreme Judge of the world for the rectitude of our intentions, do in the Name and by the Authority of the good people of these Colonies, solemnly publish and declare that these United Colonies are and of right ought to be Free and Independent States; that they are Absolved from all Allegiance to the British Crown, and that all political connection between them and the State of Great Britain is and ought to be totally dissolved, and that as Free and Independent States, they have full Power to levy War, conclude Peace, contract Alliance, establish Commerce, and to do all other Acts and Things which Independent States may of right do.

And for the support of this Declaration, with a firm reliance on the protection of Divine Providence, we mutually pledge to each other our Lives, our Fortunes, and our sacred Honor.

Answers to "Fact Checkers"

Chapter 1
1. Northwest Coastal: Makah
2. California: Chumash
3. Southwest: Pueblo
4. Plains: Cheyenne
5. Eastern Woodlands: Mohawk

Chapter 2

Across
4. Raleigh
5. Coronado
6. Pizarro
8. Smith
10. Roanoke
11. Polo
12. Champlain

Down
1. Vespucci
2. Balboa
3. Elizabeth
5. Cortes
7. Drake
9. Magellan

Chapter 3
1. Jamestown
2. Pocahontas
3. Virginia
4. Mayflower
5. Plimouth
6. Wamponoag
7. Squanto *or* Samoset
8. Puritan

Period from 1609 to 1610 and 1620 to 1621: Starving Time

Chapter 4
1. b
2. a
3. c
4. a
5. b

Chapter 5
1. John Adams
2. Alexander Hamilton
3. Thomas Jefferson
4. Louisiana Purchase

Chapter 6
1. F
2. F
3. T
4. F
5. F
6. T
7. T
8. F
9. F
10. T

Chapter 7
The correct chronological order follows:

Missouri Compromise (1820)
Compromise of 1850
Fugitive Slave Law (1850)
Dred Scott Decision (1857)
Lincoln elected to first term (1860)
Fort Sumter (1861)
Gettysburg Address (1863)
Lee's surrender at Appomattox (1865)
Election of blacks to Congress (late 1860s)

Chapter 8

Across
3. negotiation
5. famine
8. textile
9. radical
11. innovation

Down
1. poverty
2. consumers
4. barons
6. investors
7. management
10. loom

Chapter 9

Archduke Franz Ferdinand: World War I
Adolf Hitler: World War II
General MacArthur: Korean War
Woodrow Wilson: World War I
Benito Mussolini: World War II
J. Robert Oppenheimer: World War II
General Ridgway: Korean War
Joseph Stalin: World War II
Hideki Tojo: World War II
Harry S Truman: World War II, Korean War
Kaiser Wilhelm II: World War I

Chapter 10

Answers will vary. Possibilities include the following:

1. What was the first human-made satellite to go into space?
2. In what country was the United States involved in an unpopular war in the 1970s?
3. Who led a bus boycott in Alabama in 1955?
4. What event almost led to war between the United States and the Soviet Union?
5. What led to President Nixon's resignation?
6. Where did African American students desegregate schools in 1957?
7. Who was assassinated in 1963?
8. What is the name of the person whose arrest led to the Montgomery, Alabama, bus boycott?
9. Who led La Causa?
10. What *age* do we say the world entered in the 1990s?

INDEX